D1035198

Freedom for Sale

Freedom for Sale

A National Study of Pretrial Release

Paul B. Wice
Washington and Jefferson College

Lexington Books
D.C. Heath and Company
Lexington, Massachusetts
Toronto   London

Library of Congress Cataloging in Publication Data

Wice, Paul B.
Freedom for sale

Bibliography: p.
1. Bail—United States.   I. Title.
KF9632.W5   345'.73'072   73-21963
ISBN 0–669–92791–0

Published simultaneously in Canada.

Printed in the United States of America.

International Standard Book Number: 0–669–92791–0

Library of Congress Catalog Card Number: 73–21963

To the memory of my father

Table of Contents

List of Figure and Tables

Figure

Table

Foreword

This book is a most useful contribution to the literature of criminal justice for two reasons. First—and I believe this is the author's primary interest—it combines careful scholarship and skillful fact-gathering to provide useful systemic insights into a complicated and important social institution. On that basis alone, this book is valuable.

Secondly, and on another level, the subject of pretrial release is a perfect example of a fascinating problem concerning social issues: What does it take to bring about reform? How does our country change its Vietnam policy; how do outraged citizens get the air clean, their cars made safe, their risky new medicines professionally supervised, dangerous toys off the market, and so forth?

In the early 1960s, a number of social scientists and legal scholars focused attention on the fact that the country's bail system operated in a scandalous way. It punished the poor. It generated discrimination against needy defendants throughout their criminal justice experiences. It gave birth to the outrageous and corrupting bailbond industry. It was manipulated by judges for improper and personal purposes. It did not even do effectively what it set out to do: to assure a defendant's presence at trial.

The subject interested then Attorney General Robert F. Kennedy; subsequently, the Justice Department sponsored and conducted a national bail conference in 1964 which appeared to generate an interest in and inclination for bail reform around the country. Model experimental programs were tested and proved efficient, economic, and practical. Popular writings picked up the theme and observers assumed that the problem was solved, or at least that it was going to be solved soon.

Finally, a federal law was passed which changed the bail system in all federal courts. Scores of notable personalities from the bar attended a White House ceremony when President Johnson signed that bill, the result of almost a decade of efforts for bail reform.

Five years later, when interested observers and students of the problem looked back to assess the extent of this reform movement, we were shocked to find how little had been accomplished. There were appearances of reform, but only a questionable amount of reform had in fact taken place. About a hundred bail reform projects were chugging along around the country, but no one was keeping records describing experiences, successes, or problems. In fact, many of the problems we had supposed were resolved still remained both under

the old money bail system (which essentially remains) and, even more patheti-
cally, under the new reformed federal system.

   This book returns our attention to pretrial release and adds more useful
and up-to-date information about what is happening in this important part
of the criminal justice system. I hope that this book will be widely read and
considered, and that it will serve to bring attention back again to an important
problem: making bail reform a reality.

                                              Ronald L. Goldfarb
                                              Washington, D.C.
                                              February, 1974

Preface

Purpose

The purpose of this book is to present a comprehensive and scientific investigation of the current pretrial release system operating in the United States. In addition to offering a detailed analysis of how this system functions, there is also a discussion of the various reforms which have been suggested for its improvement. The research is comprehensive in that 125 knowledgeable officials in eleven cities were interviewed and an additional 160 respondents from seventy-two cities completed mailed questionnaires on the administration of bail in their community. The cities were selected so as to ensure geographical dispersion as well as to represent a broad range of demographic characteristics. Throughout the study an attempt was made to remain as objective as possible on this highly controversial and emotional topic. All observations reported were based upon scientific research procedures.

The significance of the book lies in its ability to benefit the social sciences by contributing new understanding to the fields of public law and urban affairs. It is also hoped that the study may serve some practical purposes in the area of public policy formulation with regard to improving the operation of our nation's criminal justice system. Thus far the most satisfying results have been in the findings being utilized by various federal, state, and local agencies as a resource in their attempts to understand and improve their pretrial release program.

The study of bail has traditionally concentrated upon the constitutional, jurisprudential, and ethical nature of the system. In the isolated studies of bail systems in actual operation, research has been restricted to a series of case studies such as Arthur Beeley's work on Chicago and Martin Friedland's study of Toronto. The only creditable attempts at evaluating and critiquing bail on a national scale have been Daniel Freed and Patricia Wald's *Bail in the United States: 1964* and Ronald Goldfarb's *Ransom: A Critique of the American Bail System.*

Methodology

The data gathered in this study was the product of a combination of research techniques: personal interviews and mailed questionnaires. The mailed questionnaires were sent to seventy-two cities. For each city a questionnaire was addressed to a judge, a defense attorney, a prosecuting attorney, and a bail project director or a public defender if the city did not have a bail project. The rate of return was quite good with 55 percent of all respondents sending back completed questionnaires.

How were these respondents selected? The criminal court judge, prosecuting attorney, and public defender for each city was found in the appropriate American Bar Association Legal Directory for each state or region of the country. The bail project director was located from a directory compiled by the Vera Institute of Justice. The selection of the defense attorneys was from Martindale and Huebell Legal Directory and involved a more complex sampling procedure. The writer selected a lawyer from a law firm which indicated an active practice in criminal law. Care was taken to select one-third of these lawyers who had prior experience as a prosecutor, one-third who were previously associated with a public defenders office, and a final third who had not worked for either of these public agencies. It was hoped that by breaking up these defense attorneys according to previous legal experience there would be a better chance for insuring that the sample would not be skewed in their attitudes due to their previous experiences.

The selection of the cities for the survey was done with a great deal of care since the sampling of entities is a crucial element in any research design. The first step in the process was to select the bail reform cities. These are cities which operate bail reform projects. The projects provide a standardized fact-finding mechanism employed to systematically investigate an arrested defendant to determine his reliability for release on his own recognizance. The project attempts to predict the defendant's likelihood of appearing for his court date by evaluating his community ties, past record, and seriousness of the present crime of which he is accused. They will make a recommendation to the judge who usually makes the final decision. The Vera Foundation in New York City published a list of all current (1968) bail reform projects in the country. This list contained approximately fifty cities. Forty cities were chosen from this list. Ten cities were eliminated in order to achieve an equitable geographic distribution. A second reason for discarding a few of the original fifty was because it was discovered that they were presently phasing out or discontinuing their bail reform projects. At final count there were thirty-six bail reform cities in the survey because three failed to return questionnaires or did not provide sufficient information.

This list of bail reform cities was then broken down according to a number of geographic and demographic variables such as geographical region, percentage nonwhites, population, median family income, and unemployment rate. Based on the distribution of these thirty-six reform cities within these demographic variables, a group of thirty-six traditional cities were selected which nearly matched, as closely as possible, the frequency distribution of the reform cities for the specified demographic variables.

Of the seventy-two cities in the national survey, seventeen are located in the

East, twenty-two in the Midwest and Plains, eighteen in the South and Southwest, and fifteen in the Far West and Rocky Mountains. Although this presents a fairly equitable distribution into the four geographic regions, it distorts the actual population distribution across the nation. As a result of this distortion, eastern and midwestern cities are underrepresented while the Far West and Rocky Mountains are slightly overrepresented. The implications of this distortion are unclear. Because the geographic region was found to be a very weak explanatory variable whenever it was used, and also because these distortions were of such minor magnitude, the author believes that these discrepancies in distribution are of little consequence to this study.

Because of the inherent limitations of mailed questionnaires, this writer also conducted personal interviews in eleven cities chosen from the original seventy-two of the mailed survey. The purpose of these interviews was not only to validate the information obtained in the mailed questionnaires but also to ask additional questions and probe into areas which could only be examined by on-the-spot discussions.

In addition to conducting interviews in these cities, information was also obtained through a variety of other means. In each city, the investigator spent at least twenty to thirty hours in court watching. These periods of observation gave the author a better understanding of the style of criminal justice in each city. It also disclosed many informative incidents which gave the author a thoroughly realistic portrayal of the administration of bail. A complete check on the accuracy of a respondent's answers was, of course, impossible. Through these courtroom observations, however, one was able to perform a limited spot check and was thereby able to evaluate the respondent's frankness and accuracy.

The official court records were also a source of data. The author tried to spend ten to twenty hours in each city reading the criminal court dockets to gain a clearer understanding of the administration of bail, especially with regard to validating data on forfeitures and additional crimes committed while awaiting trial. The official criminal court annual (and monthly if that was all that was available) reports, as well as reports by the bail reform projects and other outside groups concerned with the administration of urban justice (i.e., The Alliance to End Repression in Chicago), were also collected.

As in the selection of the original seventy-two cities, the method for selecting these eleven cities for intensive investigation must be discussed. The following are four considerations which influenced the author's selection of cities for the intensive survey. First, the number was held to eleven because of time and financial limitations placed upon the author. A second consideration was that these eleven cities had to be from the original seventy-two of the mailed national survey. The reason for this was to afford the author an opportunity to validate the mailed questionnaire responses from these cities.

A third qualification for these cities in the intensive survey was that each had to be a large city with a population exceeding 500,000 and the administration of justice must be run as an assembly-line process. By assembly-line process, the author has borrowed a concept from Charles Work, Deputy U.S. Attorney for the Court of General Sessions in Washington, D.C., as well as the President's Commission on Law Enforcement and the Administration of Justice directed by James Vorenberg. These jurisdictions are distinguished from nonassembly-line jurisdictions because the prosecutor and the judge do not follow a case through the entire system from preliminary arraignment to trial and sentencing. In the assembly-line system of urban justice, a defendant's case is brought before a different judge at each stage in the proceedings, and the prosecution will often be represented by different attorneys at these various stages.

The reasons for placing these size restrictions on the sample of cities in the intensive survey is because the larger urban centers are faced with the most severe problems in the administration of bail and are also the most active in attempting to find solutions to these problems. Thus the author wished to go where the most activity in the field of bail and its reform was occurring. Because the assembly-line type of justice is so crucial a development in the administration of urban justice and is cropping up in even middle-sized cities, the author deemed it essential that every city in the sample conform to this process.

A fourth requirement in selecting these eleven cities was that they be distributed among the various geographical regions of the nation so that they would represent a sufficiently national sample of bail systems. This geographic spread was achieved by selecting three cities from the East, four from the Mid-west and Plains, three from the Far West and Rocky Mountains, and one from the South. The South was the only system underrepresented numerically but this can be justified by the absence of large cities of over 500,000 in this region.

After imposing the four previously listed requirements on the seventy-two cities of the national mail questionnaire survey, it was fairly easy to randomly select the eleven cities since so few were able to satisfy all the conditions. New York City was purposely omitted because of this writer's belief that the city's problems are so complex and so enormous that they do not easily allow for comparisons to be drawn from their experience to other cities. Thus New York City, particularly in its administration of criminal justice could be categorized as *sui generis*. The eleven cities selected for intensive study were the following: Washington, D.C.; Philadelphia; Baltimore; Atlanta; St. Louis; Indianapolis; Detroit; Chicago; Los Angeles, San Francisco, and Oakland.

A final consideration was the author's attempt to have these eleven cities be representative of the percentage of bail reform projects found in cities with populations of over half a million. It was discovered that in the seventy-two-city sample, 75 percent of those cities with populations exceeding 500,000 were operating bail reform projects. Therefore, eight of the eleven cities, approximately 73 percent, selected for intensive study, were also found to be

administering reform projects. The three traditional cities in the intensive
study were Detroit, Oakland, and Philadelphia.

A week was spent in each of the eleven cities with the exceptions of
Washington, D.C. and the Bay Area where two weeks were devoted to the
project. The extra week periods in Washington was due to the opportunity to
use federal agencies as well as congressional committees as an important source
of information. Also the new preventive detention legislation scheduled for
the D.C. government was an additional and unique topic of study. The interviews were conducted between August, 1970 and March, 1971.

An average of ten interviews were conducted in each city with the total
number reaching approximately 115. The author was interested in speaking
to anyone in the city who was knowledgeable on the subject of the administration of bail within his community's court system. Among the various groups
of interviewees in each city were judges, criminal court clerks, defense attorneys,
representatives from the prosecuting attorney's office, public defenders, bail
project directors, bondsmen, newspaper reporters, court administrators, law
school professors, and leaders of concerned citizens groups. A listing of all
the interviewees and their positions will be found in Appendix C.

The format for these interviews was greatly conditioned by the environment in which the questioning took place. Because of the subject matter
examined, nearly all interviews were conducted with officials who were
concerned with the administration of urban justice. This required most interviews to be held in courthouses, jails, municipal office buildings, and police
stations. With all these locations being in the heart of a criminal justice system
which is operating frenetically to keep pace with an ever expanding workload,
the author's interviews had to accommodate and bend with the exigencies of
this difficult situation. Thus, one was forced to be extremely flexible in interviewing these overworked and harrassed dispensers of justice. It would often
take an hour to merely ask five or six questions because of the constantly
recurring interruptions. There was no solution to this dilemma facing the
author except to possess a great deal of patience and fortitude while maintaining a flexible schedule to account for the inevitable delays and intrusions.
Always one had to remember that he was in search of answers to important
questions and would have to endure these difficulties in order to gain this
information.

Most of the interviewees were helpful and were apologetic about the persis-
tent interruptions. The average interview would last an hour and result in three
to four pages of handwritten notes. By allowing a full week per city, the author
had a sufficient amount of time to meet with each of the informants at their
convenience. It was important also to have at least two to three hours between
interviews because of the uncertainty of length of the interviews or delays during
them. Despite all of the aforementioned hazards and inconveniences, over 100
interviews were conducted. The author strongly believes that the total output

from these interviews gave the project a complete and reliable collection of data on the administration of bail.

Did the results of the personal interviews in the eleven cities agree with the mailed questionnaires sent to those same cities? The author found that the responses were in virtual agreement. This was an important and reassuring discovery since there were so many opportunities for distorting the information gathered by either technique.

Acknowledgements

It should first be noted that every endeavor of this type is a collective venture, dependent upon the help and wisdom of many individuals. I am deeply indebted to the many judges, lawyers, journalists, and other concerned citizens without whose cooperation this book would never have been possible. I sincerely regret that this debt can be repaid only through the meager medium of this acknowledgement.

I must first state my gratitude to the Law Enforcement Assistance Administration of the Department of Justice whose research grant allowed the author to travel extensively throughout the country and gather the necessary information. The views expressed in this book however, are solely those of the author and represent neither the many individuals who aided him nor the Justice Department whose generous aid was so important.

I should like particularly to thank the following individuals to whom I owe a special debt of gratitude: to Stuart Nagel, my advisor whose wisdom and encouragement were essential to the completion of this work, to Oliver Walter and Karl Johnson upon whose patience, friendship, and methodological expertise I could always depend, to Richard Max Bockol and Stephen Franklin whose good hearts and good minds continually served as an inspiration, and most of all to my wife, Marsha, whose love and understanding allowed me to finish this work.

Freedom for Sale

1

An Introduction to the American Bail System

There are currently 160,000 adults behind bars. Nearly half of these individuals have been denied their freedom without having been convicted of any offense. Their only crime was that of poverty.[1] These 78,000 detentioners, because of their inability to raise the required bail, had to await their trials behind prison bars. They are often detained with criminals already convicted and serving sentences. They may be confined on the average in our larger cities from three to six months. These unfortunate individuals are the losers in our system of bail, a system which has its roots in England and as Lord Devlin has pointed out is "as old as the law of England itself." They are losers because they do not possess the financial resources to purchase their pretrial freedom. Why should they be denied this freedom simply because of their financial condition? Let us look at what the legislators and judicary have to tell us about the purpose of this seemingly oppressive system.

The Purpose of Bail

The purpose of bail is indicated to the judiciary, who are the primary administers of the bail system, by their respective state statutes and criminal codes. Although the judiciary varies widely in their implementation of these statutory guidelines, every jurisdiction surveyed in this study with a single exception,[2] was directed to use bail for a singular purpose. This purpose is simply to have the court set bail at an amount which they believe will insure the presence of the defendant at the requested time.[3]

The Georgia statute which controls the operation of the Atlanta bail system is typical of a statutory provision explaining the purpose of bail. In Georgia, bail was found to have a twofold purpose: (1) to prevent punishing the accused before conviction, and (2) to secure his attendance at trial. It goes on to add that any person who has been arrested for any felony other than capital offenses is entitled to bail as a matter of right. For those cases involving a capital offense, bail is allowed only as a matter of discretion by a superior court judge.[4] The concluding section of the Georgia bail statute grants an absolute right to bail for any individual awaiting trial or after conviction pending appeal for a misdemeanor.[5]

As a result of this type of statutory directive, the judges in Georgia (and in most other states) have construed their bail instructions to mean that the amount of bail assessed in each criminal case is left to the discretion of the court, and in the absence of a flagrant abuse, will not be altered.[6] Adding to the ability of judges to control the bail amount without fear of being overruled are the relative scarcity of cases challenging the misuse of judicial power in setting bail. This situation is probably caused by the extremely vague wording of these statutes as well as the deprived economic and social condition of those defendants who would most likely be affected by such questionable bail practices.

As an aid to the judge in setting bail, several state statutes list criteria which the judge should consider when determining the amount. The model for most of these state statutes is Rule 46 (c) of the Federal Rules of Criminal Procedure which requests the judge to inquire into the "nature and circumstances of the offense charged, the weight of the evidence against him, the financial ability of the defendant to give bail and the character of the defendant."[7]

The state guidelines are rarely as complete as the federal model and generally fall into one of two broad categories; those emphasizing the seriousness of the crime as the primary determiner of bail and those urging the courts to stress the community ties and character of the defendant. The Michigan statute is representative of the former category and specifies that the amount of bond "shall be fixed with consideration of the seriousness of the offense charged, the previous criminal record of the defendant, and probability or improbability of his appearing at the trial of the cause."[8]   The Illinois and California statutes are examples of the latter category as they recommend that the judge inquire into the defendant's background, regarding his family ties, employment record, residential stability, and financial condition.[9]

The Washington Experiment: Bail's New Purpose

Through the passage of the District of Columbia Court Reform and Criminal Procedure Act of 1970, a new purpose for bail was legislatively created. The Washington, D.C. courts were now directed not only to set bail at an amount which would assure that the defendant would appear for his court date but were also instructed to determine and detain without bail any defendant who would endanger "the safety of any other person or the community."[10]

Critics of the American bail system are quick to point out that this supposedly "new" purpose of bail which is designed to preventively detain dangerous defendants, has been operating in an informal manner in most cities for as long as courts and judges have been setting bail. Nearly 300 public officials who are associated with the administration of bail in their community, were asked if they thought their city was using an informal system of preventive detention. Such an informal system goes into operation when the judge identifies a defendant who he believes will present a threat to society if released while awaiting trial. When one of these potentially dangerous defendants is spotted by the judge, his bail will be set at an amount which the judge believes is sufficiently in excess of the defendant's financial means so as to guarantee his pretrial detention. Nearly half of the respondents (48 percent), representing seventy-two cities located throughout the country, *agreed* that such a system of pretrial detention was actually taking place in their town. It is interesting to also note that 54 percent of this national sample thought that the courts ought to be using this type of procedure more often and 54 percent believed that by increasing the use of this system, the crime rate would be reduced.[11]

The uniqueness of the District of Columbia's preventive detention system therefore does not lie in its discovery of a new approach to the bail question but rather in its willingness to clearly spell out the operation of such a system thereby endowing it with a previously unachieved air of legitimacy. Congress then, attempted to create a preventive detention system which would be able to identify and detain those defendants posing a threat to the safety of the community while also being careful not to violate any of the defendant's constitutional rights.

The bill first noted that preventive detention would be used only on certain types of defendants. These categories included defendants charged with dangerous crimes, those convicted of a crime of violence, and those accused of any offense which threatens the safety of any prospective witness or juror. All classificatory terms such as dangerous crimes or violent crimes are carefully and explicitly defined. It is against these types of defendants that the U.S. Attorney may make an oral motion for pretrial detention hearing before a judicial officer.[12] The hearing must be held within five days. This hearing will determine whether or not there is clear and convincing evidence that the safety of the community or any other person cannot be assured by the defendant's release. Present at the hearing is a representative of the U.S. Attorney's Office, the judge, the defendant and his lawyer, and all other necessary officials. The defendant is allowed to offer evidence on his own behalf and the evidence need not conform to the regular rules of admissibility. The testimony given during this hearing shall not be admissable on the issue of guilt in any other judicial proceeding.[13]

If the defendant is found by the judicial officer to require pretrial detention he may quickly appeal this decision. This is done by moving to the court having original jurisdiction over the case, where a prompt determination will be made. For those unfortunate defendants who are detained, they are placed upon an expedited calendar and are kept a maximum of sixty days from the hearing, unless their trial is in progress. After sixty days, if the defendant is still not tried, he must be placed before a judicial officer who will determine his conditions of release.[14]

After listing these elaborate procedures for pretrial detention, it is ironic to then report that nearly every public official which was interviewed in Washington, D.C., regardless of whether he was a judge, prosecutor, or defense counsel, agreed that the entire preventive detention program appeared to be a "red-herring" issue. The consensus was that these procedures were so complex and burdened down with so many due process guarantees, that it would prove an impossible addition to an already overworked and understaffed court system. The increase in manpower, time, and space necessary to administer pretrial detention hearings make these hearings impractical except in the most pressing cases. If the criminal courts of the District of Columbia were to follow the dictates of this legislation precisely, it was estimated by several public officials interviewed that the following changes would have to be made: (a) a minimum of two more courtrooms to be made available for at least sixteen hours per day; (b) an addition of one to two full-time judicial officers to supervise these hearings; (c) a staff increase of four to five U.S. Attorneys specializing in pretrial detention hearings, as well as conducting investigations related to these hearings; and (d) an annex constructed on to the present city jail to house the increased numbers of detained defendants since the present facilities are filled to capacity. Because of the necessity for all these changes if the statute was to be strictly implemented, most city officials concluded that it would be used in only the most extreme cases.

A combined research effort by the Georgetown Institute of Criminal Law and Procedure and the Vera Institute of Justice has documented the correctness of these skeptical views which minimized the impact of the preventive detention program on the city's criminal justice system. Their report entitled *Preventive Detention in the District of Columbia: The First Ten Months* arrived at the following conclusion:

> The chief finding of the first ten months of observation has been the virtual non-use of the preventive detention law. The law was invoked with respect to only 20 of a total of more than 6000 felony defendants who entered the D.C. Criminal Justice system during the period. Of the 20, nine were subjected to preventive detention hearings, and eight of the nine were ordered preventively detained. Two others were held in preventive detention at judicial initiative, without a detention hearing. Of the 10 preventive detention orders, five were reversed on review or reconsideration, and one was dismissed when the grand jury refused to return an indictment on the underlying charges. Six of the 20 defendants obtained pre-trial release, four after rescission of preventive detention. [15]

Despite the great national notoriety given to the preventive detention concept and the fact that most public officials favored use of such a procedure, preventive detention appears to be a rather localized issue (the Washington, D.C. area), no longer commanding national attention. As the author toured the country and interviewed numerous public officials and concerned citizens, it was discovered that preventive detention was viewed as a problem restricted to the crime ravaged nation's capitol. In none of the cities visited was there a movement developing to enact similar preventive detention procedures. Most informants agreed that either their court systems were accomplishing preventive detention informally without recourse to enacting formal legislation, or that it simply was not needed in their community.

The Uses of Bail

Thus far we have learned the statutory purposes of bail. Let us now examine how the courts actually interpret and implement these legislative directives. It will be shown that the courts use bail to accomplish a variety of objectives, some of which are clearly antithetical to the statutory provisions.

The most frequently articulated objective is to use the bail system as a means for ensuring that the defendant appears for trial. This objective is congruent with the statutory purposes discussed in the previous section. The theory behind this objective is that a defendant will appear for his trial in order to collect the amount of money which he has posted for his pretrial release. Thus it is believed that this fear of losing the money paid into the court will serve as a sufficient incentive to prevent the defendant from skipping town. The validity of this theory has been frequently challenged. A San Francisco defense attorney in an interview with the author offered a most persuasive argument refuting the worth of such an hypothesis by stating: "Those defendants who have the money to afford bail are also the most able to absorb the financial loss as well as have the financial capabilities to flee the jurisdiction. On the other hand, improverished defendants who could not even afford a bus ticket out of town are the very ones who cannot make bail and are detained awaiting trial."[16]

Students of the criminal justice system have been aware of this paradoxical situation for over forty years. In drawing his conclusions to his classic study of the Chicago bail system, Arthur Beeley commented in 1927 that "The present system [of bail], in too many instances, neither guarantees security to society nor safeguards the rights of the accused. The system is lax with those with whom it should be stringent and stringent with those with whom it could safely be less severe."[17]

A second use of bail is as a punitive measure. In the majority of cities investigated, the police were found to be in the habit of overcharging suspicious defendants.[18] The police defend this procedure by stating that they know the defendant has committed an illegal act, and their only problem is in determining exactly which act. The police realize that because of constitutional guarantees they can only delay and interrogate the defendant for a brief period of time. They also realize and are angered by the fact that the defendant often posts bail so rapidly he is out on the street before the patrolman has completed the arrest report. A final irritant to the police, which encourages them to engage in this overcharging tactic is their belief that because of current plea-bargaining practices the defendant is frequently able to have his original charge significantly reduced in exchange for a guilty plea.

Due to these various irritations and fears that the defendant is "beating the system" and thereby humiliating the police, the police therefore seek to punish the defendant by charging him with a serious crime. These serious charges usually result in the judge setting a very high bond and so the defendant is often unable to raise the required amount. The defendant must then remain in jail until either the charge or bail amount is reduced, or have his friends or family raise enough money to pay the designated bond. Since most judges assume that anyone in their courtroom is guilty of something, or else they would not have been arrested by the police in the first place, they are willing to go along with this informal system of preventive detention. By setting a bond which the defendant is unable to raise or at least will cause him some temporary financial hardship, the judge is able to join the police in punishing selected defendants. The documentation of such pretrial detention as "punishment" will be presented in Chapter 5 where the horrible conditions currently found in our nation's pretrial detention facilities will be described.

A third purpose of bail is found in the premise underlying the Washington, D.C. preventive detention program. This purpose is to protect society from defendants who are likely to commit additional crimes or threaten to harrass witnesses and jurors. As noted previously, most judges use an informal preventive detention system. The judges are able to alter the amount of bail in most cities because they are given complete discretion in felony cases as to the amount of bail. Many judges interviewed frankly admit using these arbitrary procedures. A judge, in reputedly progressive Alameda County, California, told the author in an interview that "if a guy is before me and I think he is a bad risk I simply won't let him out. I will keep raising the bail to an unreachable amount. The difficulty is that there is no way to know what he'll do once released." [19] An excellent study of the Detroit criminal justice system by Donald McIntyre entitled *Law Enforcement in the Metropolis*, reports how Detroit judges manipulate the bail amount to detain a defendant wanted by another jurisdiction:

> When the three defendants were arraigned on the warrant, the judge had several dozen requests from other police departments throughout the U.S. to hold the defendants. The judge set the bond for each one of them at $25,000, feeling sure that none of them

would be able to make it. The gangster's moll, however, was almost ready to post this large bond when she was again called into court and the bond was raised to $30,000. She did not post the bond.[20]

The purposes of bail thus far discussed have been punitive and protective. A fourth, though less frequently used, purpose is rehabilitative and primarily reserved for juveniles or first offenders. A small minority of judges believe that bail may be manipulated so as to detain these youthful offenders for a short period of time. By giving these inexperienced defendants a taste of the harshness of pretrial detention, they may be intimidated into following more law abiding paths upon release from detention.

All of our previous uses of bail have been adopted primarily for use with defendants accused of felonies and the more serious misdemeanors. A final use of bail is its manipulation in misdemeanor cases as a pressuring device to force defendants into waiving their right to an attorney and thereby unclog the typically overcrowded and heavily backlogged calendar. This process begins with the defendant being brought before the magistrate or judge for his initial appearance. The defendant is notified by the judge that if he does not have an attorney (which is the condition of the large majority of defendants at the initial appearance), he will be granted a continuance of approximately two to three weeks in order to obtain one. The judge, however, also takes great care in notifying the defendant that if he chooses to waive his right to an attorney, he can take care of the case at this initial appearance and terminate the entire proceeding within ten minutes.

In most cities the judge makes it perfectly clear that he favors the defendant going to trial immediately, waiving his opportunity for having a defense counsel argue his case. Because of the judge's control over the defendant's bond, there is little doubt in the defendant's mind that a substantial bond will be set if a continuance is requested. Thus a defendant may have an opportunity to obtain a lawyer, but it is at the expense of probably losing his pretrial freedom. Rumors also circulated throughout these criminal courtrooms that if you were found guilty after requesting a continuance, your sentence would be much more severe than if you were found guilty at the initial hearing. Most defendants grasped the significance of the judge's control over their pretrial release and agreed to have their case disposed of at the first opportunity, willingly relinquishing their chance for legal counsel in exchange for more lenient treatment by the judge.

This distorted use of bail appears to be a national phenomenon. It was observed taking place in every city visited, and was especially visible in Atlanta, Georgia and Indianapolis, Indiana. The following is a typical scenario at these initial appearances and was noted by a Pittsburgh, Pennsylvania, journalist as he discovered three haggard defendants in the city's night court, listening to the statement: "If you want a lawyer and qualify, then you can wait for the public defender in the morning, the magistrate says. But he warns that they will have to post bond if they do not want to spend the night in jail. None has the money for bond. They waive their right to an attorney and after the five minute hearing are found guilty of obstructing traffic."[21]

Methods of Obtaining Pretrial Release

Cash Bail

A defendant may obtain his pretrial release through one of a wide variety of procedures. The most frequently used method is cash bail which simply means that the defendant raises the required bond either through direct payment to the court of the full amount or with the help of a bondsman. The amount required is determined primarily by the specific crime which the defendant is accused of committing. The following are the basic ways in which the amount of bail is set: (a) it can be set through reference to a fixed bail schedule, where the defendant merely has to find the crime he is accused of on this list, and next to it will be the amount of bail necessary to gain pretrial release for that charge; (b) the judge may have complete discretion to set bail at any amount he desires as long as it is not found to be "excessive or unreasonable"; (c) a judge may have the use of a bail schedule as a guideline which recommends upper and lower limits for bail on a particular offense but the judge maintains the authority to select the exact amount within these limits.

Once the defendant has learned the amount of bail required for his pretrial release, he can use his personal savings as well as loans from family and friends to raise the full amount of the bond. If he shows up in court for all of his required appearances, the entire amount will usually be given back to him. However, if the defendant cannot raise the full amount himself, he may go to a bondsman and pay him a fee to put up the necessary bail in his behalf. The bondsman has complete discretion in deciding whom he will select as clients, just as any other businessman. If a defendant is turned down by a bondsman, his only recourse is to attempt to raise the full amount himself.

Through the author's seventy-two-city survey, it was found that 65 percent of all defendants arrested for misdemeanors and felonies were able to obtain their pretrial release through the use of cash bonds. Of this total, 44 percent used a bondsman while the remaining 21 percent raised the money themselves. Since these figures are based upon estimates provided by knowledgeable officials, an attempt was made to travel to selected major cities and collect accurate court statistics from official documents in order to replicate the earlier estimates and see how close the two sets of figures were in agreement. Table 1-1 presents the percentage of defendants utilizing cash bail in four of the cities visited where exact records were kept.

Table 1-1
Release on Cash Bail: Four-City Comparison (1969 Figures)

	Released by Surety Bonds	Released by 10% Plan	Detained
Washington	15.2%	4.5%	23.8%
Chicago	52.1%	29.0%	16.1%
Detroit	41.3%	–	25.8%
Indianapolis	55.0%	–	16.0%
National Average (From 72-city study)	65.0%	a	15.0%

[a]10% Plan in use in only Illinois and Washington, D.C. in 1969.

Ten Per Cent Bail Deposit Provision

In 1964 the state of Illinois, in an attempt at improving the defendant's chances for pretrial release and also striking out against the bail-bonding industry, enacted the Ten Per Cent Bail Deposit Provision. Since that date at least two additional jurisdictions have developed similar procedures (Washington, D.C., and Pennsylvania). In 1969 in Chicago, 36 percent of the defendants were able to obtain their pretrial release using the state's Ten Per Cent Plan.

This Bail Deposit Provision allows the defendant to gain his release by paying a percentage of the total bond to the court. For example, in Illinois it is 10 percent while Pennsylvania has selected an 8 percent rate. Thus a defendant who has his bail set at $1000 need only pay $100 to the court to obtain his release. If the defendant fails to appear for court appearances he owes the court the entire $1000. However, if the defendant does show up in court at the appointed time, 90 percent of his original payment to the court (90 dollars) will be refunded to him and the remaining 10 percent (10 dollars) will be used to cover costs of administering the program.

The defendant therefore only loses 1 percent of the original bond if he appears in court. If a bondsmen would have been used, the entire 10 percent bonding fee, which is usually charged, would be lost. In our example, if the defendant would have gone to a bondsmen instead of raising the Bail Deposit Provision himself, he would have lost $100. This Bail Deposit Provision clearly represents a direct threat to the bail bonding industry. It is interesting to note that in Illinois where the bondsmen have been statutorily eliminated from operating, they are now often switching hats and becoming small loan agents charging defendants inflated interest rates on the money needed by the defendants to raise the 10 percent of the original bond. Although many bondsmen adopted this new profession following passage of the Illinois act in 1964, in the last few years they have given up their temporary small loan agencies and have drifted into a wide variety of new professions.

The continued use of the Ten Per Cent Bail Deposit Provision in Illinois is threatened by a pending federal court case, despite its apparent success throughout the state. In 1971 the United States Supreme Court granted certiorari on a case raising the issue of whether the 10 percent plan was in violation of the equal protection clause of the 14th Amendment (*Schilb v. Kuebel* 264 N.E. 2d. 377). The controversy surrounds the 1 percent payment of the bond which the Illinois plan uses for court costs while the cash bond is completely returned to the defendant if he appears in court. Thus it is argued that a defendant who is wealthy enough to pay the court the full cash bond will eventually have it all returned to him, while the poorer defendant who can only raise the 10 percent deposit provision will still lose 1 percent of the total value of the bond even if he appears in court. There is then charged to be a violation of the equal protection clause of the Fourteenth Amendment because the wealthier defendant who can afford the total cash bond is being financially favored by the Illinois court system.

Property Bond

In three-quarters of the cities studied, the local court will allow for a defendant to be released through a property bond. This method of release provides for property of the defendant, his family or friends, to be offered as bail in lieu of a cash payment. The following rules of the Supreme Bench of Baltimore City regarding property bonds are representative of judicial rules regulating the use of such bonds:

1. Property shall not be accepted as bail in one case while pledged in another.
2. Property offered as bail, must be situated in Baltimore City.
3. Property shall not be accepted as bail if all liens and encumbrances thereon exceed 50 percent of the said tax assessed.
4. The total value of unencumbered property offered as bail shall be 50 percent more than the amount of bail required; if such property is encumbered, its value shall be 75 percent over and above such encumberances. [22]

Although most cities do have court rules providing for the use of property bonds, only two cities visited were found to use this method of release with any regularity. They were Atlanta and St. Louis. Interviews in both cities, however, indicated two basic problems associated with the use of property bonds. The first problem is what to do if the defendant fails to appear in court and the property is supposed to be seized by the city or state. In an interview with members of the St. Louis Criminal Court Clerk's Office, the author was told that forfeiture on property bonds creates a moral dilemma for their office. The difficulty is caused by naive and altruistic individuals who are willing to sign a property bond in order for the defendant to gain his pretrial release. These good-hearted individuals never consider what the possible consequences will be if the defendant fails to appear. Because these are usually respectable citizens who are unfamiliar with the operation of the criminal courts, they never look into the sanctions for forfeitures which allow the courts to hold liens on their property which may be claimed by the city at any time. The unintended result of this situation is to pressure the clerk's office into ignoring enforcement of the law, for fear of having to remove the property of these well-intentioned but naive citizens. Currently, state legislators are trying to correct the administration of property bonds in St. Louis and throughout Missouri by clarifying the procedures and sanctions. Like most other attempts at reforming the bail system, especially those which challenge the bondmen's financial condition, it is a long way from discussion to enactment. [23]

The second problem created by the use of property bonds is most prevalent in Atlanta, Georgia. An Atlanta bondsmen told the author that several of the city's businessmen had misused the property bond procedure by manipulating one piece of property to be used for several bonds. These businessmen had become pseudo-bondsmen, without being threatened by the traditional risks inherent in the bonding industry; the payment of the total bond in cases of forfeiture. The businessmen, who usually own several pieces of real estate in the city, would contact defendants arraigned on high bails and offer to sign property bonds for them if they would pay them a fee which was much less than that charged by the bondsmen. The businessmen were shrewd enough to realize that because of the enforcement dilemma noted previously, they ran no real risk of losing their property even if the defendant decided to skip town. Even though the Atlanta District Attorney's Office was found to be quite rigorous in collecting forfeitures from bondsmen on sureties, there is no record of their office calling for a lien on someone's real estate due to a forfeiture on a property bond. The understaffed clerk's office was unable to cross-check the illegal practice of multiple use of a single property. It is safe to predict that with their potential political clout, the bondsmen should soon be flexing their lobbying muscles and putting an end to this illegal procedure which is undermining their industry. [24] Private individuals are not the only group which was found to be misusing property bonds. In Baltimore, bondsmen may use property bonds in lieu of surety bonds, and it has recently been discovered that several of them are using the same piece of property to cover several defendants. [25]

Conditions of Release

Conditions of release may be categorized as both a traditional method of release as well as a reform procedure. In most cities where the judge is allowed a great deal of discretion in setting bonds, he may on occasion replace or supplement the surety bond (also termed cash bond) with the imposition of a series of conditions placing certain restrictions on the defendant's pretrial conduct. Examples of such court-ordered restrictions are directives forcing the defendant to return to work or school or prohibiting him from certain areas of the city or associating with particular individuals thought to be exerting a bad influence.

In Washington, D.C. the Court of General Sessions imposes these conditions with great regularity. The *Report of the Judicial Council Committee* indicated that these nonfinancial conditions were set in 48 percent of the cases.[26] In addition to the types of conditions described in the preceding paragraph, judges in the District's criminal court system have formulated conditions forcing defendants to be tested for drug addiction. The primary weakness of this program of conditional release is the inability of the court, in conjunction with the D.C. Bail Agency, to enforce these conditions in a meaningful manner. Presently the Bail Agency is given responsibility for enforcing these conditions of release and they are simply unable, given their plethora of additional responsibilities, to adequately supervise all of these defendants during this pretrial period. The result is a rather haphazardly administered program. When a violator is finally apprehended, and this is a rare occurrence, the court is usually too busy to take any meaningful action on the case, and he is returned to the streets after a new bond is set or additional conditions imposed.[27]

Personal Bond

Personal bond is a method of release whereby the judge determines the defendant to be of such a reliable character and possessing sufficient community ties, that he may be released on his own signature without having to raise any financial security. A minor adaptation of this procedure is to release the defendant to a third party who agrees to be responsible for him and becomes his personal surety. In this instance, both the defendant and his surety must be approved by the judge. This method of release has a different name in nearly every city but all follow the basic procedures just outlined. In Detroit it is called personal sureties, in St. Louis and Philadelphia it is nominal bond, while in the California cities it is termed own recognizance release.

The basic principle is identical with that of the bail reform projects to be discussed in Chapters 6 through 8. The major difference is that in the traditional system, personal bond release is the product of the judge's inquiries into the defendant's background and the decision to grant a personal bond is continually under the sole control of the judge. In distinction to this, the bail reform projects operate as an objective fact-finding mechanism to uncover and verify a defendant's background and then make its recommendation to the appropriate judge who makes the final decision as to whether or not to grant a personal bond.

Most of the personal bonds which are offered to defendants are for those accused of the less serious crimes. This is also caused by the fact that approximately 80 percent of the country's bail reform projects handle only felonies and serious misdemeanors, leaving the misdemeanant to the mercy of the court. In only one city visited has the court refused to follow a policy of personal bond. In the Circuit Court of St. Louis City the judges voted *en banc* that in their interpretation of the state judicial rules, they did not have the authority to release a defendant on his own recognizance. The most common explanation for this unique stand is that the St. Louis judiciary have been under an uncommon amount of criticism from the local newspapers whenever one of the defendants they release commits an additional crime, during the pretrial period.

Overview of the American Bail System: Variations and Distinctions

So far we have discovered that the narrow statutory objectives of bail are twisted and contorted by those individuals who control the nation's pretrial release system. The results are a system used to punish, rehabilitate, and control defendants during their pretrial existence. In order to more fully understand the complexities and variations in this system, eleven of the nation's largest bail systems will be briefly described. Special attention will be paid to the unique features found in each city. Together, these eleven sketches form a composite picture of the realities of the administration of bail in our major urban centers.[28]

Indianapolis

An interesting feature of the Indianapolis bail system is found in its pretrial detention facility where all defendants are forced to use a special phone system. Both ends of the conversation are broadcasted loudly throughout the entire facility. The rationale offered for this blatant invasion of privacy and resulting cacophony, is that it is necessary for maintaining security. One must wonder how many jail escapes and other threats to the building's security are actually thwarted by these measures. One can only imagine what happens when some poor unsuspecting visitor brings a specially baked cake to a prisoner.

The administration of bail for felons in the Indianapolis Criminal Division

Court is in sharp contrast to the flexible treatment of misdemeanants. Unlike most cities, the judges have not been given discretionary power to determine bail in felony cases. The amount is fixed by a fee schedule for each felony. Although these figures have not been revised in fifteen years, they are still quite high in comparison to most cities. Any attorney wishing to challenge this amount will take his petition to the bailiff or court clerk who turns out to be the key administrator of the city's bail reduction program. The attorney supplies the clerk with as much background information on the defendant as possible. The clerk then checks with the detective assigned to the case as to the prior record and arrest report of the defendant. After all this information is collected, it is turned over to the judge who can rule or call all parties in for an evidentiary hearing. This entire process of bail reduction is used very sparingly and usually dominated by the court clerk rather than the judge.

Probably the most interesting aspect of the bail system in Indianapolis is the activities of their bondsmen. Simply by perusing the city's newspapers during the past year (1970-71) one receives the distinct impression that the city's bondsmen must be either buffoons or criminals. Million dollar bonding companies becoming liquidated by the state, bondsmen having their licenses revoked, bondsmen being indicted for tax evasion, bondsmen indicted by the grand jury in linkage with an underworld crime empire, are but a few of the nonprofessional involvements of Indianapolis bondsmen during this period. Despite adequate legislation in the state statutes, the bondsmen are very poorly supervised and are frequently able to avoid paying the state treasury on client forfeitures.

Atlanta

Atlanta contrasts sharply with the Indianapolis system in the great degree of flexibility and informality with which the amount of bail is determined in each case. From the police station officer to the superior court judge, each public official, working with or without the help of a bail schedule, possesses some discretionary authority to set bail at any amount which he chooses. There are of course practical limitations upon this power to alter the bail figure but relative to other cities the Atlanta system seems to place a great amount of discretion in the hands of judicial and police officers.

The police department, which usually assumes no role in the administration of bail in most cities, plays a most significant role in the determination of the amount of bail set for an individual during his initial appearance in court. At this commitment hearing the defendant charged with a felony will be notified by the judge as to whether his case will be bound over to the Fulton County Superior Court and if so, the amount of his bond. This amount is determined by what the police officer recommends to the presiding judge. The author had the opportunity to sit next to the judge for three consecutive days of commitment hearings and in each felony case the judge would either ask the arresting officer for his recommendation on the amount of bail or if the policeman was unable to offer a specific amount, the judge would state an amount, and then turn to the policeman for his approval.[29]

The District Attorney's Office, another organization which is usually not associated with the administration of bail, also performs several key functions in the Atlanta bail system. First, the D.A.'s Office is responsible for supervising bail bondsmen and collecting all forfeitures. The bondsmen are given only four weeks in which to locate their clients who have failed to appear in court. If the bondsmen can show that they have honestly tried to find their forfeiting clients, they will be given a 25 percent discount on the amount of the original bond. The D.A.s also are quite influential in convincing the judge to raise or lower the amount of bond after a defendant has been formally indicted.

Oakland

The Oakland bail system operates fairly smoothly with no real problems or distinguishing features. The only difficulty which continues to complicate the city's administration of bail is the large number of transients who fall within the city's jurisdiction. This group is consistently involved with the courts. Their excessive number may be explained by the proximity of Berkeley and other attractions in the Bay Area such as its comfortable all-year climatic conditions which allows these people to live out of doors. When these transients are arrested, frequently for narcotics violations, they are unable to make bail either because they have no money or family to raise the required amount or because many bondsmen refuse to take them as clients. With no fixed address and an unverifiable background, these defendants are poor risks for both the judge and the bondsmen. As a result, over 50 percent of all felons in Alameda County are unable to gain pretrial release and are detained prior to their trial, a percentage more than twice the national average for detained defendants. This has put a great strain on their already overcrowded detention facilities.

San Fransicso

Similar to Oakland, the bail system in San Francisco was characterized by most informants as being generally fair and effective. The ability of the San Francisco bail system to allow for the speedy release of defendants was one of its strongest assets. Although there has been no predetermined felony bail schedule since January 1970, and the judges may exercise complete discretion in assessing the amount of bail, very few complaints were heard about excessive or arbitrary bail amounts. The only occasion for a high bail was when a case had received a great deal of notoriety and the public was thought to be overconcerned. This type of case appeared to be a rather rare occurrence. As succeeding chapters will indicate, the San Francisco bail system and its bail reform project were the most effective and equitable operations of the cities investigated.

Keeping with these high standards, the city's regulation of bondsmen is superior to nearly every other city in the country. The state insurance commissioner works closely with several judicial officials to closely supervise the bondsmen. The records of each bonding company are carefully scrutinized and the abundance of forms required for each transaction allows the city and state officials to maintain a tight rein over the bondsmen. As a result of this bureaucratization of the bonding industry, nearly all of the prior collusive activities between bondsmen, policemen, and various court officials have been eliminated. The sole remaining problem for the bondsmen, apart from the great amount of time spent filling out these forms is that it still takes a substantial bribe of certain policemen to enlist their help in rounding up clients who have forfeited bail and are hiding out in some corner of the city.[30]

St. Louis

The operation of the bail system in St. Louis appears to be an extremely visible and political phenomena when compared with the other cities visited. The visibility is caused by a very active pair of municipal newspapers whose conservative editorial policy has resulted in a very tough law and order position. Any crimes which were committed by a defendant released on bail received a frontpage headline coverage by the press. The result of this media concern and focus has been the creation of a very cautious judiciary who are unwilling to risk their prestige and reputation for any defendant's pretrial freedom. The city's circuit court bench has recently decided *en banc* that they cannot release a defendant on his own recognizance under the existing state rules controlling court procedures, despite the fact that judges in other parts of the state have been ROR'ing (releasing on their own recognizance) defendants for several years.

The political aspect of the situation becomes evident when one realizes the great amount of political efficacy possessed by the city's bondsmen. The names of St. Louis bondsmen are to be found in key Democratic party positions at the city, state, and congressional levels. The necessary legislation to provide for the circuit court's releasing defendants on their own recognizance will probably fail to materialize because of the bondsmen's political clout as well as the timidity of the city's judiciary to confront the newspaper's criticism.

Washington, D.C.

The most distinctive aspect of the District of Columbia's bail operation is the extensive use of nonfinancial conditions placed upon the defendant during his pretrial release. In 1969 it was reported that 48 percent of the defendants were given these conditions.[31] In comparison with the other cities evaluated, the District's system, while it appears to have the most humane objectives, is also plagued by the worst administrative control and resulting mistakes. Having to work under so many jurisdictions and tiers of authority as well as receiving their defendants from a pair of overlapping court systems are the primary explanations for this confusing state of affairs.

It may still be too early to offer a definitive pronouncement as to the effectiveness of the city's preventive detention program. It will be interesting to see if the numerous court officials interviewed who termed the preventive detention statute a "red-herring" issue were correct in their diagnosis. The high rate of crime committed while defendants were released and awaiting trial continues to be a debatable issue despite the finality of the Bureau of Standard's report on the subject which supposedly laid the question to rest. Their $60,000 investigation revealed that the District had an 11.7 percent rearrest rate for the four-week period studied.[32]

Balitmore

The Baltimore Municipal Court system differs from most because of its regionalized structure. There are nine police districts with a municipal court housed in each district station. Until 1970 this arrangement provided the police with an opportunity to influence the administration of bail. The police rarely abused this privilege and usually offered only arrest reports and prior criminal records if available. Beginning in 1971, as a result of a 50 percent increase in the size of the State's Attorney's Office, they are now able to have an assistant state's attorney in each of the police district courts. Besides serving as a filter for the police department's background information, they may also help to curtail the overcharging tendencies of the police which occasionally occur. It is hoped that by placing these assistant state's attorneys so close to the point of initiation of the criminal justice system, the courts may have the necessary legal sieve to unclog the system by removing weak arrests as soon as possible.

The municipal court judges rely heavily upon a fixed bail schedule for both felonies and misdemeanors. The amount of bail assigned to felonies has been acknowledged to be quite inflated. The supreme bench of the city, which tries the felony cases, is aware of this problem and frequently accepts bond reduction petitions. The weakness of this review procedure is that by the time the defendant has his case presented to the supreme bench he has already been detained in jail three to six weeks.

Detroit

One of the key problems in the Detroit bail system is that it is occasionally administered (at least for felonies) by visiting judges from jurisdictions outside of Detroit. These judges have been accused by the black community of failing to possess the necessary degree of empathy and understanding of the defendants and their backgrounds. The visiting judges were called in to Detroit because of the city's extreme shortage of criminal court judges and the ever-increasing caseload.

Following a weeks observations in the preliminary arraignment court which sets bail in all felony cases, it was discovered that a detective sergeant was the dominant figure in the determination of bail. His specific title was arraignment officer and his job was to represent the complaining witness, who was usually the detective in charge of the case. By having an arraignment officer permanently assigned to this court, the detectives were able to avoid having to take time out from their busy schedules and waste a half day sitting in the courtroom. The arraignment officer controlled the flow of all relevant information to the judge as he wrestled with the question of determining the amount of bail. It was observed that not only did the arraignment officer have complete control over this information but he frequently went so far as to offer a recommended bail amount to the judge in most cases. One of the judges was found to accept this recommendation in virtually every case, rarely asking the defendant anything. Even though the arraignment officer appeared to be extremely fair and competent, this procedure which displaced the traditional role of the court is a questionable practice and easily open to abuse.

Philadelphia

A unique feature of the Philadelphia system is the extremely important role played by the District Attorney's Office in the administration of bail. In addition to the procedural rules establishing the District Attorney's Office as a key functionary in the bail system, the present District Attorney (Arlen Specter) is a powerful political personage. This involvement in the bail system may be seen as simply another manifestation of his department's pervasive interest in all aspects of the city's criminal justice system.

Most criticism of the city's pretrial detention facility focuses upon the jails where the defendants must spend their many months awaiting trial.

In Philadelphia, the Holmesburg Prison was in such deplorable condition that it sparked a riot in 1969. Additional indications of the hardships facing a detained defendant in Philadelphia was a recent expose by a prominent city lawyer, Alan Davis, which showed a large number of inmates being raped and beaten by fellow prisoners as they were being transported in police vans from the Holmesburg Prison to City Hall for their court appearances.[33]

Los Angeles

Similar to Philadelphia, the Los Angeles District Attorney takes a very active part in the administration of bail. Their office will make a formal written recommendation to the judge in all serious cases as to the amount of bail. In contrast to Philadelphia, the Los Angeles judges do not have to follow this recommendation and are ultimately free to set any amount which they decide.

One surprising development in the Los Angeles bail system is the interest of the court bailiffs in the various municipal courts in administering an Own Recognizance program for misdemeanors (The present OR unit handles only felonies). A representative of the D.A.'s Office surmised that the bailiffs reform tendencies were sparked by the fear that their jobs were soon to be swallowed up by the County Sheriff's Department. The bailiffs were thus seeking to create a new rationale for their continued existence.

Chicago

The Chicago bail system is presently under the state of Illinois' Ten Per Cent Bail Deposit Provision which has also served to eliminate the bail bonding industry. Despite the good intentions of this act, it has backfired on many poor defendants whom it was designed to help because of an inflationary rise in the amount of bail required for certain crimes. Without the financial aid of bonds-men and facing rising bond costs, defendants are forced either to hope to be released on their own recognizance or wait in jail for their trial. The Ten Per Cent Provision is still used by many defendants and in 1969 over 100,000 defendants were able to obtain their pretrial release through this procedure.

The city of Chicago has provided the annals of judicial bail bond abuse a legendary character in the infamous Judge Louis Kizas whose heroics are pre-served for posterity in the 1968 Chicago Crime Commission's Annual Report. It should be noted that Judge Kizas was suspended from the bench in May 1967 but he had sufficient time in office to build a legacy that will never be forgotten. One example of this man's unique style, was his notoriety as the only member of the city's judiciary to advertise his ability to perform marriage ceremonies in the yellow pages of the telephone directory.[34]

2

The Administration of Bail: The Procedures

From Arrest until First Judicial Appearance

The administration of bail commences when the defendant is arrested by a police officer. If the arrest is made on the basis of a warrant, the defendant can often find the amount of his bail stated on the warrant. Once the defendant is taken into custody and booked, he should be able to obtain his pretrial release by simply posting the required bond with the police officer in charge of the stationhouse. The decision as to the amount of bail has been previously made by the judge who authorized the warrant. The majority of arrests, however, are made by a police officer without a warrant. They are based upon the officer's belief that there is reasonable cause to suspect the defendant of violating the law. These defendants usually must wait until they appear before a judge or magistrate for their bond to be determined.

How long must a defendant wait before he will see a judge and be notified as to the amount of his bond? Most states follow the requirement found in the Federal Rules of Criminal Procedure that states that the arraignment should be "without unnecessary delay." In the Mallory case the Supreme Court of the United States clarified this vague guideline by finding that a ten-hour police interrogation following apprehension and prior to arraignment was a violation of this federal requirement.[1]

Despite the general acceptance of this doctrine, several police departments have objected vigorously to the Mallory rule. They view it as another example of judicial interference limiting police effectiveness. Specifically, it poses a serious limitation upon their ability to interrogate suspects. In an attempt to circumvent these judicially imposed restrictions, several police departments were found attempting to delay as long as possible the actual "booking" of the suspect.

In St. Louis, after a defendant is arrested he is taken to the nearest station-house where the police have twenty hours to decide whether or not to turn him over to the Circuit Attorney's Office (prosecuting attorney) and allow them to place formal charges. The police use the twenty-hour period to complete a rigorous investigation of the case and conduct an intensive interrogation of the suspect. It is hoped that by the conclusion of this interrogation period, the police will have uncovered sufficient evidence to allow the Circuit Attorney to prosecute the defendant for a specified charge.

21

Detroit policemen attempt to evade the Mallory Rule by making "arrests for investigation." This seemingly unconstitutional practice finds the police taking into custody any suspect whenever there is a possibility of criminal act due to the defendant's possession of certain suspicious objects, his resemblance to a wanted fugitive, or simply being in the wrong place at the wrong time. A person arrested for "investigation" is not charged with a crime and his arrest is designated as "preliminary" in police records. Once detained, the suspect is referred to the detectives in the precinct where he was arrested. The detectives proceed to question him until the suspicions surrounding the defendant's arrest are satisfactorily verified. If the suspect is kept in this "investigative detention" for more than twenty-four hours, higher police officials must be notified. In cases involving holdups, car thefts, or any crime involving specialized police units, the defendant may be sent to the particular unit involved for an additional twelve to twenty-four hours for clearance by them.[2] As the Defender's Association of Detroit has stated, the real harm of these investigative arrests is to sanction and indirectly encourage weak or harrassing arrests of suspects who are then allowed to wait in jail for a day or two with no opportunity for release through bail or any other means.[3]

Bail cannot be determined until the defendant has been told the specific crimes of which he is accused. Thus, by postponing the booking procedure where the defendant should be notified of the charges against him, the police have an opportunity to question the defendant for several hours before he can obtain his pretrial release through the payment of the required bail. The only way to expedite this booking procedure is for the defendant to have his lawyer file a writ of *habeas corpus*. Even this procedure may prove to be of little consequence since it requires many hours to complete the necessary procedures. Morris Wexler commenting in the *Chicago Bar Record* on the difficulty of using these writs to force the Chicago police into booking the defendant writes: "An additional problem with this procedure (securing writs of *habeas corpus*) is it is only available while the criminal court is in session or approximately 10 a.m. to 4 p.m. on weekdays and 10–12 a.m. on Saturday."[4]

The typical defendant is not usually affected by these prebooking detention procedures. Following his arrest, he is taken either to the nearest stationhouse or driven directly to the central police headquarters where he is booked, fingerprinted, photographed, and placed in a temporary jail cell. Those defendants who were initially transported to the neighborhood precinct are removed and placed in the city jail or police headquarters within twenty-hour hours after their arrest. Detention in these neighborhood precincts is kept to a minimum of time because of their inadequacies as well as the necessity for placing the defendant in close proximity with the municipal courts where the preliminary arraignment will soon be conducted.

The effect of these procedures following arrest, on the administration of bail, is to place the stationhouse and its leadership in a key position. They are the first institution which can offer the defendant an opportunity for early pretrial release. They also usually have the responsibility of communicating to the defendant what his bail will be, and how to communicate with his family, friends, or selected bondsman, in order to raise the required bond and obtain his release. The police are instructed by a fixed bail schedule as to how much bail to set for a specific offense.

A fixed bail schedule (or an emergency bail schedule as it is referred to in several cities) is a precise statement of exactly how much bail is required to release a defendant arrested for a particular crime. The fixed schedule is a means of allowing a nonjudicial officer, the desk sergeant in most instances, to set bail and release defendants upon payment of the required amount. It is a convenience to the defendant because it permits his rapid release from detention, often within an hour or two after his arrest.

The fixed bail schedule is also used by judicial officers at the initial appearance which is the customary occasion for setting bail. Even defendants released earlier from the stationhouse will have to reappear in court for this initial appearance before the judge who has the authority to review the previous bail amount set from the fixed schedule, as well as notifying the defendant of the charge. It is true that in nearly all felony cases the judge is given complete discretion as to the amount of bail he wishes to set, as long as it is "reasonable." The judges, however, may make use of the fixed schedule in two additional ways. First, it can be used as a guide in selecting the amount of bail in the more serious cases. Several cities recognize this function of the fixed schedule and will offer a sliding scale as a guide in felony cases. For example, bail for armed robbery may be recommended by the schedule to be set somewhere between $2500 and $7500. Second, the fixed bail schedule is a great aid in misdemeanor cases. They allow the rapid processing of these cases which seem to be so plentiful in our criminal court system. The judge need merely refer to the fixed schedule and inform the defendant of the required amount of bail which is determined solely by the category of crime of which he is accused. The judge does not have to ask questions, review prior records, or peruse the present arrest report.

In 84 percent of the cities surveyed, a fixed bail schedule was being used. As noted previously, however, its use could either be as a mere guideline for felony cases or its more common use as a specific requirement in misdemeanor cases. The presence of such a fixed schedule was found to be totally unrelated to the size of the release rate. Fifty percent of those cities not using a fixed bail schedule were able to release a percentage of defendants above the national average (65 percent), while 54 percent of those cities having bail schedules were also releasing a percentage of defendants above the national average.

The most important variable in determining how quickly the defendant can obtain his pretrial release is the seriousness of the offense of which he is accused. If he is charged with a misdemeanor, the defendant is able to obtain his release from the stationhouse or initial detention facility within an hour or two after arrest. He learns the amount of his bail from the desk sergeant who simply refers to a fixed bail schedule.

If a defendant is being charged with a serious misdemeanor or felony, he discovers many more obstacles blocking his path to pretrial freedom. Only about 25 percent of the cities studied were willing to allow the police to release defendants accused of these more serious crimes. In Baltimore and Indianapolis the police or custodial officer has a fixed bail schedule which includes felonies, while in Atlanta the police use a discretionary schedule for all categories of offenses.

In the majority of cities, when a defendant is arrested for one of these serious crimes, he is transported from the local stationhouse (also referred to as the neighborhood precinct) to a central detention facility. This is usually located near the courthouse where the defendant will soon have his initial appearance before a judge. In 75 percent of the cities surveyed, a defendant accused of a felony or serious misdemeanor will have his bail amount set by a judge at this initial appearance (also referred to as preliminary arraignment). Whether the judge may have a flexible bail schedule with a sliding scale or more simply relies upon his own experience and common sense, he is permitted to impose any bail he deems necessary as long as it is not blatantly arbitrary or excessive.

In addition to having the courts impose higher bail amounts, a second important consequence of having been charged with a felony is the greater period of confinement while awaiting this initial appearance. Even if a defendant is financially secure and confident of raising the required bond, he must still wait for his initial appearance and the formal statement by the judge as to the amount of bail. Several cities guarantee that a defendant will be before a judge within twenty-four hours. Forty-three percent of the cities studied were conducting this initial appearance within a twenty-four hour period while 40 percent of the cities estimated that the defendant would have to wait till the next day after his arrest. The national average was estimated to be between twenty-four and thirty-six hours. The remaining 17 percent of the cities were detaining their felony suspects from two to five days before giving them the opportunity to obtain their pretrial release. Although this time period is fairly short for most defendants, it is an uncomfortable situation and especially traumatic for the youthful offender or the defendant experiencing his first serious confrontation with the criminal justice system. It is during this period that the initial shock of the arrest begins to wear off and the reality and consequences of confinement present themselves.

Another important factor influencing the length of time the defendant must wait to see a judge is the day or time of day when he is arrested. Approximately 50 percent of the nation's cities do not operate a weekend court. Therefore any defendant arrested Friday night or during the day Saturday will have over a two-day delay until bail will be set. If the defendant is arrested after the court closes, which is usually at 4:30 P.M., he will be confined until the next morning before he can see a judge. It is ridiculous that the courts operate at the most inconvenient hours for their clientele since three-quarters of the defendants are arrested after the courts have concluded their daily operations.

Chicago is one of the few cities to operate a twenty-four hour bond court. It also operates a special holiday court which sets bail during the weekends. If a defendant is arrested after the regular district police courts have closed at 5 P.M., he will be held in one of the twenty-one police district stationhouses. Each stationhouse is electronically linked with central police headquarters where a bond-setting court is in continuous operation. Through television cameras the judge can question the defendant and set bail, no matter what time the arrest was made.[5]

The overriding concept which affected the operation of the traditional bail system during these crucial initial stages was the seriousness of the charges against the defendant. As will be seen in subsequent chapters, the author's research will clearly refute this reliance on the seriousness of the charge as a valid predictor of the defendant's pretrial behavior.

Table 2-1 serves to summarize the variations in bail-setting procedures during this initial phase.

The Judiciary and Their Bail-Setting Decision

As one attempts to examine the process by which a judge reaches his bail-setting decision, it is necessary to discuss this process separately for felonies and misdemeanors. Looking at misdemeanors first, when the defendant appears before a judge or magistrate he has already had his bail set previously by a responsible police officer at the stationhouse or city jail. The defendant may decide to have the judge try his case at this time, thereby eliminating the issue of bail, or he may request a continuance of a week or two in order to obtain counsel and gather witnesses. If the defendant elects to postpone his case in order to prepare his defense, the issue of bail again presents itself. The judge has the authority to review the bail which was initially set from the fixed schedule. The judge may permit the original bail to continue to be in force until the case is terminated in his court or he may choose to revise the amount or conditions of this original bond.

Because of the tremendous backlog of cases jamming the lower courts which try the misdemeanor cases, the judges of these courts do everything in their power to clean up their docket as quickly as possible. One of the greatest drags on this attempt is the irritating delay caused by the failure to dispose of these cases at the initial appearance. The judges in many of these lower courts use their authority to control the amount of bail as a pressuring device to

Table 2-1
The Initial Bail-setting Stage

City	Who Sets the Bail		Where it is Done		How it is Done	
	Misdemeanor	Felony	Misdemeanor	Felony	Misdemeanor	Felony
Washington	Desk Sergeant	Judge	Stationhouse	Court of Gen'l Sessions	Schedule	Discretion
San Francisco	Clerk of Criminal Court	Judge	Hall of Justice	Hall of Justice	Schedule	Discretion
Los Angeles	Police Captain	Judge	Stationhouse	Regional	Schedule	Discretion
Oakland	Police Captain	Judge	Stationhouse	Courthouse	Schedule	Discretion
Detroit	Desk Sergeant Arresting Magistrate	Arresting Magistrate	Police Station	Hall of Justice	Schedule	Discretion
Chicago	Desk Sergeant	Judge of Bond Court	Police Station	Bond Court or electronically	Schedule	Discretion
St. Louis	Desk Sergeant	C.C.C. Judge	Police Station	Police Station or Courthouse	Schedule	Flexible Schedule
Baltimore	Desk Sergeant	Judge	Police Station	Police Court	Schedule	Schedule
Indianapolis	Turnkey	Turnkey	City Jail	City Jail	Schedule	Schedule
Atlanta	Police	Police	Police Headquarters	Police Headquarters	Discretion Schedule	Discretion Schedule
Philadelphia	Desk Sergeant	Magistrate and District Attorney	Stationhouse	Police Headquarters	Schedule	Discretion

force defendants into deciding not to request continuances beyond their initial appearance.

In every city visited, the power of the judge to control the initial bail amount is most evident in felony cases. Over 80 percent of all officials surveyed found the judge to play the most significant role in the setting of bail. In felony cases this significance is manifested through his ability to set the initial bail amount. This was found to be the case in 91 percent of the cities surveyed. In the small percentage of remaining cities, the judge has an opportunity to revise the initial bail decision if it was made by the police or custodial officer at some earlier time.

What considerations and guidelines are offered to the judge in making these difficult pretrial decisions? Judges realize that the basic purpose of bail is to insure that the defendant will appear at trial, but the difficulty arises in attempting to decide which criteria are most closely related to this objective. We should also remember that lurking in the back of many judicial minds are several additional objectives which were discussed in Chapter 1 such as protecting society and punishing the defendant. Table 2-2 lists the pretrial release criteria considered by judges and presents an assessment of their importance by judges representing seventy-two-cities.

The criterion which nearly all judges assign the greatest importance is the seriousness of the offense. The author believes that the criterion is used most frequently because it is so easy to apply. No questioning of the defendant is involved, nor does it necessitate the court's having to verify any of the defendant's responses. With the tremendous workload facing most lower courts, this clear-cut criterion is ideal. Many experienced judges who were interviewed,

Table 2-2
Pretrial Release Criteria: An Assessment of Importance

Criterion	Unimportant	Slightly Important	Moderately Important	Extremely Important
Present charge	1(1%)	6(8%)	28(39%)	34(47%)
Previous record	2(3)	6(8)	22(31)	38(54)
Past app. record	3(4)	14(19)	29(40)	25(35)
Likelihood of a future crime	6(8)	18(25)	24(33)	22(31)
Character References	16(22)	30(42)	20(28)	4(6)
Community Ties	8(11)	25(33)	28(40)	10(16)

stated that after several years on the bench, they had a predetermined bail amount for each category of crime. Table 2-2 clearly shows that the overwhelming percentage of judges (86 percent) believe that the seriousness of the present charge is the most important pretrial release criterion. The assumption underlying this belief is that defendants accused of the more serious crimes will experience a greater urge to skip town and therefore the financial costs of this flight, as reflected in the loss of the posted bond, must be severe enough to deter the defendant.

Use of this criteria, however, does not result in a uniform bail setting policy because each judge has his own conception of the relative seriousness of various offenses. These conceptions are tempered by the personal experiences of each judge. The author found judges in every city reacting in a variety of highly individualistic ways on the question of which particular crime appeared most offensive to their own system of values.

This variation in bail setting behavior was lucidly brought to the public's attention by Lee Silverstein as part of his excellent study entitled *Defense of the Poor*. His findings reveal an accurate assessment of the tremendous variations in the amount at which bail is set. Silverstein goes on to comment on this point by offering the following documentation:

> For example in Chicago 77 per cent of the defendants had bail set at 5000 dollars or more, including 35 per cent having bail set at 10,000 dollars or more; while at the other extreme in Philadelphia, 83 per cent of the defendants had bail under 3000 dollars and only one per cent had a bail of 5000 dollars or more. In Los Angeles, where the proportion of defendants released on bond is near the large county median, 81 per cent of the defendants had bail set at less than 3000 dollars, while 16 per cent had bail set at 3000 dollars or more, including 12 per cent at 5000 dollars or more. These representative examples provide considerable evidence to support the common sense notion that the amount of bail will largely determine the percentage of defendants who make bail.[6]

The amount of variation is not only caused by having a great number of different judges setting bail at their own discretion or using broad guidelines. As Table 2-3 indicates, even where fixed bail schedules are used, there may still be variation between the schedules found in different court systems. Even though both St. Louis and Baltimore use these fixed schedules, it is obvious from this table that a defendant's chances for pretrial release is much greater in St. Louis.

Table 2-3
Variations in Fixed Bail Schedules

	Arson	Att. Burg.	Rape	Sodomy	2nd Murder	Assault W/ITR
St. Louis	2,500	1,500	5,000	2,500	7,500	2,500
Baltimore	No Bail	3,500	No Bail	3,000	No Bail	5,000

A second criterion considered relevant to the question of determining a defendant's chances for pretrial release is his prior criminal record. Although the judge is theoretically limited to the facts of the case before him, he is frequently influenced in the setting of bail by the defendant's past criminal activities. An overwhelming majority of judges surveyed (85 percent) support the use of this procedure and find it an important release criterion. Only two percent of the judges were willing to disregard a defendant's previous encounters with the law and believe that bail should be determined solely by the present facts and future possibilities. One of the reasons why judges chose to rely on the defendant's criminal history is because it is so readily accessible to them. The police provide these "rap sheets" to the judges immediately upon request and in most cities it is automatically presented to the bail-setting judge as part of his essential materials.

A third criterion used, in close conjunction with the previous two, is the strength of the state's case against the defendant. The greater the surety of a conviction, the higher the bail, since the defendant will realize the inevitability of his ultimate plight and be more inclined toward leaving town. This information (concerning the state's case) is presented to the judge through a variety of sources. In Oakland the judges are presented a statement from the prosecutor's office outlining the evidence, interrogation information, and facts surrounding the arrest. In Atlanta the prosecutor will come to the judge's chambers or his courtroom to present this information. The judges will also listen to the police officer during the commitment hearing so as to be advised of the facts surrounding the defendant's arrest.

These first three criteria are considered by the judiciary to be the most crucial factors in setting bail as over 80 percent of the judges attested to their importance. It is interesting to note that none of these three criteria have ever been proven to be related to being able to predict a defendant's proclivity toward forfeiting or committing additional crime (See Chapter 4). One of the most ironic aspects of this entire bail-setting procedure is that the criterion which the judge inquires into least frequently has the greatest effect on his obtaining his pretrial freedom. This is the question of the defendant's financial condition and the amount of bail which he believes he will be able to raise. Only two judges out of the more than thirty who were actually observed setting bail, were found to be making inquiries into the defendant's financial capabilities, particularly with regard to the amount of bail he could raise. Another criterion which also was rarely pursued was the question of whether the defendant had appeared in court on past occasions when he was released prior to his trial. Despite the logic of this inquiry, only one-third of the judges believed this to be an extremely important criterion.[7]

The likelihood of a defendant committing additional crimes while awaiting trial is an additional release criterion and was the primary reason for the District of Columbia's preventive detention statute. Sixty-four percent of the judges surveyed stated a belief in the importance of considering the possibility of a defendant committing an additional crime during this pretrial period. As mentioned earlier, while the nation's capital is the only city to statutorally construct a preventive detention system designed to detain those defendants adjudged likely to commit these pretrial crimes, most cities have informally devised preventive detention systems without resort to legislative decree.

Beginning with the Vera Foundation and their Manhattan Bail Project, two additional criteria have been added to the list: community ties of the defendant and character references. The purpose of these inquiries into the defendant's lifestyle is to establish a sufficient pattern of stability and reliability to merit granting him his pretrial freedom. These community ties standards usually refer to the defendant's employment stability, family and marital stability, residential stability, and character references.

All of these considerations relating to the defendant's background were rarely pursued by judges at the initial hearing. The only point where the judge and defense attorney were found to discuss these questions was at a later hearing where the defendant's bail was being reviewed and possibly reduced. This usually occurred several weeks after the initial bail hearing was conducted. Only one-third of the judges thought that character references were a useful criterion, while slightly over one-half (56 percent) believed the community ties standards to be important. What types of cities produced judges who were most sympathetic toward the use of these community ties criteria? This survey found no satisfactory answer to this question as no demographic characteristic could be significantly correlated with the belief by the judiciary in the community ties standard.

Why are the judges so unwilling or unable to utilize the community ties criteria as a consideration in their pretrial decision-making? There seem to be several possible explanations. First is the simple pressure of time caused by an overcrowded docket. Many judges simply are too harried and overworked to have an opportunity to question the defendant as to his background. Judges claim that they are barely able to go over the charges, glance at the rap sheet, and hear a word about the case from the arresting officer before being urged on to the next case by the clerk who apprehensively views the plethora of cases having to be completed that day. The President's 1968 Commission on Law Enforcement documented this gross disparity between personnel and caseload by stating, "Until legislation last year . . . the D.C. Court of General Sessions had four judges to process the preliminary stages of more than 1,500 felony cases, 7,500 serious misdemeanor cases, and 38,000 petty offenses and an equal number of traffic offenses per year. An inevitable consequence of volume that large is the almost total preoccupation in such a court with the movement of cases."[8]

A second explanation is that the author found throughout his interviews with lower court judges a pervasive dislike and cynicism toward the defendants appearing before them. These judges believed it would be a waste of time to make these personal inquiries because the defendant could not be trusted to give truthful responses. A judge in St. Louis said that unless the information is carefully verified one cannot take these people at their word. He specifically opposed any type of personal bond which allowed the defendant to be released solely on his signature which was to him a worthless gesture endangering society.[9] A third reason is that the judges simply prefer the first three criteria and believe them to be the most valid predictors of the defendant's pretrial behavior. These other humanistic and sociological questions are considered a waste of time and an unnecessary extravagance.

Because of the ambiguity of the state statutes and the variety of criteria available to the judiciary in setting bail, the performance of the judge is often in sharp contrast to these legislative guidelines. One of the most blatant examples of such a contradiction between prescribed rules and actual practices was found in Chicago. Presiding Judge Boyle has written that the Chicago bail system is among the fairest in the nation because its judges operate under a state criminal code which instructs them to observe the following rules: (1) Bail should be sufficient so as to assure compliance with the conditions set forth in the bail bond; (2) not oppressive; (3) consideration of past criminal conduct; (4) commensurate with the nature of offense charged; and (5) consideration of financial ability of the accused.[10]

How does the judge actually determine bail in Cook County? The results of a study by the Cook County Special Bail Project of the Chicago Holiday Court and Night Bond Court indicated that the judges are unable to follow any of the guidelines listed in the Illinois Criminal Code. The two-month survey reported the following findings:

1. Bonds were set for hundreds of people without legal representation.
2. The average bail hearing lasted less than one minute.
3. In the great majority of cases no inquiry was made into the financial capabilities of the accused person.
4. Too few persons were released on their own recognizance.
5. At Night Bond Court the accused was rarely present when bail was set.
6. Judges seldom were given enough information on which to base their bail decisions.[11]

The judges in Detroit's Recorder's Court who administer the initial bail decision in felony cases offer the reader a more typical example of this contradiction between rules and reality. The Michigan statute specifying the criteria to be used by Detroit judges in setting bail lists the identical three considerations listed in the California statute which was noted in Chapter 1. As one observes the judges in this Detroit Arraignment Court, it is obvious that there has been no effort to enforce usage of these criteria or standardize bail-setting procedures

among the various judges. The most important consideration was the seriousness of the offense, although the judges interviewed, differed as to what was the
order of seriousness. In the more serious felonies such as armed robbery, bail
was found to be set between $5,000 and $15,000, without the judge ever inquir-
ing into the defendant's background or any other criteria related to his likelihood
of appearing for trial. The next most important consideration was whether the
defendant had a previous police record. If a history of criminal activity was discovered, a high bail was set, regardless of the seriousness of the present charge.

The judge does not make this important bail-setting decision in a vacuum.
In addition to the general commotion found in most courtrooms, the judge's
bail decision is influenced by a variety of outside influences and pressures. The
most significant of these influences are the following groups of nonjudicial
actors: police officers, prosecutors, defense attorneys, court officials, and
bondsmen. A detailed analysis of the role played by each of these outside
groups in the traditional bail system will be presented in Chapter 3.

Beyond the pressures exerted upon the judge by this collection of public
officials, he may also find his decision-making process affected by subtle, and
more pervasive types of pressures. One example of this type of pressure is the
amount of influence wielded by the community's dominant political faction and
their interest in the court system. The basis for this interaction is probably
associated with the current importance of law and order as a top priority
political issue. One could expect that in those cities where the judiciary is the
most responsive to political forces, it would be more cautious in its bail-setting
policies. This responsiveness could be defined as a judiciary whose members
owe their nomination and ultimate election to office, to the dominant political
party. Cities with a low responsiveness in their judiciary will have judges
appointed in a professional and apolitical manner. It may also be hypothesized
that such judges will take a more balanced and generally softer stand on pretrial
release because they would be less concerned with the political ramifications of
their judicial decisions.

Chicago is the most obvious example of a city where the judiciary is highly
responsive to the predominant political forces in the community. Each judge in
the Chicago system clearly understands his allegiance and the party's desires,
which definitely overrides any other factor in his judicial performance. The
pretrial release system in Chicago is therefore closely geared to the desires of
the mayor and his representatives on the bench. This study found the Chicago
bail system to be one of the most resistant to viable reform. The city tolerated
a malfunctioning bail system which was herding defendants through their initial
bail hearing at the rate of 57 seconds per defendant.[12]

At the other extreme is Washington, D.C. where it was found that the
judges were the least responsive to political pressures and operated one of the
nation's most effective and humane pretrial systems. Their unresponsiveness
is due to the fact that they are appointed and are not concerned with reelection

or additional political demands. With this political freedom, the Washington judiciary has been a leader in experimenting with a wide variety of reforms. The city's Project Crossroads is one of the few bright spots in the bail reform movement. It is also important to note that Washington is releasing the largest percentage of defendants on their own recognizance of any city surveyed while also maintaining a very low forfeiture rate.

A second type of societal influence pressuring the judge as he attempts to decide a defendant's chances for pretrial release is the amount of organized community activism which is concerned with the city's criminal justice system. In cities where there seems to be a large number of community organizations pressuring the city government for reform, one is most likely to find judges who are interested in improving the quality of justice. The converse was also found to be true; where cities seem to be apathetic and lack such reform groups, the bail system operates under the strict control of the judiciary and city hall, experiencing only isolated instances of improvement or reform. Thus the pretrial release issue is one of several important potential problems facing lower class communities. Until these communities can organize themselves into active pressure groups or win the support of middle-class or other reform organizations such as the ACLU (American Civil Liberties Union) or the Urban League, these problems will not be solved.

Los Angeles offers an excellent example of a city whose community activism has spurred some of its citizens to attempt to improve the operation of the bail system. The Community Justice Center, funded by HEW and operated in the Watts section of the city, is just one of the groups helping to improve the pretrial release system. Detroit seems to be the most apathetic of the cities visited. There is a noticeable absence of community organizations, and as a result, the Detroit bail system is one of the least effective systems studied. It has the highest forfeiture rate while still detaining an above average percentage of defendants during the pretrial period.

In several of the cities the mass media, particularly the local newspapers, were able to influence the judge's bail setting practices. Three categories of newspapers were found to exert pressure on the bail system. The first type were the hard-line newspapers which were a negative influence on the ability of the court to operate an equitable bail system. By publicizing any instance of a defendant misbehaving while awaiting trial, these papers were able to force the judiciary to adopt a very cautious position on pretrial justice. The *St. Louis Post Dispatch* and the *Chicago Tribune* are two papers of this type. It did not appear to be a mere coincidence that the judiciary in both of these cities are among the most recalcitrant toward bail reform.

The second category is neutral newspapers such as the *Baltimore Sun* and the *Los Angeles Times*. They do not take an interest in urban judicial matters and therefore exert no real influence on the operation of the bail system. Two city newspapers, the *Washington Post* and the *Indianapolis Star*, could be classified in a third group, reforming newspapers. Both have run exposés on the problems of pretrial release and appear to have educated the public successfully as to the difficulties in the operation of bail. The Indianapolis paper, in addition, has done a community service in exposing a scandal involving a criminal syndicate's control over the city's bail-bonding industry.

From Initial Appearance to Trial

After the judge has determined the amount and type of bond or granted a personal bond, the court must then notify the defendant of his next court appearance. Table 2-4 lists the variety of techniques currently employed by court systems in their attempt to clarify this upcoming court appearance. These techniques, whether done orally or in writing, have been found to be grossly ineffective procedures. The chaotic situation found in most courtrooms, where the cases are hustled along in an assembly-line style, appears to be the prime cause for the inadequacies of the notification process. It is conceded by most judges that this malfunctioning notification system is more responsible for defendants failing to appear than the more publicized willful attempts by defendants to leave town. The most commonly used notification technique is a personal letter (used in 35 percent of the cities) while 21 percent simply make an oral statement, and 18 percent go to the trouble of telephoning.

The notification is usually carried on at the courthouse. Thirty-eight percent of the cities, however, do go to the bother of attempting to notify the defendant after he leaves the courthouse. This is usually done by a mailed notice which often becomes merely a token effort. The inadequacy of this system is caused both by the transient lifestyles of many of the defendants as well as the extremely long period between arrest and trial which frequently stretches to over six months for felony cases in large cities.

Table 2-4
Notification Procedures

Technique	Number of Cities
Personal letter	25 (35%)
Oral statement	15 (21%)
Telephone call	14 (18%)
Formal notice to appear	8 (11%)
Personal visit	5 (7%)
Other	5 (7%)
Oral means of notification	33 (48%)
Written means	34 (52%)
Notification at court	25 (38%)
Notification after court	39 (62%)

With the exception of the few cities who mail notification letters after the defendant has left the courtroom, the criminal courts do not in any way supervise the defendant during this pretrial period. It is only through the defendant's own conscience and memory, as well as the pressures applied by the bondsmen and bail reform projects, that he will appear on time for his court appearance.

After the initial bail decision has been made, the defendant may still be affected by revisions of this decision, up until his final appearance in court. The review of his bail amount may be either detrimental or beneficial to his chances for pretrial release. One of the most irritating types of revisions for a defendant is to have his bail set by a police officer at the stationhouse from a fixed schedule and after raising this amount, to report the next day to the courthouse for his initial appearance and have the judge increase the amount of the bond. The defendant will then have to raise an entirely new amount of money and come to the sad realization that he had only purchased twenty-four hours worth of pretrial freedom on the first bond at the stationhouse.

Although this practice of "double bonding" has caused a great deal of psychic and financial strain on the defendant, the courts rationalize the necessity for such a procedure on several grounds. The most common justification is that a revision has been necessitated by the prosecutor or the police uncovering new information either on the case or the defendant's background. The most regular time for these revisions to be made are not at the initial hearing but rather at the preliminary hearing, which is usually the following week. Several officials, critical of the traditional bail system, believe that double bonding is simply the product of collusion between the judge and the bondsmen. By setting multiple bonds at various stages the judge is driving additional business in the bondsmen's direction. Appreciative bondsmen, in turn, will often make sizable campaign contributions the next time the judge is up for reelection. Although difficult to document, it appeared that cities which shackled the defendant with a system of multiple or double bonding also were found to have a group of bondsmen who possessed a great deal of political clout.

The easiest way to eliminate the hardship of multiple bonding is to simply have a court ruling that one bond will be in force for the defendant throughout the entire pretrial period. In approximately half of the cities visited the court system had established rules which have eliminated double bonding. In the remaining cities, the courts usually hold the procedure in abeyance for the more serious cases where they are making a concerted effort to detain the defendant prior to his trial. Chicago was able to partially eliminate double bonding through the initiative of Judge Powers of the Criminal Division of the Cook County Circuit Court. If a defendant is held for the grand jury in Chicago and is indicted, this case will then be processed through Judge Powers' office. He has set a policy of allowing the original bond to stand in nearly every instance, thus removing any chance for double bonding to occur. Prior to his action Chicago felony defendants were often forced to obtain numerous bonds at great financial expense.[13]

The only city where defendants are still seriously plagued by double bonding is Atlanta, Georgia. Once a defendant's case has been bound over to the superior court by the committing magistrate of the municipal court (where bail is initially set), the District Attorney's Indictment Section reviews the case and decides if the bond should be revised. They also make a more thorough check of the defendant's prior criminal record. If the defendant is found to have a history of criminal activities and the present case seems rather strong, they will recommend to the judge to increase the bond. The defendant is brought in, notified of the revision, and then allowed to attempt to raise the new bail or be detained in jail. The judge will nearly always follow the recommendation of the District Attorney's Office although it may be challenged by the defense attorney. All this occurs shortly after the preliminary hearing.[14]

It is a much more common occurrence for a defendant to have his bail lowered rather than raised, following its initial determination. Most motions for bail reduction usually originate with the defense attorney although in Oakland the district attorney has been known to recommend OR (release on the defendant's own recognizance) or reduced bail after the defendant has been detained over a week. As the judge reviews a case bound over from the lower court, he will review the amount of the bond and may reduce it on his own initiative.

Baltimore and Philadelphia use investigators from the local bail reform project to expedite the bond reduction process. In Philadelphia the Defender's Association utilizes Villanova Law School students to help administer their routine bail reduction program. Each of the association's attorneys files a bail application for his client if he indicates he will be unable to post the initially required bail. This application contains information on the defendant's background, community ties, and a brief factual statement about the present case. Each application is given to a law student, designated as a bail clerk, who attempts to verify the information in the application. After completing verification, the bail clerk advises the D.A.'s Office that an informal application for bail will be made on a specified date. On this date the bail clerk delivers the application to the defense counsel and is available to be called as a witness. Prior to this hearing, the assistant D.A. in charge of the case reviews the application and may decide to make the recommendation for reduction or nominal bond, negating the need for a full hearing, since the judge is certain to go along with his recommendation. The results of this program for April, May, and June of 1970 are as follows:

Bail reduced after hearing	246
Bail not reduced after hearing	85
Nominal bail received by D.A.	103
Bail reduced by D.A.	7
Pending	103[15]

In Baltimore, the Supreme Bench of the City sponsors the reduction program. When a judge of this court is requested to have a bail reduction hearing he will notify the Pretrial Release Project to run a thorough background check of the defendant. The investigator from the project will appear at the hearing as an objective fact source for the judge on any question concerning the defendant's background.

Two additional procedures designed to review and possibly reduce the defendant's bond are found in San Francisco and Indianapolis. In Indianapolis the defendant petitions the court to reduce his bond by having his attorney present to the appropriate court bailiff a collection of information relating to the defendant's background and character. The bailiff then checks with the detective assigned to the case who gives him the defendant's past record. All of this information is then given to the judge who can either rule on the matter himself or call in all parties for an evidentiary hearing.[16] In San Francisco, the author was told by a prominent defense attorney that the easiest way to get a bond reduction in his city was to go in and see the judge personally. All that need be done is present the facts of the case to the judge and if you have a legitimate presentation, your client's bond will be reduced.[17]

It is impossible to state exactly how frequently bond reductions are sought and the degree of success. Cities simply do not maintain any statistics on this subject. After questioning judges in several cities, one is left with the impression that these motions for reduction are not attempted very frequently and only about one-third are successful. In most cities these applications, motions, or writs for bond reduction can be initiated almost as soon as the original bail has been set and there seems to be no problem with securing a speedy review by the judge since there are so few applications for reduction. This is especially true in cities where the decision is made at the discretion of the judge without a formal hearing specifically for that purpose. Little attention has been focused upon the intricacies of bond reduction and consequently there has been virtually no discussion of improving its operation. The only recommendation heard on this subject was to have each city provide for automatic review of the bail amount in cases where the defendant was unable to secure his release within a week. It was discovered, however, that nearly all cities provide for this review on an informal basis without the benefit of specific court rules guaranteeing such a procedure.

One simple reform which could greatly improve the bond reduction procedure was a common-sense proposal of a Chicago public defender. He was opposed to the seemingly endless motions for bond reduction which occupies too much of the attorney's time. The lawyer should contact someone from the defendant's family or a friend of his to come in to the public defender and tell him exactly how much they know they can raise for the defendant and then ask for this amount in a reduction motion. It is a meaningless gesture to ask for a bond reduction without knowledge of precisely what the defendant's financial limits are. Even if a bond reduction motion is granted the defendant may still not be able to raise the revised amount.[18]

The Backlog and Bail: The Deleterious Effects of Court Delay

The length of time a defendant must wait between his arrest and the determination of his guilt or innocence is an important variable in the analysis of the administration of bail. This delay in most cities is between three to six months. This lengthy period is commonly blamed by judicial reformers as being the root cause of most of the problems plaguing the urban criminal justice system. As Judge Spaeth of the Philadelphia Court of Common Pleas related in an interview, "You cannot lick any of the present problems of bail until you get rid of the backlog."[19]

The defendant who has obtained his pretrial release is benefitted by the long delay from arrest to trial, and is often a contributor to increasing this delay. The reasons why defendants released on bail are in no hurry to have their trial was expressed by a San Francisco Deputy Public Defender in the following statement:

> When a defendant is out on bail, he returns to his normal life style. He is at home, maybe with his wife and kids. . . . The last thing in the world that he wants to do is to go to jail, and he will do just about anything— including going to trial—to stay. But a guy who has been sitting in jail for 2 or 3 months begins to think of only one thing: how can I get out of here as soon as possible? His most certain option is to take a deal, get credit for time served, and get out in a few months.[20]

Charles Work, U.S. Attorney for the Washington, D.C. criminal court system (formerly referred to as the Court of General Sessions) must battle with these recalcitrant defendants everyday as they attempt to extend their pretrial freedom for as long as possible. Mr. Work found that some experienced defendants who were familiar with the variety of desultory tactics available, were experts at making their case "fall between the cracks" of the criminal justice system. That is, by their use of continuances and tardy appearances, they prove so frustrating to the prosecution and witnesses as well as outwitting a pitifully gummed-up calendar, their cases are often tossed out since they appear to be more trouble than they are worth.[21]

With so many serious hardships resulting from the failure to provide a prompt trial, how long do our cities actually take to arrest and try a defendant? Table 2-5 indicates the results of a national survey of seventy-two cities which shows the average city to be experiencing a sixty-day period between arrest and trial.

Table 2-5
Time Period from Arrest to Trial

Length of Time		Number of Cities
Less than week		4 (5.5%)
1 week to a month		11 (15%)
30 days to 60 days		11 (15%)
61 days to 90 days		14 (20%)
91 days to 120 days		5 (7%)
121 days to 180 days		4 (5.5%)
Over 6 months		3 (4%)
No response		20 (28%)
Average	60 days	

Are those cities which are plagued by the most prolonged periods of court delay recognizable by certain demographic characteristics? Table 2-6 identifies large northern cities as being the most prone toward experiencing these extreme delays in their criminal court system. It was rather surprising to find that the seriousness of a city's crime rate was not significantly related to the speed with which a defendant is brought to trial. It would seem that in cities with higher crime rates, more arrests would be made, resulting in more cases for the court system, and thereby causing increased periods of time from arrest to trial and the development of an expanding backlog.

Table 2-6
Court Delay and Demographic Explanations

		Length of Delay	
		0–60 Days	61 Days and Over
Population:	−200,000	15 (63%)	13 (50%)
	+200,000	9 (37)	13 (50)
Region:	North	13 (57)	22 (85)
	South	10 (43)	4 (15)
Median income:	−Natl. Avg.	11 (50)	12 (57)
	+Natl. Avg.	11 (50)	9 (43)
Poverty level:	−Natl. Avg.	9 (48)	12 (46)
	+Natl. Avg.	10 (52)	14 (54)
Nonwhite pop.:	−12.5%	10 (55)	14 (56)
	+12.5%	8 (45)	11 (44)
Crime rate:	−Natl. Avg.	8 (45)	10 (52)
	+Natl. Avg.	10 (55)	9 (48)

Because the survey was based on only estimated periods of delay by knowledgeable officials, an attempt was made to obtain more precise information on
this controversial topic. By traveling to eleven cities and speaking with numerous
judges and court clerks as well as collecting official documentation whenever
possible, a fairly accurate picture of court delay in our major urban centers was
constructed. The results of this intensive investigation are compiled in
Table 2-7.[22]

The courts recognize the hardships which those defendants detained in jail
are suffering during this pretrial period. Their solution, whether it is in the form
of a specific court rule or an informal policy, is to give priority in scheduling
cases for trial to those defendants detained in jail. This advantage in scheduling
over defendants released on bail is usually a savings of several weeks. Since the
defendants released on bail are rarely in a hurry to come to trial, no one is in
opposition to this policy.

Despite this attempt to speed up the scheduling for detained defendants,
many defendants are still forced to wait for a number of months before going to
trial. The most detailed study of this problem was carried out in Philadelphia,
after a prison riot gave national notoriety to the extremely long periods of time
defendants were detained awaiting trial. A high ranking member of the District
Attorney's Office revealed that eighteen defendants had been incarcerated for
over two years awaiting trial. This shocking figure was disclosed in a jail inventory following the riot which also uncovered a few detained individuals whose
cases had been dismissed over three months earlier and the court had failed to
notify the prison authorities to release the men. The District Attorney's Office
is presently organizing a unit to ferret out these embarrassing cases while also
working on giving priority to scheduling trials for detained individuals.[23]

Table 2-7
Time from Arrest to Trial

City	Length of Time from Arrest to Trial		Size of City	Crime Rate (FBI Crime Index)
	Misde. (wks.)	Felonies (mos.)		
Washington	4–6 wks.	5–6 mos.	763,000	94,085 (3416)
Baltimore		4–5 mos.	939,000	89,926 (4419)
San Francisco		3 mos.	738,000	138,000 (4669)
Los Angeles		3 mos.	2,479,000	290,000 (4717)
Oakland		3–4 mos.	400,000	89,926 (4419)
Philadelphia	6 wks.	5–6 mos.	2,000,000	73,900 (1563)
Detroit			1,670,000	151,700 (3611)
Chicago		4–5 mos.	3,550,000	166,000 (2457)
St. Louis		3–4 mos.	750,000	62,000 (2884)
Atlanta	1 wk.	2 mos.	487,000	31,000 (2431)
Indianapolis	1 wk.	2–3 mos.	476,000	28,000 (2652)

The Pennsylvania Prison Society, also interested in this problem, discovered through a phone conversation with Philadelphia's Sheriff Ed Hendrick, the following statistics on defendants awaiting trial in his prison: As of May 31, 1970, out of a total of 2,231 inmates, 200 had been in detention over a year, and 472 others had been detained from four to twelve months.[24]

A final difficulty to be mentioned with regard to these detained defendants is that in nearly all cities this period of pretrial detention may very possibly be dead time. *Dead time* means this period of pretrial detention will not be counted toward the final sentence which the defendant receives. Some cities, such as Indianapolis, Indiana flatly refuse to count this dead time. Most cities, however, such as San Francisco and Washington, D.C., leave it up to the discretion of the individual judge who sentences the defendant as to whether to count this pretrial time. Aside from possible humanitarian reasons, this discretionary policy is used as a tool in the plea-bargaining process. If the defendant agrees to plead guilty he may be rewarded or induced into this "copping out" by a promise from the District Attorney's Office that they will urge the judge to count his pretrial detention period off of his final sentence.

Several jurisdictions have attempted to fight the problem of court delay by legislation requiring that a trial *must* be conducted within a specified period of time or else it will be automatically dismissed. Examples of such legislation are the 30-day speedy trial rule in Atlanta, the 120-day or 160-day rules in Chicago (depending on whether the defendant is detained or released prior to trial), the two-term rule in Philadelphia, and a 12-week rule in Oakland. Due to numerous loopholes and a lackadaisical attitude toward enforcement, these rules do not seem to be making much of a dent in this serious problem. A typical weakness in such legislation is that any time the defense asks for a continuance for any reason, the rule is no longer in effect.

Bail Pending Appeal

For those defendants found guilty and choosing to appeal the decision, the issue of bail pending appeal is raised. The rules governing the procedures for granting such bail vary greatly among the cities studied. In Atlanta, Georgia and in all of the California cities visited, the decision is completely at the discretion of the judge. This may be either the judge who did the sentencing or the judge of the court to where the decision is being appealed. A variation of this was found in St. Louis where judges follow a twenty-year old informal rule which imposes a bond of $1000 per year sentenced. The judge of course, need not set any bond at all if he so desires. In Philadelphia, Baltimore, and Indianapolis the general rule is simply to double the amount of the original bond. In Chicago most judges seemed to relate the possibility of bail pending appeal to the defendants previous appearance record. A few judges simply decide to continue the same bond. The district attorney often makes a recommendation to the judge in this matter and in Philadelphia and Atlanta, this recommendation is usually followed.

It is extremely difficult to estimate the frequency that requests for bail pending appeal are made or the success rates of these requests. No statistics are kept and the judges interviewed were rarely involved in this area of decision-making. Impressions gathered, however, indicate that most defendants are not very successful and that the entire problem does not involve a very large number of cases. The explanation offered for this stricter position on bail pending appeal is that there is now a greater chance of the defendant's fleeing and also there is no longer the chance that the defendant was innocent, at least in the opinion of the court of original jurisdiction.

3 Nonjudicial Actors

Despite the apparent dominance by the judge, the administration of bail is also directly affected by various nonjudicial actors. It is the purpose of this chapter to examine the activities of the five most important groups of nonjudicial actors: police, prosecuting attorneys, defense attorneys, court officials, and bondsmen.

The Police

The greatest influence which the police exert on the administration of bail occurs when the defendant is about to be arrested. The authority of the police to charge the defendant with a specific crime is a power which the police can use in all but a few instances where the arrest is made on the basis of a warrant. Because the amount of bail is directly related to the seriousness of the offense charged, the policeman's decision on this question is a key factor in determining the defendant's opportunity for pretrial release.

This ability of the police officer to exert a direct influence on the administration of bail is rarely mentioned in discussions of pretrial release. The author was first made aware of this phenomenon in two separate interviews with defense attorneys, one in Chicago and the other in Philadelphia. In Chicago, Marshall Patner, Director of the Businessmen for the Public Interest and former attorney for the Blackstone Rangers, commented in a memo to the Chicago Bar Association that the policeman's "decision sets the fate of the person arrested, for the state proceeds on that charge as though its attorneys had checked it out. The judges then set bail on the charge acting as though there was a presumption that the policeman's decision was correct."[1]

Patner finds this situation even more disturbing because of its potential misuse in the hands of certain police officers. He offers the following example of how this charging power can be abused when it is applied in a discriminating fashion:

> The problem arises when policemen prepare charges where witnesses are mistaken, where no crime was committed, or where they prepare charges for felony mob action or aggravated assault, for example, when the lesser misdemeanor charges are all that could ever be proved. The problem is compounded where the police are not acting for a lack of knowledge or legal advice but are

43

using the power to charge as a club against one defendant and feather against another. The white construction workers in the Custom House mob scene were charged with violation of a city ordinance of disorderly conduct. On the other hand protesters at welfare offices, or at food stores in the grape boycott, unpopular youth groups in peaceful protest marches are charged with mob action, felony or misdemeanor or state disorderly conduct, as a regular and consistent policy.[2]

Vincent Ziccardi of the Defender Association of Philadelphia mentioned a second harmful effect resulting from the policeman's charging authority as it effects the administration of bail. He found that in Philadelphia the police were not sufficiently interested in investigating the defendant's explanation at the time of the arrest. Their attitude was that once the police officer believed there was probable cause for the arrest, the defendant could wait and explain his side of the story to the judge. The police felt it was not their job, but rather the district attorney's and the judge's to verify this information and determine the innocence of the defendant. The attitude has resulted in countless bad arrests which are frequently thrown out of court at the preliminary hearing or before. With these dubious arrests clogging up the calendar, more defendants are forced to wait longer periods in jail for their trial and the entire criminal justice system suffers. Also, many of these defendants who will soon have their cases dismissed will have to be detained in jail because of their inability to raise the required bond. This high dismissal rate is substantiated by figures from the Philadelphia Defender Association's *1969–70 Annual Report* which pointed out that of 920 cases handled by their office, over a third were either "nolle prossed" or adjudged innocent and discharged.[3]

Once a defendant has been arrested he will be taken to the stationhouse. The desk sergeant or some other police officer is granted authority to set bail for the defendant at this point. In most cities the police officer has to set bail either from a fixed bail schedule or has to call up a judge to set the amount. At the stationhouse the police officer lacks discretion to alter the amount of bail which is set by either authority. The only conceivable influence which the police can exert at this time is in the selection of which judge to call to set bail, if a choice is possible. Since each judge has a reputation for maintaining a certain predisposition toward the amount of bail necessary in specific crimes, the police officer's selection process will effect the amount of bail. The infamous Judge Louis Kizas used to be kept busy all hours of the day and night driving from his South Side Chicago home to police stations all over the city in order to set "reasonable" bonds for certain notorious acquaintances. The linkage of these early morning phone calls to the Chicago underworld eventually led to the judge's forced resignation from the Cook County bench.[4]

In ten of the eleven cities visited, the police were able to exert only an indirect influence on the judge's bail decision. The police serve as a supplier of information to the judiciary, concerning the defendant's past criminal record, present arrest description, and additional background facts. This apparently neutral position as a provider of necessary information about the defendant is subject to manipulation by the police. This can be done by pointing out certain detrimental facts about the defendant, while omitting information which might be advantageous. This procedure was observed in virtually all courtrooms across the country. The only point of variation was in the frequency with which the judge asked the police officer for information as compared with directly questioning the defendant himself. Even within a city, there was great variation in the receptivity of judges to relying on the police officer's help in learning about the defendant's background.

The police officer's role in the administration of bail, compared to his influential position a decade or two ago, seems to have declined. The principal explanation appears to be the growing influence of the District Attorney's Office. Assistant D.A.s in both Los Angeles and Baltimore are now being placed in all regional police courts where bail is initially set by the judge. With their presence and expertise, the prosecuting attorneys have replaced the policeman as a fact source for the judiciary. The Baltimore State's Attorney's Office offers a good example of the tremendous growth of these agencies in recent years. Through the help of federal funds, the State's Attorney's Office has had its funding doubled in one year (1969–70). Plans for the placement of these new prosecutors are to concentrate them in the screening, plea-bargaining, and pre-grand-jury sections. All these functions are obviously designed to supplant the police department's pretrial influence and also to weed out bad arrests and correct overcharging.[5]

The final chance for the police to become involved in the administration of bail is when a defendant fails to appear in court and a bench warrant is issued for his arrest. In a few cities the sheriff's office has responsibility for attempting to retrieve forfeiting defendants, but in the majority of cities studied, the police department is called on by the court. Unless the forfeiture is unintentional (such as the defendant was mistaken about the date of his appearance), the police are rarely successful in apprehending bail jumpers. This inability to recapture these fleeing defendants is caused primarily by the jurisdictional limitations placed on police operations, particularly with respect to the complex problem of extradition. One public official interviewed, however, did not believe this inability to recapture defendants was a serious problem. He found that these defendants would either skip town and become another city's problem or if they remained they would probably be arrested for another crime within a few months.[6] An assistant district attorney in Philadelphia estimated that there are currently 6000 unserved bench warrants for forfeitures in his city.[7]

The District Attorney's Office

A second nonjudicial participant in the administration of bail is the prose-cuting attorney and his staff. Although his role in affecting a judge's bail-setting decision has been deemphasized, and rarely publicized, it was surprising to find that 70 percent of a national sample of public officials commenting on their city's pretrial release system, believed the prosecuting attorney played a signi-ficant role in determining the size of the bond.[8]

Like the police officer, the district attorney can directly effect the size of a defendant's bond by the selection of the charge against him. The district attorney in St. Louis and Philadelphia becomes involved in the charging decision very quickly and may review the original charge and therefore force the reconsideration of the bail amount at the preliminary hearing, which is usually a week to ten days after the initial bail decision. The Prosecuting Attorney's Office in both Washington, D.C. and Atlanta appeared to make frequent use of this chance to amend the charge by the time of the first bail hearing. Usually the change in charge by the district attorney is to the defendant's advantage, but there are many exceptions to this generalization.

In several cities the police cooperate very closely with the district attorney in attempting to influence the judge's bail decision. McIntyre reports that the district attorney in Detroit will act in bail matters only when he is requested to do so by the police. A detective explained that "occasionally he will ask an assistant prosecutor who is assigned to the court hearing *habeas corpus* writs, to explain to the court why the defendant should not be released and the necessity for a high bond, or for that matter, no bond set at all."[9]

In Frederic Suffet's excellent article, "Bail Setting: A Study of Courtroom Interaction," he observed 1,437 bail settings in New York County Criminal Court, and he found that the judge and the prosecuting attorney were recipro-cally supportive. They both seemed to follow the same bail setting guidelines and tended to gang up against the defense attorney's recommendations. The suggestions of the prosecutor were found to carry much weight and were a strong influence on the judge's final decision.[10]

The most influential District Attorney's Office affecting the administration of bail is found in Philadelphia, Pennsylvania. It is directed by nationally prominent crime fighter Arlen Specter. The individuals interviewed in Philadelphia believed that the District Attorney's Office unusually extensive involvement in the administration of bail (in relation to the other cities studied) does not represent a special interest in pretrial release but rather is indicative of his interest in a wide range of topics which are in the public limelight, but do not fall within the traditional bailiwick of the District Attorney's Office.

An assistant district attorney is always at the preliminary arraignment court where bail is set by a Court of Common Pleas judge. The assistant D.A. will make a recommendation as to the amount of bail, based mainly on the seriousness of the present charge and the defendant's past criminal record. The judge will usually follow this recommendation. For certain serious offenses the judges may not set bail without the consent of the District Attorney's Office. These crimes are burglary, robbery, arson, rape, murder, and mayhem. After reviewing the case, the D.A.'s Office will send a recommendation to the judge, who almost always comply. The judge was also prohibited from setting bail *lower* than the amount recommended by the District Attorney. Where the D.A. recommended "no bail" the question was terminated and the judge could not alter the D.A.'s ruling.

In all categories of crimes, the Philadelphia D.A.'s Office plays a crucial role in handling appeals for bail reduction or nominal bonds (release on recognizance). All of these appeals are made directly to the D.A.'s Office and are handled by Deputy District Attorney Michael Rotko and his staff. The appeal may be made formally through a petition or letter of intent or informally through an application for a change in bail by the defense attorney who will come in to try to work out a compromise. As a result of this discussion or merely on the basis of making a decision on a formal petition, the D.A. will then recommend to the proper judge what the new conditions of release should be. If no compromise can be struck between D.A. and defense counsel informally, the counsel can request a formal bail hearing before a judge. In all maneuvers to appeal the initial bail decision, the D.A.'s recommendation to the judge is the deciding factor.[11]

Like the police, the prosecutor has the advantage of controlling the data on the case and the defendant. Even more than the police, the prosecutor is able to indicate to the judge the strength of the state's case against the defendant. This fact is often interpreted by the judge as being a strong indication of the defendant's probable guilt or innocence. It is a crucial factor in determining the amount of bail because judges commonly believe that the more obvious it appears that a defendant is guilty, the more likely he will be to attempt to avoid prosecution by fleeing the city during this pretrial period. With this increased likelihood of flight, a sufficient bail must be set to guarantee his presence at the trial.

In most cities there is very little difference between the position taken initially by the police on a defendant's bond and a later decision by the prosecutor. The prosecutor would usually agree with the initial amount, or in some instances take an even harder stand on the issue and request a higher bail. As noted earlier there is close cooperation between the police and prosecutor on the issue of bail.

The district attorney is the sole representative of the prosecution at subsequent bail hearings on an appeal of the original bail decision. Their main job at these hearings is to counter the defense attorney's arguments for lowering bond. They are also able to provide the judge with insights into the defendant's past criminal activities. After observing these bail appeal hearings in Los Angeles and Baltimore, it became even clearer that the prosecutor was able to dominate these hearings in a manner consistent with Suffet's findings vis-á-vis the initial bail hearing.

The prosecutor may also be engaged in an assortment of additional bail related functions. In Atlanta, the district attorney is in charge of supervising the city's bondsmen and is responsible for collecting all surety bond forfeitures. In Oakland the district attorney also is constantly on the lookout for indiscretions by bondsmen. They believe they must supplement the state's insurance commission which has the primary responsibility for regulating bondsmen because it is often difficult to spot irregularities in Oakland from the commission's offices in Sacramento. In Indianapolis it was learned that the prosecutor can use the judge's discretionary authority about whether to count the time detained prior to the trial toward the amount of time which the defendant will be sentenced. In other words, the prosecution may decide that if the defense attorney will convince his client to accept a guilty plea, they can promise him that when the defendant is to be sentenced they will recommend to the judge (who nearly always follows their wishes) that the defendant's "dead time" during pretrial detention be counted toward the sentenced time.[12]

Defense Attorney

Of all the nonjudicial actors discussed in this chapter, the defense attorney is the least influential in the operation of the bail system. This is unfortunate since his client's pretrial freedom is so important and also because the defendant may be relying upon his lawyer to aid him in securing his release. Of the twenty-five attorneys interviewed, only two mentioned they ever engaged in the practice of lending their client money in order for him to pay the required bond. These attorneys perceive their function vis-á-vis the setting of their client's good character. If they can prove to the judge that their client will not pose any threat to the community if released, then they can expect at best a nominal bond, and at worst a bond set at a reasonable amount which the defendant can be expected to raise.

One of the main limitations on the defense attorney's ability to improve the defendant's chances for release is the fact that he usually comes into a case after the initial bail has been set. The defense is therefore forced to change a decision which was formulated without his presence. This is not to say that the defense is always absent from the initial bail hearing. In the large majority of cities visited, a lawyer was present at the initial bail hearing in about 25 percent of the cases. In a small number of cities which operate large public defender systems (i.e., Philadelphia and Washington, D.C.), a defendant was able to have his lawyer present at this initial hearing in approximately half of the cases.

The mere presence of the counsel does not guarantee a modest bail or release on recognizance, but it appears to greatly improve one's chances for achieving these goals. The defense attorney can bring relevant facts about his client's background to the judge's attention. An awareness of such beneficial information can have a positive effect on the judge's bail-setting decision. The author attempted to test the hypothesis that defendants with counsel received more favorable treatment in the pretrial release issue than those without, by observing the preliminary arraignment court in Detroit for a full week. Here the initial bail decision was made for all felony cases. A total of 345 cases were observed. In 105 (30.4 percent) of these cases, the defendant was represented by counsel, while 240 (69.6 percent) of these defendants were unable to have counsel present. Of the 105 defendants represented by a lawyer, 50 (74.6 percent) were able to obtain release on their own recognizance without having to pay any money. The remaining 55 were forced to raise the required bonds which ranged from $500 to $2000. The 240 defendants without lawyers were not so fortunate. Only 25 percent were released on their own recognizance with monetary bond being set for the remaining 75 percent with 25 percent (45) having bond set at $5000 or above. Thus a defendant who has a lawyer has twice the chance of being released on his own recognizance. Also, if a monetary bond is set, he will have a much better chance of having a lower, more reasonable bond if he has his lawyer present.

These figures are representative of most large cities where a defendant must rely upon private bar rather than a public defender's office as a source of representation in criminal cases. The type of counsel, public versus private, seems to be an important variable in explaining the significance of counsel at the initial bail hearing. In Washington and Philadelphia, and other cities which operate large public defender programs, nearly all defendants will be able to have a representative of this program as their counsel during this hearing. The drawback to this type of program is that it dilutes the manpower of the public defender program and ultimately diminishes its effectiveness. A public defender assigned to the preliminary arraignment court will serve as counsel for indigent defendants, only at this procedural point. He knows nothing about the defendant and therefore can offer the court little information as to why his client may be a good risk for a personal bond or bond reduction. Many of these public defenders work more as officers of the court than advocates for their clients in a supposedly adversarial system of justice.[13]

The defense counsel appears to be most important in the administration of bail, whether he is a public or private lawyer, in the attempted appeal of the original bond requesting a reduction or a recognizance release. This motion or application is not made until a week after the defendant's arrest and is usually timed for the preliminary hearing. By this time the public defender assigned to the defendant's case or the privately hired attorney has had an opportunity to meet with the defendant. He now knows the defendant's background as well as the strength of the state's case. At the preliminary hearing the attorney will then be able to present a well-documented motion to the judge for a bond reduction.

Court Officials

In close working proximity to the judge is another group of officials who play an essential role in the administration of bail. These are the various court officials such as clerks, bailiffs, secretaries, and court reporters who are responsible for the tedious and difficult job of ensuring that the assembly-line operations of their city's criminal justice system does not break down. They are given a plethora of titles, but they all owe their allegiance to the court and usually devote themselves to the thankless job of its survival. Anyone who tries to confer with the judge will have to first fight their way through this bastion of officials who are protecting the judge and his court from any and all outside intrusions. The greatest influence exerted by one of these officials was noted in the Detroit Recorder's Court where the arraignment officer collected all the relevant information on each case and actually made a recommendation to the judge on the question of bail.

The Bondsmen

The major source of information on the bondsmen was collected through interviews with bondsmen in ten cities, as well as by conferring with many other public officials who were knowledgeable on the topic of the bail-bonding industry in their community. Because the majority of bondsmen interviewed would talk only upon the assurance of confidentiality, the names used for most bondsmen are fictitious.

The bail bondsman is the only nonpublic official whose activities have direct effect upon the administration of bail. Relative to the other nonjudicial actors, the bondsmen probably exert more of an influence on a defendant's ability to obtain his pretrial freedom than any of the other groups discussed in this chapter. Seventy percent of the national sample of public officials surveyed in this study are in agreement with the statement that the "bondsmen plays a crucial role in the administration of bail."

Bondsmen have traditionally been pictured as heavy-set, cigar-chomping, sinister individuals who are social parasites, living off the misfortune of others. They lurk in the courthouse corridors with only an alleyway or a phone booth for an office. Usually associated with the underworld, they are one step ahead of the law and frequently discover that they need the services of a bondsman for themselves. Though many bondsmen may be responsible businessmen, this unflattering image still persists. Nearly 60 percent of the public officials thought it was necessary to reduce the power of the bondsmen. When one adds on the high percentage of respondents who were undecided on this question, there remains less than 20 percent of the sample who were willing to defend the bondsmen and oppose the reduction of their power.

How accurate is this tarnished image today? Are bondsmen plagued by a special genetic mutation which forces them into this degrading profession? The contemporary bondsmen no longer fit the stereotypical image just described. This is not to imply that one would easily confuse a bondsman with a corporation executive or a college professor. Their offices have moved out of the alley and phone booth into quarters considered to be only a relative improvement. They are now located in one- or two-room offices which are usually found across the street from the courthouse. The typical office is furnished with chairs that appear to be refugees from a deserted bus terminal. A single file cabinet or pile of whiskey cartons are used for storage. On top of an isolated desk is located a row of telephones, obscured by a mountainous collection of phone books from various cities. The floor is rugless and carpeted only with a bed of cigarette butts and trash. This depressing habitat, however, does not occupy very much of the bondsmen's time since he is usually to be found either at the courthouse or at his private residence. They will have an answering service or an assistant to take messages and contact him at home.

On either extreme of this typical bonding establishment are found the following two examples. In Detroit, the Epstein brothers operate a classy bonding company which is acknowledged to be the most successful in the city. As one enters their spacious offices, he is greeted by a lovely receptionist and directed to the waiting room which is luxurously furnished in tasteful Danish modern furniture. One crosses over thickly carpeted floors to speak to one of the partners in their pine-paneled private offices. If one did not read the sign on the outerdoor, he would have thought he was entering the offices of a successful lawyer or financier.

At the other extreme is the offices of a bondsman interviewed in Baltimore, Maryland. His office is located on East Baltimore Street, referred to by local denizens as the "block." It is a mecca for lonely men in search of thrills and illicit adventures. The bondsman's office was sandwiched between a burlesque house and a pornographic bookstore. The front of the office was unlit and filled with trash, broken chairs, and empty boxes. The back wall contained a one-way mirror, with the actual office located through a hidden door and behind a false front. Inside this second room the author found the bondsman surrounded by four of his cronies, engaged in a spirited game of cards. The small room was crammed from wall to wall with people and was permeated with cigar smoke and other acrid odors. The few pieces of furniture served only as footrests and were in a high state of deterioration. The bondsman was sitting behind a desk, with his feet propped up and majestically puffing on one of the four cigars currently polluting the limited air space of the cramped quarters.

Turning to the possibility of a common hereditary gene linking all the bondsmen investigated, no such genetic unanimity was discovered. By examining a wide range of backgrounds from which these men evolved prior to entering the bonding business, one clearly sees the fallacy of the initial stereotype. Like most professions, the bondsmen were attracted to their vocation by a variety of motives, pressures, and circumstances. The most common explanation offered for going into the bonding business was that their fathers had been in the business before them, and they felt a family obligation to continue the operation. Two of the three bondsmen who "grew into" their father's occupation frankly stated their distaste for their business. They felt trapped into continuing in the profession because of financial necessity or familial obligations. The third bondsman, Al Freeman, who inherited his family's business, engaged in the job as only a sideline and spent most of his time as one of the Boxing Commissioners for the State of Indiana. He is also a fight promoter and brought a heavyweight championship fight to his city.[14]

Two bondsmen were influenced into going into the bonding business on the advice of policemen. Both were young and out of work, and were told it was a "good hustle" supplying a regular source of income. One of these men came from a police family, his father being a former captain on the force and his brother currently serving as an officer.

Most of the bondsmen were drawn into the business at a fairly early age. All three bondsmen from Washington, D.C. commenced their bail-bonding experience in their early twenties. One was a vacuum cleaner salesman earning decent wages before he was drawn into the bonding business. A second bondsman borrowed money from his father to help bail friends out of jail during prohibition. In the following months his friends, many of whom were lawyers, talked him into becoming a full-time bondsman. For the third Washington bondsman it was the financial strains of temporary unemployment while attempting to earn money to pay for his last semester of college. All he could find at the time was a job with a bondsman. He never returned to college and soon went into the business for himself.[15]

The most interesting entrance into the bonding industry was by Hank Edwards of Atlanta. The son of a wealthy insurance executive, he decided in high school he wanted to "make it on his own." He moved into a boarding house as he worked his way through high school, saving every cent he earned. By the time he entered college he was able to put a down payment on a small home for himself. He continued his conscientious working habits and by completion of college he was able to purchase additional pieces of real estate. Within ten years after graduation from college he was a wealthy man with numerous real estate holdings, a bowling alley, and a chain of liquor stores. Becoming restless for some new endeavors, and confessing to increasing boredom with real estate transactions, he sought a new sideline to keep him busy. The bail-bonding business at that time (1960) was monopolized by whites in Atlanta. This additional challenge of breaking the color line spurred his decision to enter the bonding business. Even though it is only a sideline, since the large majority of his revenue still comes from his liquor stores and apartment houses, he spends most of his time working out of his bonding offices, a small shack across the street from the county jail.[16]

With bondsmen depending on a predominantly black clientele, it is important to examine the racial breakdown of bondsmen. Seventeen percent of the bondsmen interviewed were black. This seems to mirror fairly well the national percentage, although no one has ever bothered to tabulate it. The two black bondsmen in this sample, one from Washington, D.C. and the other from Atlanta, were the two best-educated bondsmen in the study's limited sample. They are also two of the most successful bondsmen in terms of professional prestige and financial security. The major distinguishing feature between the two men was their conflicting lifestyles which were best exemplified by their contrasting manner of dress. The explanation for this difference is probably caused by their respective geographic locations. Michael Lewis made what he believed was a needed attempt at bolstering the image of bondsman by his mod dressing. He is easily recognized in the courthouse corridors by his flare pants and wide flowery ties. Edwards, however, dresses like a day laborer, wearing khaki work pants, and a beat-up hat. He explains his purposefully chosen drab wardrobe by stating that in the South it is much easier for a black to deal with a white if he fits their sartorial stereotype and does not appear to be an "uppity nigra" even though he may be much wealthier than the whites he must deal with in the Sheriff's Department.[17]

In this age of women's liberation movement an obvious question to be raised is the availability of bondswomen. Although none of the eleven major cities visited possessed a bondswomen, a recent Associated Press release has revealed that such an individual operates out of Clearwater, Florida. Described as blonde and buxom, Robin Harris, armed with chemical mace, leg irons, pink phones, and hot pants, is a prosperous bondswoman currently having custody of 1900 clients and wrote nearly two million dollars worth of bonds in the first ten months of 1972. Asked why she entered the bail bonding business, Miss Harris is quoted as saying, "Because I thought it was a good place for a woman's touch. . . . I just thought this was a business where I could do some good."[18]

The bondsmen generally agreed that business was down. Blame was placed on bail reform projects as well as increasing numbers of forfeitures. In Washington, D.C. the number of bonding companies has been cut in half, from ten to five, in the past five years. Six of the eleven bondsmen interviewed were visibly distressed over the current financial condition and two of them were making plans to enter a new vocation within the year. Mickey Lewis of Washington is already making plans to work solely in civil bonds and abandon all criminal bond work. Forced by economic pressures to resort to outside sources of income, several bonding businesses are on the verge of economic collapse. The largest bonding enterprise studied, the United Bonding Insurance Company based in Indianapolis, but with operations in forty-five states, was recently liquidated by the Indiana Department of Insurance. An audit revealed that United had assets totaling $2,848,000 and liabilities of $4,144,000.[19]

One of the most obvious and significant trends of the last decade, reported by all bondsmen, is the ever-increasing amount of state and local regulation of the bonding industry. A few states for the first time have enacted laws which impose certain entrance requirements on anyone wishing to become a bonds-man. The most common requirement is that the bondsman cannot have a felony conviction or a past history of criminal activity. Michigan and California seem to be the only states where the entrance requirements are rigorously enforced.

An additional method of supervison is to periodically audit the bondsman's records or force him to qualify on a periodic basis for continued operation as a state or city authorized bonding company. In St. Louis, bondsmen are required to submit their records on a monthly basis and can be forced into discontinuing bonding activities if the required corrections are not made. Outside the cities regulated by the strict California Insurance Commission, the bondsmen of the remaining jurisdictions experience very little regulation. This is not to say that these cities do not presently have sufficient legislation covering the regulation of bondsmen. The problem is in getting the responsible state and local officials to enforce this legislation. Al Freeman, an Indianapolis bondsmen, discussing the difficulties of adequate legislation stated: "The present state rules are modeled after those of Florida, which are considered to be comprehensive and fair. Unfortunately the law is unenthusiastically enforced. With so many links in the chain of a bonding operation, the state has given 'loose reins' to the problem, deferring to the insurance companies who have historically been lax in controlling their agents." The only phase of implementation which the state has undertaken with any degree of regularity and rigor is the requirement that the state must have $75,000 in escrow from each insurance company in order to cover forfeitures owed by their agents.[20]

As noted in the Indianapolis example, bonding regulations are most often controlled at the state level by the insurance commissioner or comptroller. Individual cities have attempted to control the behavior of bondsmen by placing severe restrictions on when and where they are to be allowed in the courthouse. The typical court rule allows bondsmen inside a courtroom only when they have a case coming up, such as one of their clients failing to appear. They may visit potential clients at the detention facility only *after* they have been called by the defendant. The rationale behind the creation of much of this legislation is to eliminate opportunities for collusion and kickbacks between bondsmen and public officials. The problem of collusion has been greatly reduced in recent years, but this is due more to the inability of the financially strained bondsmen to pay kickbacks, than to the elaborate reporting procedures which are so lackadaisically enforced.

With this plethora of rules and regulations governing the bail bonding business, how does a bondsmen obtain his clientele? The main problem is not with the multitude of seldom enforced rules, but rather the intense competition with other bondsmen for the best clients. Better clients mean to bondsmen those defendants who appear to be most likely to show up for their various court appearances with the minimum amount of supervision. As bail reform projects continue to release the best potential clients, the competition among bondsmen for the remaining defendants becomes even more intense. One amusing manifestation of this competition is the desire for each bondsman to be listed first in the telephone directory. The result is the listing in Detroit of over 50 percent of the city's bonding companies beginning with the letter *A*. The assumption behind this maneuver is that when an inexperienced defendant turns to the yellow pages to select his bondsmen he will naturally look at the first company listed. The intensity of this competition has also shown an ugly side which is all too frequently brought to the public's attention. One Atlanta defense attorney commented on this tarnished image by stating that bonding companies give the impression of engaging in corrupt activities designed to "screw each other out of business."[21]

There are five major sources of clients for the bondsmen. These five groups which notify the bondsmen of their need of his services will be discussed in descending order of the frequency of their use. The first group is the defendant's family and friends. After a defendant is taken into custody and is permitted one or two telephone calls, he will invariably notify a relative or friend of his difficulty and request their help in gaining his pretrial freedom. It will then be the relative or friend who will seek out a bondsman to help get the defendant out of jail. The second group are the defendants themselves. Especially if a defendant has had prior experience in such situations, he will know how to directly contact a bondsman without bothering his family. He may have had a satisfactory previous relationship with a particular bondsman and prefer to renew their association. The third source group is the defendant's lawyer. The bondsman often feels more confident in securing the defendant's appearance at court if he can work in conjunction with his lawyer. The fourth group are court officials such as the court clerk or the bailiff. If both the bondsman and the clerk are "old-timers," a suggestion may be made to the bondsman as to a potential client. If the bondsman is amenable, the clerk or bailiff may contact the defendant and tell him to quickly call the bondsman whom they believe will give him a fair deal. The police and custodial officers comprise an ever-decreasing fifth group. Out of sheer helpfulness or with the thought of future favors in mind, these men recommend specific bondsmen to the recently apprehended defendants. If the bondsmen discover that specific police officers and jailers are consistently referring clients in their direction, certain rewards are usually offered in gratitude. A final group are of a highly specialized nature. They are professional criminals who will have trusted friends notify a bondsman in the city where they are moving in to commit a crime to be on the lookout for the defendant in case he slips up and is arrested. This procedure was revealed in an Atlanta interview but is engaged in on a national scale. It should be noted that all groups must initiate contact with the bondsman. The bondsman is unable to visit the defendant in his cell and therefore must wait passively to be notified by one of these groups.

Once a bondsman learns that a particular defendant wishes to use his services, he must decide whether he is willing to take a chance on him as a client. The bondsman must be an adroit judge of the defendant's future behavior, since he stands to lose a great deal of money if the defendant willfully forfeits. The common bonding fee of 10 percent means that the defendant pays the bondsman $100 on a $1000 bond and if the defendant fails to show, the bondsman owes the court a thousand dollars. With such grave financial stakes in the offing, bondsmen have formulated many criteria and guidelines to help them in this decision.

Little agreement was found among the bondsmen as to how best to ensure that they are selecting a reliable defendant. Most bondsmen admit using the same types of criteria utilized by bail reform projects, which emphasize the defendant's community ties and past criminal record. Bondsmen seek to supplement this basic information by going to the police or prosecutor's office in hopes of ascertaining the strength of the state's case against the defendant. Most bondsmen distrust their clients since they are so involved in their own problems that they are unable to objectively and honestly supply the necessary information. The bondsman therefore relies most commonly on discussions with the family or lawyer. One bondsman interviewed in Detroit disclosed that he will consult *only* with the family since they are the ones who must be trusted to make sure the defendant will appear in court.

Like most officials concerned with the administration of bail, the bondsman believes that the most important variable affecting the defendant's pretrial release, is the nature of the crime of which he is charged. The categories of crimes which bondsmen classify as either poor risks or good risks is not based, however, on the seriousness of the offense, but on the following collection of guidelines, premonitions and idiosyncracies. Examining first the best risks, the bondsmen frequently listed any professional criminal as being the most reliable client. These are experienced criminals who believe that the arrest is merely an occupational hazard. They have frequently employed the services of bondsmen in the past and have worked out an acceptable arrangement. The defendant knows that if he forfeits and causes the bondsman to lose money, word will be circulated and he will be unable to secure his pretrial release by any bondsmen if he is arrested in the future, which of course, is a distinct possibility in the lifetime of a professional criminal. A second category of good risks are defendants arrested for crimes such as gambling which are usually run by organized crime. In this case there will be a reliable source of money and the defendant's sponsoring organization will be a persuasive force in ensuring his return for trial. If the organization is interested in getting the defendant out of the jurisdiction, they will often cover the entire bond with the bondsman, rather than pay the money directly to the court themselves.[22]

Who do the bondsmen consider bad risks? One unlikely group which most bondsmen are reluctant to have as clients are first offenders. Their explanation is quite logical. They reason that first offenders have a greater fear of a possible prison sentence since they have never experienced incarceration before. Thus there seems a greater possibility that they might panic as their court date approaches and, fearing the worst, run away. Another category of poor risks are those defendants categorized as recidivists whose crimes seem to carry the defendant into deeper trouble and eventually force him to flee the city. Examples of these types of criminals are prostitutes and junkies. Mickey Lewis, Washington bondsman, commented on the habits of both groups by stating: "Prostitutes and gypsies. They come into town for a while and get arrested. They get out on bond and they take off for another town. . . . The junkies are hazardous because even they don't know what they are going to do. The pushers are going to stay in town but you don't know about the users."[23]

A third category of crimes which most bondsmen are apprehensive about are those involving guns or physical violence. Armed robbery was always mentioned as one of those violent crimes which bondsmen try to avoid. Another seasoned Washington bondsman spoke out on why he steers away from armed robbers:

> A guy that takes a gun and goes into a store or a bank must have it in the back of his mind that he'll use it if he has to. Now if I bail him and can't produce him in court, I've got to go get him. He didn't hesitate to pull a gun when he held you up and I make a good target, big as I am. Besides that the bonds in these cases run high, making the potential losses greater. Taking someone who has gone to the gun just isn't worth the risk. Besides a guy charged with that kind of offense knows he may be going away for a long time and that increases the chances he'll skip.[24]

The bondsmen have often been criticized for being very loose or irresponsible in whom they select as clients. This criticism seems unjustified based on this study's observations. Most bondsmen are plagued by a potential clientele composed of less than ideal citizens. The bondsmen interviewed were filled with no desire to empty the jails and to write bonds for anybody. They are usually operating on shaky financial foundations and must exercise caution in order to avoid complete economic collapse. If they can be accused of anything, the

bondsmen can be chastized for turning down too many defendants, causing
them to be detained in jail.

The amount a bondsman can charge a client is usually regulated by state
statute. The customary amount is 10 percent of the total bond set. Because of
rising forfeiture rates and a less desirable clientele, the bondsmen have attempted
to require additional collateral from the defendant or his family. This is usually
a mortgage or liens on property or businesses. Several states prohibit this type
of maneuver, but it is rarely if ever enforced despite the fact that it is an
extremely common practice among bondsmen. Another frequent state prohibition is against bondsmen working on credit but this is also rarely enforced.

The 10 percent fee which the bondsman charges represents his profit before
operating expenses are deducted. From this figure must be subtracted losses
due to forfeitures as well as additional expenses and licensing fees which permit
him to take less than half of the original figure. A Detroit bondsmen frankly
stated that if it was not for a few big bonds in the $20,000 to 25,000 range
from professional criminals or organized crime, he would not be able to
remain in business.[25]

In a few jurisdictions bondsmen are permitted to write bonds on property.
In Washington, D.C. a bondsman is allowed to write bonds on clients in the
amount of three times the value of the property. Once the bondsman's limit is
reached he cannot bail out anybody else.

After the bondsman has decided to accept a defendant as a client, the crucial factor determining whether a forfeiture will occur is the degree of supervision which the bondsmen exercises over the defendant (provided of course, that
the defendant has not initially made up his mind to skip town, even before
seeing the bondsman). Although several bondsmen worked long and hard at
maintaining adequate contact with their clients, the majority seemed to be lax
and merely assumed that the defendant would appear for trial. It was only
when the defendant failed to appear that the bondsman would spring into
action and work through his network of informants and "skip tracers," modern
day bounty hunters, to retrieve the missing defendant.

The bondsman usually repeats the oral and written statements of the court
notifying the defendant of the date of his next court appearance. For many
bondsmen their contact with the defendant ends here, unless there is an
attempt to forfeit. Among the procedures followed by the more conscientious
bondsmen are a series of phone calls, letters, and visits to the defendant and his
family. Several bondsmen sneered at such "pampering" and believed that if the
defendants really required that much supervision, they should not have been
accepted as clients in the first place. One bondsman in Washington who realized
the necessity for this continuous supervision complained of the long hours
required by such procedures: "You work from 8 to 5 at your office and then
you have to run your people for the next day. Since many of them don't come
home regularly, you have to go down to 14th and U Streets or wherever they

may be hanging out. It takes up to 18 hours a day."[26] Another Washington bondsman complained that the long hours ruined his marriage and robbed him of having any kind of home life.

The bondsmen's caseload varied a great deal depending on the size of the operation. In the most typical small two- and three-man operations, it was estimated that they usually are working with about a hundred clients at a time. The size of the bonding company seemed to have no effect on the degree of supervision, although the two largest companies appeared to have the most complete system of client supervision.

The judgment of bondsmen concerning their clients is not infallible. The question of how many defendants which they bond who eventually forfeit is obscured by the poor record-keeping by both the bondsmen and the state and local authorities. Only six of the eleven cities visited were able to provide estimates of the forfeiture rate of bondsmen. Table 3-1 indicates the figures that were available and their source. The national bond forfeiture rate has been estimated to be between 3 and 4 percent.[27]

If the defendant is willfully avoiding his court appearance and cannot be located in a day or two, the bondsman must turn to his "skip tracers." These men work on commission of approximately 10 percent of the bond. They are usually armed and very often have prior records. No state has actively sought to regulate these men who are operating within the penumbra of the criminal justice system.

The legal authority for allowing the bondsmen to return their clients from any jurisdiction in the country is a document entitled the "bail piece." The bail piece is like a contract between the bondsman and his client. The critical section of this contract is the stated agreement by the defendant that he is willing to waive his extradition rights and authorizes the bondsman or his agent to retrieve him from wherever he has fled. The bondsman obtains the bail piece

Table 3-1
Forfeiture Rate for Bondsmen

City	Forfeiture Rate	Source of data
Baltimore	5%	Estimate by public officials and bondsmen (1970)
Philadelphia	4%	Estimate by Court Admin's Office (1970)
Indianapolis	5.4%	Survey by Indianapolis Bail Report Project (1969)
Detroit	8%	Recorders Court Annual Report (1969)
Atlanta	7%	Exact figures from D.A.'s Office (1970)
St. Louis	5%	Exact figures from Clerk of Circuit Court (1970)
Avg.	5.7% = 6-city avg.	

from the court after his client has fled. This document, along with the bench warrant is presented to the local police department wherever the fugitive is recaptured. The bondsmen in most states are permitted official assistance from these local authorities in their efforts at recapturing the fleeing defendant. The bondsmen often delegate their power to the skip tracer who is in possession of the bail piece and the bench warrant.[28]

Some states have tried to impose restrictions on the more blatant offenses of bondsmen and skip tracers in their attempts at recapturing defendants in other jurisdictions. Unfortunately most of their legislative endeavors are short-sighted in that they only restrict the obnoxious activities of bondsmen from other states trying to drag out citizens from within their state boundaries, while no attempt is made to prohibit similar activities by bondsmen from their state going into other states to recapture fugitives. Such a legislative defect was discussed in a California Law Review article which stated "that the state [California] encourages or at least condones the use of tactics by California bondsmen operating out of state which it would not tolerate if the bondsmen committed them within the state. While California authorities are not aware of incidents of physical or psychological abuse of California fugitives recaptured outside the state, other jurisdictions have reported incidents of such abuse."[29]

The abuses referred to in the previous quote, although infrequent, still occur too often. Two bondsmen from Atlanta, Georgia, were recently jailed in Memphis, Tennessee, in an attempt to return a Memphis man to Georgia. They had vowed to return the man to Atlanta "dead or alive," and had been found threatening him with a pistol.[30] In an even more bizarre incident involving bondsmen, a skip tracer from Chattanooga, Tennessee, had burst into the bedroom of an Atlanta citizen at two in the morning and ordered him to return to Chattanooga with him. The man refused and was shot to death. The shocking thing was the skip tracer had made an error in the address and an innocent victim was murdered.[31]

Despite the abundance of stories concerning the exploits of bondsmen recapturing fugitives, these tales appear to be greatly exaggerated. Bondsmen generally view the retrieval process as a very expensive proposition which is more often than not, unsuccessful. As a Washington bondsmen related: "Going to get a bond jumper means paying for information to locate him, the cost of driving to wherever he is and back, meals and the 425 a day cost of hiring the gun, the man who'll guard the jumper on the return trip. A recent four day trip to Akron cost $750."[32]

One of the major improvements in the administration of bail is a willingness on the part of responsible state and local officials to collect from bondsmen all forfeitures in the full amount of the original bond. The significance of this improvement in collection enforcement is that it will force bondsmen to keep closer contact with their clients so they will show up for trial. Bondsmen must be made to realize that they will be taking the risk of actually having to pay the forfeiture bond if their client flees. Judge Murphy of the District of Columbia's Court of General Sessions symbolizes this new attitude. He recently stated in an interview that "bondsmen have always been in a position where they just assumed nothing was going to happen to them. But I just don't have this club house attitude about bondsmen."[33]

The reader should be cautioned against being overly optimistic about overnight changes. There are still many cities where the bonds are not collected on a regular basis. In St. Louis, for example, records of the Circuit Court revealed that of the 318 forfeitures in felony cases in 1970, 304 were set aside. This tremendous number of unpaid forfeitures casts serious doubts as to the manner in which these bonds are being collected.[34]

The bondsmen are usually helped by the city if they have honestly attempted to recapture the fugitive. They are also provided aid in the form of extended periods of time in which to relocate their clients. This length of time varies from 10 to 14 days for Detroit bondsmen to 180 days for bondsmen in San Francisco. The average time to return the defendant and pay the forfeiture is 90 days, and is found in both Atlanta and Baltimore. In nearly all cities studied, if the bondsmen can convince the judge that the forfeiture was not his fault and that he diligently attempted the recapture of the defendant, the judge will set aside all or a part of the forfeiture amount due. In Atlanta the District Attorney offers a 25 percent discount on all forfeited bonds if their office can be convinced of the effort made to recapture the fugitive. A few cities employ a sliding scale where the sooner the bondsmen can recapture the client, the less he will have to pay on the forfeited bond.

As noted, the sinister character commonly ascribed to bondsmen is largely a fictitious creation when compared to the behavior of bondsmen who were interviewed and observed at work. Most important, there was sufficient variation in their personalities so that it was impossible to construct a valid stereotypical image of the group. Nevertheless, it was discovered that bondsmen and their skip tracers still occasionally engaged in illegal activities.

In Indianapolis, bondsman Al Freeman believed that a few bondsmen were engaged in illegal activities such as narcotics and gambling. One bondsmen was believed to be forcing many of his attractive female clients into going to bed with him before he would agree to put up their bail.[35] Another bondsman finally had his license revoked because of his numerous illegal extracurricular activities.[36] Also in Indianapolis, bondsman Norman Z. Flick was arrested in July 1970 for theft and three counts of failure to file a bond affadavit.[37]

An additional difficulty for bondsmen is the reputation of their clientele. The general public often indict bondsmen through guilt by association. Unfortunately, bondsmen have sometimes formed business alliances with organized crime figures which have discredited the entire profession. Judge Moylan, former Baltimore State's Attorney, commented that bondsmen seem to be involved in every type of conspiracy and underworld activity in the city, with a special interest in gambling.[38]

The most common complaint lodged against bondsmen by their clients was that they failed to return part of the 10 percent bonding fee when the case was quickly dismissed prior to trial. The decision not to prosecute is often made by the time of the preliminary hearing and means that the defendant may be paying several hundred dollars for only a week's freedom. A similar irritation is caused by the bondsman changing his mind about being willing to stand behind a client. The bondsman may go to the client's home and drag him back to jail, usually not returning his initial payment. This type of behavior may occur when the bondsman learns something new about the defendant or his case and decides that on the basis of this new information his client is no longer a desirable risk. It is presently undecided precisely what legal protections are offered to the bondsman's client from these two unpleasant practices.

The bondsmen do not function in a vacuum. Their interrelationships with officials and agencies involved with the administration of justice are essential to their livelihood. These relationships however, have often led to alarmed cries of collusion and serve as another example of the bondsmen's illegal activities. It is impossible to arrive at an impartial and scientific estimation of the amount of collusion actually taking place.

The most frequently named group to be accused of engaging in collusive activities with bondsmen are defense attorneys. It was a charge heard in most cities that bondsmen receive a 10 percent kickback from lawyers recommended by bondsmen. In St. Louis one attorney went so far as to state that bondsmen have made several lawyers wealthy by referring cases to them.[39] Blame can be placed upon the local bar association which fails to control these men and permits these collusive enterprises to continue.[40]

A second group charged with collusive endeavors with bondsmen are judges. There was an investigation in Philadelphia in 1964 on charges that judges were receiving money from bondsmen to set bail in all cases regardless of their seriousness, so they would have more potential clients. According to a defense attorney interviewed, this practice still persists, although to a lesser degree. He commented that a few judges will allow bondsmen to stand behind them and tell them how much they believe the defendant can afford.[41] The bondsman may attempt to improve a working relationship with a judge by contributing to his campaign fund. The bondsmen of Detroit and St. Louis seem to be the most politically active in this respect. One bondsman is a party chairman of a congressional district.

A third group accused of illegal dealings with bondsmen are the police. This relationship is supposedly founded upon the arresting officer or someone in the stationhouse recommending a particular bondsmen to the defendant. At the end of the month the policeman could expect to receive a kickback from that bondsman, based upon the number of clients referred. It was learned through interviews and many hours of observations of stationhouses, lockups, and jails, that this practice has sharply declined in the past five years, although it still continues on a sporadic basis. The reasons given for the abatement of a seemingly lucrative practice for both parties are twofold. First is the increasing supervision over the operation of bail-bonding companies by state and city agencies. Second is the decreasing profit margin of bonding companies which have been forced to curtail expenditures, such as kickback payments. These financial pressures have reduced their clientele and forced bondsmen to be more selective in whom they choose to represent.

4

Pretrial Misconduct: Forfeiture and Additional Crimes

One of the most publicized and troublesome problems facing the administrators of the nation's criminal justice system is the misconduct of defendants released prior to their trials. This pretrial misconduct is manifested in two types of illegal activities: failing to appear for trial and committing additional crimes during this pretrial period. This chapter will not only examine both of these problems but will also analyze what types of controls and procedures may be best utilized in order to curtail such undesirable behavior.

Forfeiture Rate

Dimensions of the Problem

The failure to appear for trial is reflected in a forfeiture rate. This statistic is of vital importance in evaluating the effectiveness of a system of pretrial release. A high forfeiture rate indicates that those judicial officials responsible for making the decision to release defendants have been very poor predictors of the defendant's future behavior. Once this high rate has been publicized, it can usually be expected that those defendants unlucky enough to face the judge in the immediate future, will find themselves forced to raise exceedingly high bail amounts.

An equally important consequence of a high forfeiture rate is that the court system is made aware of the failings of its present methods of notification and supervision. This means that many defendants failed to appear because the court simply failed to give them clear notice of their next appearance date or was unwilling or unable to communicate this information to the defendant during his pretrial release. Since this pretrial period often reaches four to six months, it is imperative that defendants receive additional supervision and communication during this time. It has been estimated that nearly half of all forfeitures are involuntary and caused by the defendant's either forgetting about the court date or never being adequately notified.

A final significance attached to this forfeiture statistic is that it may be used as a means to discredit the bail-setting practices of certain judges who are releasing

65

defendants on their own recognizance or nominal bond. By being able to illustrate the high forfeiture rate associated with either of these release procedures, public pressure can be mounted against the continued use of such practices.

Although the forfeiture rate appears to be a critical statistic in evaluating and ultimately operating a bail system, there are several difficulties in relying upon these statistics as they are offered to the public. Like any statistic, they are easily manipulated to indicate whatever the court system or reform group wishes to emphasize. The forfeiture rate is even more prone to these machinations since it is a highly discretionary decision by the court system as to when a forfeiture has actually taken place. In cities wishing to reform their bail system and permit increasing numbers of defendants to obtain their pretrial release, they will liberally interpret when a forfeiture has taken place. They may stipulate that a forfeiture has occurred only after the defendant has had a day or two in which to come to court and has been reminded of his tardy appearance. This approach will usually result in a city having a low or at least a respectable forfeiture rate.

In other cities which may be wishing to discredit these liberal efforts and stress the need to stop coddling criminals, the forfeiture rate will be strictly interpreted. A defendant who appears one minute late for his court appearance, regardless of any possible excuse, will be counted as a forfeiture. Such a narrow literal interpretation will raise the forfeiture rate to its optimal level. An example of a city court system utilizing this strict interpretation is the Recorder's Court of Detroit, Michigan, which seems intent on pressuring judges into not releasing defendants on their own recognizance. The annual report of the Detroit Recorder's Court in 1969 presented the alarming figures that 40 percent of the defendants ROR'd (released on their own recognizance) had forfeited. This figure is nearly ten times the estimated average reported for the nation in this study. By using the following two techniques, the recorder's court was able to inflate this statistic to the highest degree possible: First, the court used an extremely strict definition of forfeiture so that every defendant who failed to appear at the exact time was counted as a forfeiture. As we have noted, half of the defendants would eventually appear within forty-eight hours so that we can cut the 40 percent to a more realistic 20 percent rate, Secondly, if a defendant did willingly forfeit, every required court appearance was counted as a *separate* forfeiture. In other words, a defendant skipping town after his initial appearance in court would miss his preliminary hearing, grand jury indictment (or information), arraignment, trial, and finally, the sentencing. In Detroit this defendant would be counted as having committed five forfeitures. Now when we reexamine the 20 percent figure and realize that it may comprise up to five forfeitures per defendant who has voluntarily left the city, we can arrive at a much more reasonable 4 to 7 percent forfeiture rate which is consistent with the national figures.

An additional difficulty in relying upon these forfeiture statistics is that

most court systems either do not keep these figures, or if they do, it is in a
rather careless fashion and not scientifically valid. Even the state of California,
which is so often pictured as having the premier court administration in the
country, does not collect these forfeiture statistics. It should also be pointed
out that this entire discussion of the difficulties in obtaining reliable and valid
forfeiture rate statistics is found to an even greater degree when one attempts to
evaluate the amount of additional crimes which are committed by defendants
awaiting trial.

With all of these caveats in mind, let us now see how many forfeitures are
currently taking place around the country. Turning first to the large urban
centers which were personally visited and where court reports were inspected,
the eight cities listed in Table 4-1 have an average forfeiture rate of 7.8%. This
table not only indicates an exact percentage for each city but also presents the
exact source of the figure.

Since Table 4-1 reported the exact forfeiture rate in only eight cities, all of
which are major urban centers with populations exceeding half a million, it was
necessary to conduct a mailed survey of an additional seventy-two cities encom-
passing a wide range of sizes, if one were to obtain a truly national picture of
the problem. Judges, prosecutors, criminal lawyers, and bail project directors
were asked to estimate the percentage of defendants in their community who
forfeited bond. A forfeiture rate was determined for each city by averaging the
estimates of the public officials who completed the questionnaire.

The overwhelming majority of cities (80 percent) reported that between
0 to 9 percent of all released defendants failed to appear for their trial. There
were also twelve cities (17 percent) which estimated that between 10 and 19
percent of their defendants forfeited their appearance. These forfeiture rates
seem to correspond with other studies which have estimated them to be
between 3 and 7 percent. In comparing the estimated forfeiture rates of

Table 4-1
Forfeiture Rates

	Rate	Source of Statistics and Clarification
Chicago	8.7%	Clerk of Circuit Court of Cook County (1969)
Philadelphia	4.0%	Estimate by Court Administrator (1970)
Indianapolis	5.4%	Survey by Indianapolis Bail Project (1969) Surety Bonds
Detroit	24.0%	Recorders Court Annual Report (1969) 8% for Surety Bonds, 40% for personal bonds
Baltimore	5.0%	Estimate by public officials and bondsmen
Atlanta	7.0%	Exact figure from District Attorney's Office
St. Louis	5.0%	Exact figure from Clerk of Circuit Court, Criminal Division
Washington	3.7%	Exact figure from the Report of the D.C. Judicial Court, Report on the Operation of Bail (1969)

defendants ROR'd with those released through payment of bail, the ROR defendants were only slightly more responsible. Sixty-three cities (87 percent) estimated that 0 to 9 percent of all ROR'd defendants failed to show up for their trial. Fifty-eight cities (80 percent) estimated that 0 to 9 percent of all money bail defendants failed to appear. The one difference between the two groups, and it was minor, were the estimates in three cities that they had forfeiture rates over 30 percent for defendants released on money bail. In either case, the problem of forfeiture occurs in only about 5 percent of the total number of cases. Even this figure of 5 percent is subject to revision on practical grounds. It was stated previously that approximately half of those recorded forfeitures are merely technical or involuntary, and the defendant eventually appeared when notified of his tardiness.

In judging whether the amount of forfeitures has changed during the past five years, the results of the survey indicate that, like the crime rate, most cities have also experienced a dramatic rise in forfeiture rates. This increase has occurred for both ROR'd and money bail defendants. Only 1 percent of the responding cities thought there had been a reduction. Fifty-four percent of the cities found increasing forfeiture rates for bailed defendants, while 52 percent of the cities experienced increasing forfeitures for ROR'd defendants.

The study was unable to identify any significant explanatory variables derived from the demographic structure of a city to explain its forfeiture rate. This in itself indicates that the problem of defendants failing to appear for trial is truly national in scope, plaguing all types and sizes of cities. The only demographic variable which appears to hint at a possible relationship is a city's crime rate, but even this is an extremely weak correlation (0.2019).

Once a forfeiture has occurred, the judge before which the missing defendant is supposed to appear will sign a bench warrant for the defendant's rearrest. The bondsmen as well as the police then spring into action hoping to recapture the tardy suspect. Most cities studied were unable to successfully recapture very many of the defendants who willfully avoided their court appearance. The large majority of defendants who are located and reappear have usually unintentionally failed to show. Their excuses range from illness to poor memories. The small group of willful forfeitures who are recaptured are primarily those unfortunate defendants who were apprehended for an additional crime during the pretrial period. If a defendant purposely forfeits bail he will usually "skip town," and there is almost no chance of recapturing him. An explanation of this inability to serve these bench warrants for forfeitures was offered by Paul Michel of the Philadelphia District Attorney's Office, which currently has 6000 unserved warrants for failure to appear. He believes that those agencies attempting to serve these warrants usually have no idea where these missing men are and possess no adequate staff to locate them. The problem has reached its present proportions because the courts and the bondsmen have failed to keep close contact with released defendants during the pretrial period.[1]

Because of the muddled state of record keeping and the jammed court calendars, even a defendant who forfeits unintentionally by reporting late, has caused irreparable harm to the functioning of the urban criminal court system. Experienced criminals soon realize that it is more advantageous to simply show up late than to try to evade the police by skipping town or going into hiding. This tardiness causes great confusion and often results in a case being dismissed. In an attempt to rectify this situation, Judge Tim Murphy of the District of Columbia's Court of General Sessions recommends that a foolproof warrant squad be created. They would be notified the second the defendant failed to show up and would immediately move out after him. He would then be returned to court so quickly that his case would not have to be continued.[2]

One of the continuing controversies in the administration of bail is how many of these forfeitures are technical or unintentional and how many are willful. Officials interviewed on this subject agreed that the majority of forfeitures were unintentional. The only attempt to scientifically study this question was done by the Cook County Special Bail Project which found that well over half of the I bonds (personal bonds for release on recognizance by the judge) forfeited in 1968 were of a technical nature. Once bonds were vacated for illiness, misunderstanding, and a long list of other excuses, the forfeiture rate was cut in more than half.[3]

Two of the main reasons for these technical forfeitures is the fault of the court system rather than the defendant. The first is the extremely poor notification system used by the courts to inform the defendant of his court date. In many cities the defendant is notified of his next appearance by the judge, or more commonly by the court clerk. This notification is simply an oral statement made at the conclusion of the proceeding. Remembering the lower intelligence of most defendants, the noise and confusion of the courtroom, and the strangeness of the entire proceeding, it is little wonder that more defendants do not fail to appear. In a few of the more conscientious cities, this oral notification may be followed by a written reminder mailed to the defendant's last known address. The court, which mails this note several weeks after the initial appearance, never finds out whether this notice is ever received.

A second reason is the poor quality of the clerical administering of this notification system. Exacerbating this problem even more is the confusion and strangeness of the entire judicial process. Public Defender Hooley of Oakland, California, commented that since so many defendants are transients and indigents, they are hampered by a poor sense of timing and reliability which also contributes to their negligent behavior.[4] Commenting further on the difficulty of reaching these transient and impoverished defendants, Judge Davis of Indianapolis believes that many of these defendants cannot be reached because they have no phone, and move around a great deal without leaving a forwarding address. The Judge warns, however, that all the blame should not be placed on the courts. He and several other judges interviewed in other cities believe that the bondsmen have not been doing their job. They are failing to keep close enough contact with their clients to guarantee their appearance.[5]

Once it is certain that a defendant has forfeited, the city must collect the total amount of the bond from the surety. A great deal of confusion exists in the various cities studied as to exactly when the courts have officially declared a forfeiture to have occurred and demand payment of the bond. Even as the bond is collected, many courts allow the bondsman an opportunity to convince the judge that the cause of forfeiture was not their fault and that they had made a diligent and honest effort to recapture the defendant. If the judge is convinced, he may set aside the entire forfeiture, or a percentage of it.

In nearly every state and city it is a crime to forfeit one's bond. These forfeitures are usually categorized as a serious misdemeanor, frequently carrying a one or two-year maximum prison sentence. It is argued that rigid implementation of these criminal statutes would help to reduce the forfeiture rate. When one closely examines the current operations of our court systems, it can be seen that merely adding on an additional penalty would have little effect. With our criminal justice system plagued by a tremendous backlog of cases and all court officials devoted to the important task of moving these cases through this assembly-line process, the plea-bargaining system has developed as the only feasible solution to the current dilemma. The addition of one count of bail forfeiture to the already existing plethora of charges against the defendant, who is manipulating to have a reduced charge and light sentence in return for a guilty plea, is insignificant at best. All such charges, it should be remembered, are usually permitted to run concurrently.

How Can It Be Reduced?

So far our discussion of bail forfeitures has dealt with the magnitude of the problem and only tangentially focused upon the important question of how to reduce their numbers. This question which we must now squarely face is, given the present administration of bail, what procedures and measures can be adopted for eliminating (or at least controlling) this problem? Examples of operational procedures which may affect the forfeiture rate are the following: (1) how the defendant is notified of his next court appearance; (2) where and when this notification is made; (3) the presence of a bondsman; (4) the presence of a system to validate the information about the defendant; and (5) the presence of a system to supervise the defendant during his pretrial release. Table 4-2 indicates that of these five procedures, only the presence of a supervisory system during release and the place of notification are related to a reduced forfeiture rate.

The procedures found to be most significant were the operation of a system to supervise the defendants during their pretrial release. These supervisory

Table 4-2
Forfeiture Rates and Operational Procedures

Procedural Variables	The Forfeiture Rate	
	Below the National Average	Above the National Average
1. Place of Notification		
At the Court	7 (77%)	21 (37%)
At a later date	2 (23%)	35 (63%)
2. Method of Notification		
Oral Notice	12 (63%)	17 (55%)
Written Notice	7 (37%)	21 (45%)
3. Presence of a Bondsmen		
Absent	6 (21%)	8 (22%)
Present	23 (79%)	28 (78%)
4. Verification System		
No	24 (67%)	26 (76%)
Yes	12 (33%)	8 (24%)
5. Supervisory System		
No	15 (31%)	14 (64%)
Yes	33 (69%)	8 (36%)

programs were found primarily in cities operating bail reform projects. The supervisory function is manifested through certain requirements placed upon the defendants. The most common requirement was to have the defendant report in to the bail project or court clerk on a periodic basis, usually every two weeks. The defendant reported in by phone in most cities although a few required an occasional personal visit. If the defendant failed to report in on one or more occasions, the court system and the bail project would attempt to use informal means to locate the missing defendant before issuing a bench warrant for his rearrest. The importance of such a supervisory system can be seen from the statistics in Table 4-2 which show that nearly 70 percent of the cities operating a supervisory program are experiencing a *below* average forfeiture rate while 65 percent of those cities plagued by a forfeiture rate *above* the national average have failed to install such a system.

A second procedure related to the forfeiture rate is the place where the defendant is notified of his next court appearance. It was found that cities which notified defendants at the courthouse rather than at a later date (and usually done through the mail), were able to maintain a below average forfeiture rate in nearly 80 percent of the cities surveyed. Only 23 percent of those cities notifying defendants after the bail hearing were able to possess a below average forfeiture rate. The necessity for notifying the defendant, before he leaves the courtroom of his next appearance date was emphasized in several interviews with court officials. Many defendants are transient, and once they depart the courthouse, they are very difficult to locate. Their lifestyle involves frequent changes of address, often without leaving any forwarding notice. Many of these defendants are also nearly impossible to locate by phone. Many who are indigent or are temporary boarders in a rooming house cannot afford the luxury of a phone. A final complication is the unwillingness of many to follow the normal work schedule of middle-class citizens and who therefore, cannot be reached at a regular scheduled time. All these difficulties simply reinforce the fact that it is imperative that notification, if it is to have any value, must be done before the defendant leaves the courthouse and supervision must be carefully planned and rigorously implemented.

A second set of explanatory variables related to a city's forfeiture rate is the type of release criteria which the local court system uses to determine if the defendant is to be relased or the amount of bail to be set. The officials in each of the seventy-two cities were asked to evaluate the importance of each of the following criteria used to determine pretrial release: present charge; past criminal record; likelihood of committing a future crime; strength of community ties; and his past appearance record. It is frequently hypothesized by defenders of a strict law and order system that the seriousness of the present charge and the defendant's past criminal record are the most important criteria in attempting to predict a defendant's pretrial behavior and should therefore be stressed by those cities attempting to decrease their forfeiture rates. Table 4-3 relates

Table 4-3
Release Criteria and the Forfeiture Rate

Release Variables	*Forfeiture Rate*	
	Below the National Average	*Above the National Average*
1. Present Charge		
Unimportant, Slightly Important	9 (48%)	15 (30%)
Extremely Important	10 (52)	35 (70)
2. Past Record		
Unimportant, Slightly Important	8 (42)	14 (27)
Extremely Important	11 (58)	37 (73)
3. Likelihood of Future Crimes		
Unimportant, Slightly Important	8 (38)	14 (33)
Extremely Important	13 (62)	28 (67)
4. Community Ties		
Unimportant, Slightly Important	6 (33)	26 (61)
Extremely Important	12 (67)	17 (31)
5. Past Appearance Record		
Unimportant, Slightly Important	8 (36)	29 (58)
Extremely Important	14 (64)	21 (42)

these criteria to the forfeiture rates of each city in the survey and arrives at some rather unexpected results for the law and order advocates.

As critics of the traditional bail system have continually advocated, there seems to be no relationship between the seriousness of the charge against a defendant and his proclivity toward forfeiting his bail. Table 4-3 indicates that the defendant's community ties and his past appearance record are the most reliable pretrial release criteria used to predict a defendant's appearance in court. Sixty-seven percent of those cities who considered community ties to be an extremely important pretrial release criteria had a forfeiture rate below the national average. It should also be noted that 64 percent of those cities stressing the importance of the defendant's past appearance record also experienced below average forfeiture rates. Turning now to the traditional criteria of seriousness of the present charge and past criminal record, one finds them to be of very little predictive value. Seventy percent of those cities considering the seriousness of the charge to be an extremely important release criteria experienced *above* average forfeiture rates. In a similar vein, 63 percent of the cities stressing the defendant's past record had *above* average forfeiture rates. The results of Table 4-3 conclude that judicial systems wishing to control the forfeiture rates of pretrial releases should emphasize the defendants community ties and past appearance record, rather than maintaining faith in the traditional criteria of a defendant's present charges and past criminal record.

Are any types of cities more prone to be suffering from excessive forfeiture rates? The results of this survey, after controlling for city size, percentage black, percentage engaged in manufacturing, median income and geographic region, concluded that these demographic characteristics were not statistically related to the forfeiture problem. It may therefore be inferred from this finding that the forfeiture problem is nationwide and not concentrated in any particular category of city. Based on the information derived from Tables 4-2 and 4-3, if we are to successfully fight the forfeiture problem, we must attack it in all types of cities, stressing the need to create viable supervisory programs and convince the judiciary to emphasize the community ties and past appearance record of defendants when they are considering a defendant's pretrial release.

Additional Crimes: The Rearrest Rate

Dimensions of the Problem

An even more serious type of pretrial misconduct by the defendant is when he commits an additional crime while awaiting his trial. These incidents are frequently well publicized and indict the entire criminal court system. They are also the death knell for any attempt at initiating bail reform projects in a community. These additional crimes are not only significant to the administration of bail by their inherently serious nature, but also because they have been used as a rationale for enacting preventive detention legislation. Presently only the District of Columbia Criminal Courts have such a provision, but former Attorney General Mitchell recently sent a new legislative proposal to Congress that would allow federal courts to hold without bail persons accused of specific dangerous or organized crime acts. How many crimes are actually committed by defendants awaiting trial? This question cannot be answered accurately on the basis of the present state of available statistical data. The author discovered that reliable statistics on the rearrest rate during pretrial release were an even more elusive statistic than the forfeiture rates just discussed.

Because of the current controversy surrounding preventive detention, the seriousness of this problem (additional crimes during pretrial release) is of great importance to policy decisions related to the pretrial activities of defendants. If it can be determined that large numbers of defendants are actually committing additional crimes during the pretrial period, this fact will serve as a justification for future preventive detention statutes. With this important policy question at stake, it is no wonder that so much confusion surrounds the issue of exactly how many additional crimes are actually committed by defendants awaiting trial.

The recent statistical warfare in Washington, D.C., which occurred just prior to the passage of the city's preventive detention provision, is an extreme example of this confusing state of affairs. It began with the finding of the D.C. Crime Commission that between January 1963 and October 1965 out of a surveyed 2,776 defendants held by the grand jury, 7.4% percent were charged with a felony while on bond. In December of 1968 this percentage increased to 7.6 percent in a study by the U.S. Attorney's Office for the first nine months of 1968. The Metropolitan Police Department, believing those statistics seriously underestimated the amount of crime committed by defendants during their pretrial release, conducted their own study which indicated that a shocking 35 percent of the defendants had committed an additional crime while awaiting trial. The Police Department's findings alarmed the public and served as a catalyst for a movement to enact a preventive detention statute for the District in order to detain these dangerous felons behind bars. Liberal skeptics attacked the department's study. A careful review by legal scholars and statisticians either discredited its accuracy or raised several crucial questions as to whether it could be relied upon as an objective analysis of the problem.[6]

In a final attempt to produce a definitive and reliable measure of the amount of crime committed by defendants on pretrial release, the National Institute of Law Enforcement of the Department of Justice financed a study by the National Bureau of Standards. This 208-page study was to be the last word on this subject—an unbiased statement of exactly how serious the problem of additional crimes on bail was in the District of Columbia. Despite limited criticism of methodological flaws, the report was accepted as an accurate and objective statement of the problem. The report found that 11.7 percent of the defendants committed additional crimes (felonies) while awaiting trial.[7] The only other city to have conducted a detailed analysis of this problem was Indianapolis which, interestingly enough, discovered a rearrest rate of 11 percent, only seven-tenths of 1 percent off the D.C. figure from the Bureau of Standards report.[8] The similarity between the results obtained in these two rigorous examinations of the pretrial rearrest rate indicates that our major urban centers are experiencing rearrest rates slightly above 10 percent.

Table 4-4 presents the results of the seventy-two-city survey which attempted to measure both types of pretrial misconduct. This national survey estimated the country's rearrest rate to be approximately 7 percent. One explanation for this figure being 4 percentage points below the scientific Indianapolis and Washington studies is that the national survey contained at least thirty cities with populations under 200,000. With so many smaller cities in the national sample, it is reasonable to expect them to have lower crime rates than the metropolises of Washington and Indianapolis. One would also expect the rearrest problem to be less severe in smaller cities. Forty-five cities in the national sample estimated a rearrest rate of less than 10 percent and fifteen cities estimated a rate between 10 and 19 percent.

Are defendants released on their own recognizance any more likely to commit additional crimes than those who have obtained their release through the traditional process of raising the required money bond? Table 4-4 refutes the claim of bondsmen as to their predictive abilities and supervisory diligence, by indicating that the ROR'd defendants had the lower rearrest rates. Though the difference was very slight, 6.4 percent for those ROR'd to 8.2 percent for those raising money bail, these figures are a challenge to critics

Table 4-4
Statistical Summary of Pretrial Misconduct

% of total Defendants	% rearrested		% forfeitures	
	1. ROR'd	2. Money bail	1. ROR'D	2. Money bail
0–9%	79% (57)	66% (48)	87% (63)	80% (58)
10–19%	13% (9)	18% (13)	11% (8)	13% (9)
20–29%	6% (4)	6% (4)	1% (1)	4% (3)
30–39%	3% (2)	7% (5)	–	3% (2)
40–49%	–	3% (2)	–	–
50–59%	–	–	–	–
60–69%	–	–	–	–
70–79%	–	–	–	–
80–89%	–	–	–	–
90–99%	–	–	–	–
National Average for 72 cities	6.4%	8.2%	2.8%	3%

of bail reform who believe that these projects are releasing many poor risks whose pretrial misconduct is a threat to society. This survey has discovered that it is those defendants released on money bail who appear to have the greater inclination toward criminal behavior, and it is therefore this group which should be screened more carefully.

What trends have taken place in the past five years with regard to this rearrest rate? Has the percentage of defendants committing additional crimes during pretrial release increased at a pace similar to the highly publicized national increase in crime reported by the FBI's *Uniform Crime Report*? It was found that half of the cities surveyed experienced an increase in the number of crimes committed by defendants awaiting trial for another crime. Of the remaining cities, thirty-three saw no change at all while two perceived a decrease in the rearrest rate since 1965. Those defendants released on bail payment seemed to be causing a slightly higher rate of increase in the number of defendants rearrested as compared with ROR'd defendants. Fifty-one percent of the cities believed there was an increasing rearrest rate for bail defendants while 43 percent of the sample saw an increasing rearrest rate for ROR'd defendants.

It appears from Table 4-5 that an increasing rate of defendants being rearrested while awaiting trial is a regular feature of our larger cities which are experiencing severe increases in their overall crime rate. With court congestion in these larger cities permitting defendants five to six months of pretrial freedom,

Table 4-5
The Importance of Demographic Variables to the Rearrest Rate

| | Defendants Rearrested | |
| | *(1)* | *(2)* |
Demographic Variables	*Below National Average*	*Above National Average*
1. Population		
a. Less than 200,000	30 (79%)	9 (21%)
b. More than 200,000	16 (16%)	17 (52%)
2. Nonwhites		
a. Less than 12.5%	23 (61%)	15 (39%)
b. More than 12.5%	20 (58%)	11 (35%)
3. Poverty Level		
a. Below national average	20 (69%)	9 (31%)
b. Above national average	23 (58%)	17 (42%)
4. Crime Rate		
a. Below national average[a]	15 (63%)	9 (37%)
b. Above national average	13 (52%)	12 (48%)

[a]The national average crime rate is a 2000 Uniform Crime Index based on the *FBI Annual Report* (1971)

Note: All numbers and percentages refer to cities in each category.

it is quite understandable that by the conclusion of this lengthy period additional crimes may be committed. A recent study by the *Temple University Law Review* has documented the fact that nearly two-thirds of those crimes committed by defendants awaiting trial were done after the defendant had been released for at least three months.[9] Thus by instituting procedures to speed up the court delay to only a two- or three-month period, the large majority of these crimes may not have been attempted. The financial situation of defendants who have lost their job or must quickly raise large amounts of money to pay a lawyer or bondsman's fee creates the type of monetary pressure which could conceivably drive a defendant to commit additional crimes.

A humorous, yet pathetic, incident related by a Detroit bondsman illustrates the kind of illogical actions which may be taken by defendants forced to exist under these types of pressures. The bondsman stated that during the previous week a client of his who was originally arrested for auto theft was late for his preliminary hearing. The bondsman knew his client from previous business dealings and immediately called him up and told him to hurry down to the courthouse. The defendant, in his haste to make his court appearance, stole a car in order to eliminate further delay. Unfortunately he was arrested five blocks from the courthouse.[10]

Which type of defendants seem to have the greatest proclivity toward committing additional crimes while awaiting trial? No consensus of these recidivistic categories of crimes was discovered, with the exception of narcotics-related offenses. Most judges had their own particular hypotheses regarding which types of criminals were the poorest risks. Examples of this range in preferences are the following: (1) Judge Freund, Los Angeles—armed robbery; (2) Judge Sharpe, Indianapolis—prostitution and gambling; and (3) Judge Little, Atlanta—shoplifting.[11]

How Can It Be Reduced?

Based on the results of the prior analysis of reducing the forfeiture rate, it is logical to hypothesize that the best way to reduce the amount of crime committed by defendants awaiting trial is to develop a viable system of supervision during the pretrial period. As Table 4-6 illustrates, those cities who do conduct some type of supervisory control over the defendants during the pretrial period are least likely to be suffering from an above-average additional crime rate. The presence of a supervisory system was the only procedure which was found to be significantly related to the dependent variable, the additional crime rate.

Seventy-two percent of cities currently using a system of pretrial supervision of released defendants have an additional crime rate less than the national average. Additional proof of the importance of this supervision in reducing pretrial criminal behavior is found in Table 4-6 which shows that nearly half of the

Table 4-6
Additional Crime Rate and Operational Procedures

Procedural Variables	The Forfeiture Rate	
	Below the National Average	Above the National Average
1. Place of Notification		
At the Court	13 (48%)	21 (47%)
At a later date	14 (52)	23 (53)
2. Method of Notification		
Oral Notice	16 (52)	19 (47)
Written Notice	15 (48)	21 (53)
3. Verification System		
No	14 (61)	28 (72)
Yes	9 (39)	11 (28)
4. Supervisory System		
No	9 (38)	18 (54)
Yes	23 (72)	12 (46)
5. Presence of a Bondsman		
No	9 (24)	8 (25)
Yes	28 (76)	24 (75)

cities not using a supervisory system experienced an additional crime rate above the survey's national average. The explanation for the effectiveness of such a system in reducing pretrial crime is the same as was offered to show its ability to diminish the forfeiture rate. By forcing the defendant to report to the court system or bail project, he believes that his conduct is under surveillance and is therefore more inhibited from engaging in criminal activities. This is not to say that all defendants have strong predilections toward a variety of illicit and illegal activities. The commission of additional crimes has been estimated as involving only 5 to 10 percent of the total number of defendants released prior to their trial.

Before the court system is forced to decide how best to control the defendant's pretrial behavior, a more basic question must be raised. What considerations should be weighed and emphasized in the determination of what types of defendants should be released, and the amount of their bond? The release criteria listed in Table 4-7 indicate that none of these criteria are significantly related to the defendant's proclivity for engaging in pretrial criminal behavior. The implication is that there is little the courts can do in accurately predicting the defendant's pretrial criminal actions.

The only variable which shows even the slightest relationship to the issue of additional crimes is the criterion of the defendant's past appearance record. In approximately 65 percent of the cities surveyed, those which considered past appearance record as extremely important possessed pretrial crime rates below

Table 4-7
Release Criteria and the Additional Crime Rate

Release Variables	Additional Crime Rate	
	Below the National Average	Above the National Average
1. Present Charge		
Unimportant, Slightly Important	8 (27%)	10 (26%)
Extremely Important	21 (73)	29 (74)
2. Past Record		
Unimportant, Slightly Important	7 (23)	9 (24)
Extremely Important	23 (77)	29 (76)
3. Likelihood of Future Crimes		
Unimportant, Slightly Important	11 (35)	14 (37)
Extremely Important	20 (65)	24 (63)
4. Community Ties		
Unimportant, Slightly Important	18 (60)	23 (68)
Extremely Important	12 (40)	11 (32)
5. Past Appearance Record		
Unimportant, Slightly Important	11 (34)	22 (69)
Extremely Important	19 (66)	0 (31)

the survey's average. Meanwhile, less than a third of those cities who considered past appearance record only slightly important could claim additional crime rates below this average. A possible explanation for this relationship is that the past appearance record seems to be the most reliable indicator of a defendant's tendency toward misbehaving during the pretrial period, regardless of whether the misbehavior is willfully failing to appear for trial or committing additional crimes. If a defendant has a history of appearing for court, this type of responsible behavior may also be manifested in a desire to avoid criminal activities during the pretrial period.

It has been continually inferred in this and other studies of the bail system that the length of time a defendant awaits trial is a highly significant variable affecting the likelihood that he will engage in criminal activity during his pretrial release.[12] The cities with the greatest backlog of criminal cases, permitting the defendant approximately four to six months of pretrial freedom, are consistently plagued by high rearrest rates. Combining this fact with the findings in this chapter which have been unable to significantly relate any procedural or release criteria to a reduction of the additional crime rate, it appears that the only avenue open to a city attempting to reduce pretrial crime is to decrease the existing period of court delay from arrest to trial by eliminating the backlog of cases.

It is interesting to note that neither the defendant's past criminal record nor his present charge were found to be criteria significantly related to a defendant's committing additional crimes during his pretrial release. This finding should come as a disappointment to defenders of preventive detention statutes similar to the one in Washington, D.C. This limited survey, however, cannot be interpreted as totally discrediting the concept of preventive detention. The Washington operation is of very short duration and is of such a cumbersome procedural nature as to be nearly impossible to implement. It seems therefore that before condemning the criterion of a defendant's likelihood of committing future crimes, the mechanism of preventive detention should be given an opportunity to clarify and streamline its procedures. Once the process has undergone a sufficient trial period, with the public being made more aware of its potential use, it can be more accurately evaluated as a viable criterion in determining pretrial release. Most critics of preventive detention point to its potential for misuse as a weapon against certain defendants deemed "undesirable" and "dangerous" by the courts. Whether or not this system can reduce the number of crimes committed during the pretrial period or will simply be improperly manipulated against selected defendants are questions only time can answer.

As with the forfeiture rates, demographic variables are of little value in accounting for the variation in additional crimes committed during the pretrial period. The only variable significantly related is the city's crime rate which had a correlation coefficient of 0.265 at significance level of 0.02. This is a rather unstartling finding since one would expect that cities bothered by high crime rates would also be experiencing a high percentage of crimes being committed during the pretrial period by defendants awaiting trial. The fact that demographic variables were not found to influence the pretrial crime rate would seem to indicate that this is a national problem, as was the forfeiture rate, and not restricted to any type of city or to be blamed on any particular type of defendant.

In concluding this chapter, two points should be remembered as being of primary importance. First, both types of pretrial misconduct involve a very small percentage of the released defendants. Secondly, the most sensible way to reduce even these few cases is not through setting higher bonds but rather through operating an effective supervisory system over the defendants during their pretrial release.

5 Pretrial Detention Facilities

Approximately 20 percent of all defendants charged with felonies or the more serious misdemeanors are unable to obtain their pretrial release either through posting bail or personal recognizance. These men must spend the lengthy time period awaiting trial in the local detention facility. The significance of a defendant's pretrial incarceration was stated in the following resolution adopted by the National Association of Attorneys General (July 3, 1963) declaring: "Many persons accused of crime are incarcerated for various periods of time because of their inability to post bail, although often not indicted for the crime or later found not guilty after trial, resulting in the loss of liberty, separation from families, and loss of employment as well as expense to the state in the costs of confinement [and] relief for dependents."[1]

The data for this chapter was gathered from four sources. First were visits to the detention facilities in six large cities (Baltimore, Atlanta, Indianapolis, Philadelphia, San Francisco, and Washington). These visits were in the form of conducted tours, usually given by members of the bail reform project or an assistant district attorney interested in the study. In five additional cities I was unable to gain entrance to the detention facility or was unable to locate a willing guide. The second source of data were over 100 interviews with responsible public officials who appeared to be knowledgeable on the topic of their city's jails. The third source was a collection of reports, hearings, and other documents on the subject of pretrial detention facilities. The fourth and final source was the results of the attitudinal study previously referred to.

Initial Detention Facility

After the defendant is arrested, the policeman may decide to take him into custody. This is the common practice for all felonies and misdemeanors, while those apprehended for petty offenses may be given a citation to appear in court at a future date. At this point, the arrested defendant may be initially detained in either the police stationhouse or at police headquarters. The former is usually a neighborhood precinct located in close proximity to the scene of the arrest, while the latter is customarily found in the downtown area adjacent to the city's criminal courthouse.

Both detention centers are operated by the police department and are only temporary holding cells until the defendant has had his initial appearance before a judge. Following the initial appearance where bail will be set or modified, the police turn the defendant over to the sheriff (or some analogous custodial official) who will be responsible for the defendant until he obtains his pretrial release or it is time for his trial. The police will only have control over the defendant for the first day or two after arrest, while the custodial officers will be watching over him for several months depending on the amount of court delay from arrest to trial. This second detention facility is the county or city jail which supervises the pretrial detention of defendants unable to afford bail. It will be the primary focus of this chapter.

A third category of detention facility is the small holding center in the courthouse. This is used to house defendants who are being detained prior to their trial during one of their several appearances in court. The defendant will be transported from the jail to the courthouse, which may be only one block as in Chicago, or fourteen miles as in Philadelphia. This is usually done early in the morning and the defendants will await their court appearance. This holding area frequently resembles a large cage with a number of subdivisions. The worst of these facilities was observed in Philadelphia. The defendants were housed on the seventh floor of the City Hall Courthouse. The room which was designed to hold twelve men but often was filled with twice that number. During the summer of 1970, several prisoners passed out from the lack of ventilation.[2]

Once a defendant is taken into custody, the police have a variety of procedures for placing him in one of these initial detention facilities. In Baltimore and Los Angeles the municipal criminal courts operate at various regional offices which are located either within or adjacent to the local police stationhouse. The defendant will spend his initial period of detention, which is usually a day or two, in the stationhouse cells. The quality of these cells varies greatly from stationhouse to stationhouse, and it is impossible to generalize about their overall condition.[3] A second procedure is used in Washington, D.C. and Philadelphia where the defendants are first taken to a regional police precinct for booking and temporary custody. As soon as the necessary paperwork has been completed, the suspect will be taken downtown to the central police headquarters which has a large lock-up facility which will hold him until he has had his initial court appearance. A final mode of operation is to take the suspect, following his arrest, directly to the central police headquarters where he will be confined until his initial court appearance. This procedure is used in Indianapolis.

The jail facilities housed in the police headquarters are frequently referred to as lockups. These lockup facilities were observed in four cities (Indianapolis, Washington, San Francisco, and Philadelphia) and were all found to be quite similar. They are usually divided into three to four large cells which each may house about forty defendants. They are furnished only with cots, arranged as double bunk beds in long rows. In the center of the room or at the back wall is the toilet, which is often only a hole in the floor. There is usually a wide aisle between the rows of bunks.

The defendants seem to spend most of their time lying on their cots. Each prisoner appears to make a conscious effort to avoid contact with his fellow prisoners. The most oppressive feature of these large cells is the stench which fills the air. There is no apparent attempt made to classify prisoners in the lockups since they will be detained for such a relatively short period of time. The lack of supervision is also noticeable, as the turnkey or guard rarely inspects the cells. A few cities use a television camera to aid in this supervisory task, but with such a large cellblock even this technique is inadequate. The absence of supervision, the indiscriminant mixing of offenders, and the large cells impose a constant threat to the safety of the detained defendant.

The most important function which these initial detention facilities can provide for the defendant is a means of communication with the outside world. A frequently heard complaint about these facilities is not the conditions in the cell but rather the need for increasing the number of phones available for use. The number of phone calls which a defendant may make after the arrest and confinement is closely regulated by the police. It was found to be limited to one or two calls. These calls are made to family, friends, bondsman, or lawyer. This list is in decreasing order of frequency, since a phone call to family or friends can be used to reach the lawyer and bondsman. To aid the defendant who wishes to select a bondsman, a list of the bonding companies, in alphabetical order, is placed over the telephone. The most unusual phone setup was in the Indianapolis lockup. For security reasons, according to the police officer in charge, the phone is attached to a speaker system so that the defendant's conversation (both his words and those of the person he has called) are broadcasted loudly throughout the jail. This security measure greatly inhibits a normal conversation and has decreased the effective use of the only means of communication which the defendant can employ.

The Primary Pretrial Detention Center

After the initial appearance before a judge, those defendants who are unable to obtain their pretrial release are taken to the city or county jail which serves as the pretrial detention center. It may be found within a few blocks of the criminal court building (as in Baltimore, Chicago, and Detroit) or many miles away as in Oakland (thirty miles), Philadelphia (fourteen miles), and Atlanta (six miles). The majority of jails are to be found over five miles from the courthouse (which is in the center of town close by the offices of attorneys and judges). The inconvenience caused by these distances between the defendant and his lawyer is another handicap in preparing a defense. The lawyer may not only be restricted by visiting hours, but must also make a long and time-consuming drive out to see his client. As a result of this inconvenience the defense attorney may be prevented from visiting his client with any degree of regularity.

It was discovered that the detention facilities in nearly every city visited were suffering from overcrowding. The main condition distinguishing these eleven city jails was merely the relative degree of overcrowding. The following figures from four of these cities will offer the reader a clear picture of the magnitude of this problem:

1. Atlanta (Fulton County Jail)—On the 29th of January 1970, when the jail was visited, it had a population of 766 prisoners. Due to its capacity of 575, approximately 190 of these men had to sleep on the floor. This was estimated to be a fairly typical figure.[4]

2. Indianapolis (Marion County Jail)—A jail inventory taken on the 4th of December 1970 by the city's bail reform project indicated 845 prisoners, 464 of which were awaiting trial. The jail was designed to accommodate 640. The excess of 205 prisoners represents a 32 percent overcapacity condition. An added note is that 114 of these men had been in the jail over three months awaiting trial.[5]

3. Philadelphia (City-County Prison)—The Pennsylvania Prison Society reported that the pretrial detention facilities were planned for 800 but are currently housing 2000 defendants. These defendants are confined in two facilities, Holmesburg and the Detention Center.[6]

4. St. Louis (City Jail)—It was reported that the city jail which is almost 100 percent pretrial detainees, is so overcrowded as to force between 70 to 100 defendants to sleep on the floor each night.[7]

Is this dilemma of overcrowded pretrial detention centers unique to our large urban jails or is it symptomatic of jails in all types of communities? This study's attitudinal survey found that two-thirds of the respondents from *all* types of cities in agreement that the pretrial detention facilities in their city or town was overcrowded. It is true that the incidence of overcrowding was relatively more common in the survey's larger cities (population exceeding 200,000) but in even the smaller cities (populations under 200,000) nearly half of the respondents thought their communities possessed overcrowded jails. (The exact figures were 81 percent of the large city respondents as compared with 45 percent of those reporting from the smaller cities and towns.)

With one notable exception, all of the professional groups surveyed expressed similar agreement concerning the existence of overcrowded conditions. This one group was the judiciary, whose agreement percentage was more than ten percentage points off the national norm. It is distressing to have such an influential group in the administration of bail be so cautious in complaining of the crowded conditions. Since the judge's decision as to the bail amount may be the most important factor in the defendant's chance for pretrial freedom, it is hoped that they would be more aware of the jail conditions facing those unable to raise the required amount.

The effects of these overcrowded conditions were summarized by the American Correction Association following their inspection of the Washington, D.C. pretrial facility: "The physical structure is such that adequate space is not available for the average daily inmate population. This has contributed along with the shortage of custodial personnel, to improper supervision of prisoners. Overcrowding, sexual perversion, idleness, gambling, and strong-arm tactics by inmates have resulted. Action must be taken now to prevent these conditions from becoming worse.[8]

In large cities the pretrial detention facilities usually house between 500 to 1000 defendants. The overcrowding is but one of the discomforts to be suffered by the prisoners in these detention centers. They are typically quite old—for example, the Washington jail was built in 1872 and the Philadelphia Holmesburg Prison opened its doors in 1896. These facilities also tend to age rather rapidly, so that even recently constructed jails soon take on the style and appearance of the older institutions. Precious few improvements were seen as most facilities weathered the past fifty years in stoic fashion. The same odors permeated the new as well as the old prisons, although there may be substituted an ammonia or antiseptic smell, similar to that found in hospital corridors, in a few of the newest jails. Nearly all the jails are arranged into long cell blocks with a number of dormitory-like cells within each block or just one large dormitory in a particular wing. Each cell will house about forty men. In addition to his bunk, each man is allowed a foot or wall locker and possibly a chair. There are a few toilets and sinks at one end of the dormitory cell. Inadequate ventilation is instrumental in creating the fetid aromas and depressing conditions.

Among the more common complaints heard about these facilities is the annoying level of noise and the sickening food. With nothing to keep the prisoners occupied there is constant bedlam as rock music is blaring while men shout to be heard above the music. The quality of food is also a constant source of anger. The following excerpt from a *Report on the San Francisco County Jails and City Prison* offers a lucid description of why these culinary complaints may be justified: "The stockpot simmers all night in the kitchen at San Bruno (Men's Jail for S.F.). Occasionally, according to one member of our staff, "eggshells and other odd looking things" bubble to the surface. The stock will provide the next day's soup. Applesauce, to be served the following evening, sits in open pans uncovered. The floor of the storeroom is filthy. The inmate trustees who work in the kitchen do not receive any medical exam before they are assigned to prepare meals. The meals are unvaried, unappetizing, and sometimes cold. Milk is diluted roughly 2 to 1; two parts water to one part milk. (According to jail staff, "the inmates don't seem to notice.") . . . Special diets, a medical necessity for diabetics, are not available."[9]

One of the eleven cities visited has had a recent jail riot resulting from the prisoners' reaction to these conditions. This riot took place in Philadelphia's Holmesburg Prison. The following description of this prison is offered to illustrate what was found to exemplify one of the worst detention facilities in the nation. There are 660 cells in the jail divided among 10 cell blocks. Each cell is about 12 feet deep, 1½ feet wide, and has an arched ceiling of about 10 feet. Each cell had a few cots, a toilet, and a wooden table. Although originally designed to hold one prisoner, today each cell has two or three occupants. Besides the overcrowding, the cells are physically unwholesome. Many skylights leak whenever it rains, causing the water to accumulate on the floor because there is no drain in the cell floor. The cots cannot be moved easily from beneath the skylight with the result that the mattresses often become soaked with no way to be dried out. A final discomfort is that the prisoners are forced to share their cells with omnipresent roaches and occasional rats. Each prisoner receives two blankets in winter and one in summer. A blanket is kept for six months and becomes filthy.[10]

Isolation cells are used in nearly all detention centers for containment of disciplinary problems. Each detention facility houses ten to twenty of these undersized individual cells where problem defendants are confined until they are willing to follow house rules. These cells are approximately 8 feet deep, 6 feet wide, and about 8 feet high. They are furnished with a mattress on the floor and a hole in the back of the cell to serve as a toilet. Many cities, Atlanta, in particular, also use these isolation cells for drug addicts while they are suffering withdrawal. Most city hospitals either lack adequate facilities to take care of these drug cases or simply do not want the security problems created by their presence. On a few occasions mentally deranged defendants will also be housed in these isolation cells if no adequate psychiatric facilities are available.

How secure are these detention facilities? Because these defendants have not been found guilty and are merely awaiting trial, critics of the present system believe that there is too great an emphasis placed upon security. The President's Commission on Law Enforcement in their *Task Force Report on Corrections* supports this criticism, finding that "unconvicted persons, as yet legally innocent, are almost invariably subjected to the tightest security and receive the least attention of any group in jails. . . . This primary concern for security imposes regimentation, repeated searches, and close surveillance on detainers. Most jails also have poor facilities for visitors, thus hampering a detainee's efforts to arrange for his defense and maintain contacts with the community."[11]

While several of the detention facilities studied have imposed severe security regulations, a majority operate with a laxness of control which totally contradicts the Task Force's findings. In Atlanta, the Fulton County Jail operates in such a relaxed manner as to result in several successful escapes. The prisoner often was able to escape by simply walking out unlocked side doors when the guards were not paying sufficient attention. The author was permitted to roam through the jail and found many doors (which may serve as possible escape routes) unlocked. The prisoners were given a great deal of freedom to walk through the halls, particularly if they were working in the kitchen or had trustee status. One of the reasons given for this permissiveness was that there is nothing else for the defendants to do but wander around and visit with other detainees. A small recreation area was constructed but not used because of the overcrowded conditions.

Atlanta is not the only city whose jail fails to meet minimum standards of security. In Philadelphia, security at the Holmesburg Prison was described in the following pessimistic terms: "This situation prevails [a situation which lead to a jail riot] because the authorities responsible for supervising the prison are helpless to do what is necessary to ensure even minimum standards of security in the prison. . . . They are helpless because they have no power to obtain the funds needed to repair the prisons, to make it habitable and to employ the additional guards, social workers, vocational teachers, and other personnel needed to bring the prison to minimum standards of security."[12] A new detention center has recently been constructed in Philadelphia which has successfully established rigorous security measures. However, because of overcrowded conditions, many defendants are still housed in Holmesburg (over 500 detentioners).

The loosest security standards were found in the San Francisco Jail System, particularly at the San Bruno Institution for housing male pretrial detainees (also referred to as County Jail, No. 2). Although it was originally to be used as a minimum security facility to house mainly alcoholics and misdemeanants, San Bruno has increasingly been filled with defendants accused of committing dangerous felonious acts. (The number of felony defendants increased almost 400 percent in the past decade.) With inadequate facilities, untrained staff, and weak administrators, one of the sheriff's staff recently told the San Francisco Committee on Crime that "the inmates are running the institution." In March 1968, the Deputy Sheriff's Association charged that "the inmates could take over the jail and free all the inmates within 20 minutes on the understaffed 4:00 p.m. to midnight shift and they knew it." The San Francisco Committee on Crime found the charge was valid "not only because of the understaffing but because of the jail's careless procedures, all the more dangerous because the jail staff is limited."[13] The following is a partial list of these careless procedures and security measures which the committee found to exist:

1. The gate to San Bruno is left unlocked and unmanned from midnight to 8:00 A.M. When manned at all, it is often inmates who are on watch.
2. Inside the jail, inmates move around freely. No organized system of checking inmate movements exists within the facility. On the night of a recent escape, it took the jailers 3½ hours to learn the identity of the escapees, long after a bulletin had been issued identifying the wrong men.

3. The facility is totally inadequate in the event of any emergency. There is no operating alarm system.

4. There is no system of key control, with the jail staff failing to know precisely how many keys there are. On two occasions investigators observed deputies carrying all the keys to the institution with them into the inmate security area while the inmates milled around them.

5. Weapons of many kinds are potentially available to the inmates. In the kitchen area, large knives, cleavers, and tenderizing mallets are easily accessible.

6. The jails had available to them, as a defensive force, four 12-gauge shot guns with a total of five shells and five 30-06 rifles with a total of nine shells. Deputies disagree as to how many of these guns are in serviceable condition.[14]

Classification of Defendants

Another side effect of the overcrowded conditions found in the pretrial detention facilities is that the jail officials are unable to classify and segregate the prisoners according to age, seriousness of crime, or any other criteria. The result is that first offenders are mixed in with hardened criminals, eighteen-year olds with sixty-year olds, felons with misdemeanants, and occasionally pretrial defendants with inmates already sentenced. With barely enough room available, and many jails forced to have detainees sleeping on floors, the jail officials cannot afford the luxury of a careful classification and placement of defendants. When a new inmate arrives he will be sent to the first available vacant cell. An additional difficulty with implementing an effective classification system is that the defendants are often housed in such large dormitory cells that it prohibits creation of specialized areas for particular classes of defendants. The American Correctional Association, after inspecting the detention facilities in Washington, D.C. and other major cities, emphasized the role which overcrowding and understaffing has played in the failure of inmate classification by commenting: "The double-decking of bunks in the dormitories, extra men in the cells, the almost impossible task of picking out potential homosexuals, psychotics, psychopaths, and agitators among so many admissions with relatively little personal data about the individual and the relatively few correctional officers available for supervisory duties at any time can spell trouble if allowed to go on for a longer period of time."[15]

Although a disproportional percentage of overcrowded detention centers were located in large urban centers, the problem of indiscriminant mixing of pretrial defendants, even with inmates already sentenced, is found in all types of cities. Fifty-three percent of the cities surveyed *do not* maintain any type of classification system. The minimum amount of discrimination among the various types of defendants is between those sentenced and those awaiting trial.

In a few cities, even this segregation is not possible. In St. Louis, for example, the overflow of pretrial detentioners has caused several of them to be housed in the workhouse where men convicted of misdemeanors are serving out their sentences. In no city, however, were pretrial detentioners forced to be kept with sentenced felons serving time, although they often must share cells with convicted felons awaiting sentence or shipment to the penitentiary. Compounding the difficulty of forcing so many disparate types of defendants to share close quarters is the great length of time a defendant must spend awaiting his trial. Even though nearly all cities make an effort to try detained defendants first, it is usually two to three months before a serious crime will be tried. Thus these dormitory companions will be in close quarters for an extremely long period of time. Such conditions often force defendants to adopt a life-style predicated solely on allowing them to survive until their trial. The testimony of Leroy Cothran before a Baltimore Grand Jury on April 24, 1970, on the conditions of the city's detention center offer a shocking example of these experiences. Cothran was sixteen years old (an adult under the Baltimore City law at that time) and had to spend sixty-five days in jail on charges of shoplifting and trespassing. He was housed in a long room, shaped like a hall, which was the size of a football field, where 50 men slept on cots. He and the others, who aged from sixteen to sixty, stayed in the dormitory all day long except to go out for their three meals.[16] The most abhorrent effect of this indiscriminant massing of defendants may be that the abuse and contamination experienced by these men during their pretrial detention will contribute significantly to developing future criminal behavior. When youthful offenders are tossed in with professionals and hardened criminals, it is little wonder that so many emerge not only unrehabilitated but even more prone toward incorrigibility than before.

Absence of Rehabilitation

What do the pretrial detentioners do during the agonizing long days while awaiting trial? Are any rehabilitative programs available for their benefit? The answers to both these questions will create an even more depressing picture of life for the detained pretrial defendant. The second inquiry can be answered by stating that no such programs are available for the pretrial detentioner during his many months of confinement. In a few cities (St. Louis, for example) where pretrial defendants are housed with already sentenced prisoners, there may be rehabilitative programs available for the sentenced defendants and occasionally the pretrial defendants are allowed to participate. Due to the overcrowded conditions, however, officials in cities attempting this combined style of rehabilitation were plagued by an overabundance of pretrial defendants who overran the program and caused it to be inoperative for both groups. The result in these institutions was then to restrict rehabilitative programs only to those defendants already sentenced, even though their stay in jail was of nearly equal length as the pretrial detainee. In summary, it was found to be the accepted policy of all pretrial detention facilities studied that rehabilitative programs were used only with sentenced inmates, while pretrial detentioners were to be provided with nothing but empty hours.

The tragedy of not having any correctional programs in jails for these pretrial detentioners is eloquently stated by the President's Task Force on Corrections in the following quote: "The lack of correctional training . . . means for one thing, that those who are least culpable receive the most inadequate treatment. . . . It also means that opportunities invaluable from the correctional standpoint are last: the chance to counsel an offender immediately after his offense, when he may be most responsive, the change to secure social services with little or no disruption of the fabric of an offender's life."[17] The explanation for the absence of rehabilitative programs for pretrial detentioners is twofold. First are the obvious shortages of resources necessary for developing a viable rehabilitative program. These shortages include low salaries, inadequate facilities, and a general feeling of apathy among prison officials. (Because these detention centers are the financial responsibility of the city or county, federal funds are usually unavailable.) The second reason offered is that many defendants are not detained a sufficient length of time to conduct a worthwhile program. It often takes several weeks to ascertain the degree of risk a defendant may present as well as the time it will take him to be socialized into institutional procedures and requirements. Because of the great amount of time spent by most pretrial detentioners in these facilities, this second explanation seems rather weak. There must be several short-range educational and vocational programs which can be completed in less than four or five months, the average period of detention in our major cities.

If a city has attempted to initiate some sort of rehabilitative or educational program, its success is seriously handicapped by countless difficulties. The education program of the Holmesburg Prison, which houses a large part of Philadelphia's pretrial detainees, offers good examples of these limitations. There is one school teacher assigned by the Board of Education to the prison during the day. He has five prisoners acting as aides. Basic courses in reading, writing, and arithmetic are offered, as well as an opportunity to earn a high school equivalency diploma. (In the past years, about 200 inmates have earned the diploma). On three nights each week for three hours per night, seven classes are held. They are conducted by seven teachers from the Board of Education and offer the same course selection as the day program. There is no vocational training in the formal sense that an inmate is taught a trade. However, defendants assigned to work in various maintenance shops incidentally may learn something useful about their particular job.[18]

Free Time and Recreation

Returning to the first question posed at the beginning of the previous section, the pretrial detentioners appear to have an unlimited amount of free time while awaiting trial. Their days are filled neither with rehabilitative programs, meaningful job assignments, or any planned recreation activities. If one is touring the detention facilities, he will find the defendants spending their time sleeping, playing cards, watching television, or engaging in idle chatter with their fellow inmates. Although these time-killing activities do not appear at first glance to be particularly oppressive, when the days stretch into months, and the months multiply, such meaningless avocations can be a great strain on the detained defendant. The ability to tolerate such ennui declines as the period of detention increases until the prisoners yearn to be tried and possibly sentenced so as to get to a penitentiary where their days might be filled with something besides the monotony engendered in their present confinement. Several prosecutors candidly admitted that the horrors of pretrial detention are one of the prime forces encouraging defendants to enter premature guilty pleas.

Because of inadequate facilities, insufficient custodial personnel, and endemic overcrowding, the defendants are rarely permitted any recreational activities, especially of a physical nature. It was tragic to see baseball fields and basketball courts vacant day after day due to these limitations. In several cities such as Balitmore the inmates were only allowed out of the dormitory cells for their three meals.

For a few fortunate pretrial defendants there are jobs around the jail to occupy their time and also give them a relatively greater degree of freedom. These jobs are usually in the bakery, kitchen, laundry, sanitary crews, or physical employment in various maintenance jobs such as in plumbing or electrical work. It is the general policy not to pay the defendants for performing any of these tasks. The only opportunity discovered in any detention facility for a defendant to earn money was in the Philadelphia detention centers. Here a defendant could volunteer to submit to tests in a medical research program conducted by the University of Pennsylvania and receive a token monetary reward.

There is an obvious need in these facilities for the development of programs designed to keep all pretrial detentioners engaged in meaningful activities. This could be accomplished by use of short-term courses in vocational as well as educational subject areas. The problems caused by the emptiness of this pretrial existence are exacerbated by the inability of the defendants to obtain help in solving their personal problems which have usually deteriorated during their confinement. There should be a counseling director to assist the defendant in resolving these problems. What must be avoided is the following description of pretrial detention given before a Baltimore grand jury by a sixteen-year-old former inmate relating his experiences during this period: "I have not learned anything over there but how to watch other people take something from other people, take their manhood from them and I don't like to see it, so I don't say nothing because I can't beat the whole jail. I hate to see young boys coming to jail, going home half men half women, scared to tell somebody that you have been in jail. When you get something good, if you can't fight they will take it from you."[19]

Preparation of the Defense

One of the most significant effects of pretrial detention is in the harm which it causes to the preparation of the defendant's defense. Numerous studies conducted in several cities have clearly shown that detained defendants are far more likely to be found guilty and receive more severe sentences than those defendants who obtained their pretrial release.

A Philadelphia study conducted by the University of Pennsylvania Law School found that out of 946 cases, only 52 percent of the bailed defendants were convicted compared with 82 percent of those jailed. Among the convicted, only 22 percent of the bailed defendants received prison sentences while 59 percent of the jailed defendants received jail terms.[20] Daniel Freed and Patricia Wald in their working paper for the National Conference on Bail in 1964 explained the impact which pretrial detention has upon a defendant's defense in the following statement: "He [the detained defendant] contributes neither money nor labor to pretrial investigation. He cannot help locate witnesses or evidence which may be more accessible to him than any outsider. His contacts with counsel may be impeded by having to plan a defense in cramped jail facilities within the limited hours set aside for visitors."[21]

With so many empirical studies indicating the serious handicaps of pretrial detention in preparing an adequate defense, it was surprising to find so many public officials unwilling to acknowledge this fact. When asking the respondents in the attitudinal survey whether they thought a defendant's chances for acquittal were influenced by his pretrial detention, 57 percent *disagreed* that such detention was harmful to the defendant's chances. Only a third were willing to agree that the defendant was handicapped by this period of incarceration. As expected, when one isolates the respondents by profession, 12 percent of the prosecutors agreed with the original statement while 64 percent of the public defenders were in support.

The detained defendant is limited in his relationship with his lawyer by several restrictions imposed on him by the detention facilities. Approximately half of the cities studied allowed the lawyer to visit his client only during regular visiting hours which were usually in the afternoon. The remaining jails operated more flexibly and would allow the lawyer to visit any time during the day. Two cities allowed the lawyer visitation privileges anytime of the day or night. By not having flexible visiting hours and locating the jails several miles from the downtown offices of most lawyers, the court system has made even more difficult the problem of preparing an adequate defense.

Once the lawyer reaches the detention center he will meet with his client in a large room or hallway which lacks the confidentiality necessary to prepare their defense. In only three cities were private rooms set aside for these conferences between lawyer and defendant. In several cities the detention facility remodeled hallways into conference areas. The lawyer was separated from his client by a screen and both had to sit on stools in order to converse. An additional threat to this already compromised privacy is the constant fear that the room is "bugged." Most lawyers skeptically believed that some electronic surveillance of their conversation with their client was occurring, although they lacked proof. In a few instances, however, defense attorneys were insistent that such illegal invasions of privacy were taking place. One lawyer in San Francisco actually showed the author a blueprint for a detention facility which indicated such eavesdropping was in progresss. A final incursion of the defendant's privacy and his ability to plan his defense is the practice of censoring mail. In Atlanta it took a court order from the superior court prohibiting information ferreted out of the detentioner's mail during the censorship process from being turned over to the District Attorney's Office. Another type of deceptive activity found was in cases where the prosecutor wished to establish the insanity of the defendant. The district attorney would arrange to place a compliant defendant in a cell next to the suspect and then have him testify in court as to his cellmate's sanity.[22]

Custodians

A distinction must first be made between the administrative officials directing a detention facility and the custodial staff or guards who are involved in the daily supervision of the inmates. In discussing the administration first, the author was handicapped in his research on this topic by his inability to interview these officials. This failure to gain access to these men was caused primarily by their extremely busy work schedules as well as a general reluctance to be interviewed. The observations presented are the result of conversations with other noncorrectional officers as well as personal insights obtained by visiting the detention facilities. Most adminstrators believed that the primary thrust of their job was to merely perform a service for the courts. This service was the custodial function of detaining the defendant until his trial. This detention period was viewed as only a temporary status for the defendant, preliminary to his being found guilty and then taken to a permanent facility where the rehabilitative process was to begin. With this attitude so prevalent among the administrative officials, it is no wonder that so few programs were provided for the pretrial detainee while he awaited trial. Unfortunately however, this "temporary" incarceration often extended into several months duration.

The universal criticism of the custodial force is that there are simply not enough members. This understaffed group are responsible for the supervision and scheduling of visits by family, friends, and attorneys, and must also control the constant traffic of inmates being released, going to court, or being sent to other institutions. These tasks, of course, are in addition to their general custodial functions of controlling the daily operation of the inmates. As a result of the serious shortage of guards and the overcrowded facilities, there is an inadequate supervision of the inmates. The safety of the inmates as well as the outside community is constantly threatened by this deplorable condition.[23]

A secondary criticism of the custodial force is their tendency to abuse and mistreat the prisoners. The tremendous numerical superiority of the prison population over the guard staff has precluded this mistreatment from becoming a regularly recurring phenomenon. Any guard who maliciously attacks prisoners will be flirting with severe retaliation the next time he is forced to walk among the inmates, which is an inevitability. Unarmed and isolated, these guards must rely on the trust and respect of the inmates, if both groups are to survive. However, documented reports from Philadelphia and San Francisco indicate that these infractions still occur sporadically. In San Francisco, according to two U.S. District Court judges and other federal officials interviewed by the San Francisco Committee on Crime, "there have been numerous complaints about the poor quality of medical care, the indiscriminate sentencing of prisoners into isolation cells, and physical abuse and beatings by the guards."[24]

Guards as well as wardens are usually poorly qualified. The low salaries and equally low status of such jobs insured the recruitment of low quality individuals. Their main concern is with discipline and fear only the loss of their jobs. If a decent jail guard does arrive on the scene, the institution will soon destroy him. This is not to say that all guards are either morons or sadists. Recently a courageous Pittsburgh journalist, in an attempt to obtain an insider's view of the city's detention center, masqueraded for three days as a guard. His article relating his experiences, reveals the basic humane instincts which these oftmaligned custodial officers fight to sustain.[25]

Safety of the Defendant

As noted previously, the shortage of guards has jeopardized the health and safety of the inmates. When one also takes into consideration the overcrowded conditions and the absence of any meaningful system of inmate classification, the situation becomes even more chaotic. The physical arrangement of the cell blocks into large dormitories also contributes to the problem. In the Holmesburg Prison in Philadelphia, for example, the guards will usually remain "at center" by the entrance of the cell block. From this position a guard cannot see into the cells, so that if a prisoner is being attacked inside a cell, or some other illegal activity is occurring, a guard "at center" cannot see it. The number of guards is so limited that in some blocks there may be no guards assigned.[26] Adding to this dilemma is the fact that even when guards are present they frequently choose not to become involved. This may be due to fear, apathy, or possibly, bribery. The true leadership and control of the cell block is therefore relegated to the inmate "bosses" who dominate their area through guile and intimidation.

The degree to which these detention centers are unsafe is manifested by the high incidence of sexual and other assaults, the availability of weapons and narcotics, and the regular occurrence of thievery. Although no accurate statistics are kept on these matters, it is believed that they occur with sufficient degree of frequency to make it a very important problem requiring an immediate solution. The increasing number of suicides by pretrial detentioners incarcerated in these facilities is tragic proof of the depravity of these conditions. In New York City there were ten suicides in the County Jail within a ten-month period.[27]

The two most frequent types of crimes committed in the detention facilities are homosexual attacks and thievery. With such poor supervision and cramped dormitory living conditions, gang rapes occur with alarming regularity. Young boys are particularly susceptible to such sexual attacks from groups of older men. With no exercise or recreation or any rehabilitative programs, men's minds can only turn to debased thoughts and, eventually, antisocial behaviors. The attacks usually occur during the day when the cells are open, and at the far end of the cell block, which is not always patrolled by guards. The victim is dragged into an open cell while a prisoner acts as a lookout. Because of the constant threat of theft, most inmates will carry their personal belongings with them. Most prisoners are skeptical of trusting guards with the safekeeping of their valued posessions, but they are not provided with any locked container to store the belongings in the cell.

Medical and Psychiatric Facilities

As a general statement, the medical and psychiatric facilities in all the detention centers were despicable. The rationale commonly given for this condition is that if any serious medical problem develops, the defendant will be transported from the jail to the proper medical facility. The typical jail will have one or two nurses on full-time duty in their dispensary. Doctors, usually privately contracted, will come in each morning to tend to the more serious problems and then leave within a few hours to attend to their regular practices. The job is a political patronage position in Atlanta, where the doctor earns nearly $20,000 a year for a few hours work a week. While the author was on the premises, the physician completed his rounds for the day in thirty minutes. The only thing an inmate can hope for is either very good health or else very good timing if he does become ill so he can catch the doctor on one of his fleeting visits. The horror stories relating to serious illnesses which were either mistreated or not treated at all are legendary and plentiful at all of the city detention facilities which were studied.

The biggest medical problem facing detention facilities today is drug addiction. The jails simply do not have the medical facilities to treat the drug cases, particularly when the defendant is experiencing withdrawal. Most jails place the defendant in isolation. The officials' attitude was generally unsympathetic to the addict's suffering since his addiction was viewed as a voluntary act brought on by his own weaknesses. Compounding the problem is that city medical facilities are also inadequately staffed to handle these drug cases and have no room for treatment. The narcotic traffic was described as being heavy in nearly all detention facilities. The only solution for most addicts is to try to make it in the regular jail population and hope he can buy a sufficient amount of drugs through the jail's "black market" drug dealers to satisfy their habits.

Conclusion

In recent years the plight of sentenced prisoners in penal institutions has steadily come under the reformer's gaze and a slow but perceptible improvement has begun to take place in several state correctional systems. This same public notice and resulting reform, however, has failed to reach those pretrial detainees confined in our city's jails. With little public concern over the problem, one must be pessimistic about the opportunity for viable reform of these pretrial detention facilities.

The criticism of these pretrial detention facilities need not be premised on only humanitarian grounds but can also be derived from pragmatic considerations. It is a very expensive proposition for cities to operate these facilities, even at the deplorable level most of them seem to be functioning. In the seventy-two-city survey it was found that the average cost of detaining one inmate one day in these pretrial detention centers was five dollars. When one controls for the size of the city, the larger cities with the greatest pretrial jail populations are spending approximately $8.50 per defendant each day. Translated into a yearly figure, a city such as St. Louis, which houses about 700 pretrial detainees in their city jail, will spend approximately $2.2 million dollars per year detaining these defendants.

Not all officials, however, share the author's pessimism. In order to end this chapter on a more optimistic note, the following quote from the *Task Force Report* of the President's 1967 Commission on Law Enforcement, and Administration of Justice is offered:

> Nevertheless there is clearly much that can be done. . . . Particularly in jails and detention centers, recreational and educational opportunities can be greatly expanded. Few detainees pose substantial security risks in supervised activities within an institution; in many other cases there is no reason for denial of access to television or reading materials that can help to relieve boredom even for those confined to a cell. In many cases further treatment can be instituted, given the resources to do so, if adequate practices for avoiding coercion and securing a suspect's full consent are developed."[28]

6 Introduction to Bail Reform

The Necessity for Bail Reform: Defects of the Traditional System

In its discussion of pretrial release, the President's Commission on Law Enforcement and Administration of Justice seemed to base its recommendations on the unstated assumption that the present system for administering bail was malfunctioning and in urgent need of repair. The large majority of public officials who were surveyed in this study agreed with the commission's assumption. Only 16 percent of these officials approved of the current money bail system, as nearly 70 percent disapproved and were in favor of an alternative process.[1]

Why are so many of the nation's judges, prosecutors, criminal lawyers, and public defenders opposed to the traditional bail system? The answer most frequently given by these officials is that the money bail system was badly in need of reform due to the human and public costs which it caused. Defendants, whose only crime is their financial condition, are placed in detention facilities whose deplorable conditions were documented in the previous chapter. As a result of this pretrial incarceration, the defendants and their families are forced to suffer severe economic hardships which may continue for months, and even years, after the case has been concluded. Their families are humiliated and the scar on relations with friends and family may never heal.

Whereas the previously mentioned hardships have been directly borne by the defendant, the fourth cost is to the public. It is the financial cost to the public, the financial cost of operating these detention facilities for defendants who would be good risks for pretrial release except for their penurious condition. This expense, which is ultimately passed on to the taxpayer, of housing, feeding, and guarding a detained defendant, has been estimated to be between $3 and $10 a day per person.[2] Several advocates of bail reform have pointed to the great savings to the already financially crippled city which are inherent in these bail reform projects. In a recent report on bail and OR release by the San Francisco Committee on Crime, it was estimated by the Committee that the city's bail reform project was saving the city a minimum of $330,000 per year. They also added that "if the O.R. project were not taking people out of jail, new jail facilities would have to be built. This could cost millions of dollars.[3]

97

A second reason offered for reforming the traditional bail system was the necessity of eliminating, or at least reducing, the influence of the bondsmen in the administration of bail. Why did nearly 60 percent of the public officials questioned believe that the power of the bondsmen should be reduced? The most significant reason given was an objection to a private businessman playing so dominant role in determining whether an individual was to be granted his pretrial freedom. Judge Skelly Wright of the Federal District Court for the District of Columbia eloquently argues this position in the following statement:

> The professional bondsmen hold the keys to the jail in their pockets. They determine for whom they will act as surety—who in their judgment is a good risk. The bad risks in their judgment, and the ones who are unable to pay the bondsmen's fees remain in jail. The court and the commissioner are relegated to the relatively unimportant chore of fixing the amount of bail.[4]

Charges against the bail-bonding business ranging from corruption to domination by criminal elements (organized crime) have provided additional reasons for attempting to diminish the influence of the bonding industry and indirectly discredit the money bail system. Bondsmen are continually being found to be in collusion with various court officials and are frequently implicated in scandals involving defense attorneys who have "kickbacked" a certain percentage of their legal fees to the bondsman in gratitude for having been recommended by the bondsman.[5]

In addition to the important pragmatic reasons just offered to explain the necessity for reforming the traditional bail system, the system can, and often is, criticized on broader philosophical and constitutional grounds. The most basic criticism is that the traditional system punishes a defendant merely because he is financially incapable of raising the required bond. What makes this blatant form of economic discrimination even more upsetting is that it is an irrational procedure for insuring that a defendant will appear for trial. It has *never* been proven that a defendant who might be considering forfeiting his bond and skipping town will be deterred simply through fear of losing the posted amount of bail. A more thorough analysis of these philosophical and constitutional failings of the traditional system will be presented in Chapter 9.

Alternatives to the Present System

Bail Reform Projects

The response to the inadequacies and injustices of the traditional money bail system by the criminal justice system has resulted in the development of a series of alternative methods of pretrial release. By far the most popular response has been the development of the bail reform project. A bail reform project may be defined as a program which systematically investigates an arrested defendant, usually employing a type of standardized fact-finding mechanism, to determine his reliability for release on his own recognizance. The project attempts to predict the defendant's likelihood for appearing on his court date by looking at his community ties, his past criminal record, and the seriousness of the current charge. Within the broad parameters set by this definition, individual bail projects exhibit great variety in procedures, results, and philosophies. Adding even more confusion to an already muddled concept is the insistence of many court systems to declare that they are operating bail reform projects, when in reality no actual program is in existence, or the program is such a watered-down version that it serves no real purpose other than allowing the particular court system to proclaim itself to be in the forefront of judicial reform.

Reform projects are not usurping authority to control the pretrial release system. These bail projects are only *recommending* to the judge that a particular defendant be released on his own recognizance and have no power of their own to grant an outright release. One final point in clarifying the capabilities of these projects is that they are nearly always held responsible for the supervision of those defendants which they recommended and the judge approved for ROR. This supervision may be nothing more than an occasional letter or phone call and has often been found to be an ineffectual means of control. A few projects, however, do attempt to do much more and have added vocational counseling and job placement to their basic program.

The concept of bail reform projects as a viable alternative and improvement to the traditional system has met with approval by most public officials. Seventy percent of the respondents to the national survey were in agreement with the use of bail projects as a needed reform to the current pretrial release system. The Office of Economic Opportunity Pretrial Release Research Program presently lists ninety-three cities and counties as having operational bail projects, while an additional six have projects planned for the near future.[6] Of the seventy-two cities investigated through this study's mailed questionnaire, approximately half are operating bail reform projects.

The first bail reform project was initiated in 1961 in New York City where the Vera Institute of Justice was created to finance its operation. The bail reform movement was given great inpetus by the National Conference on Bail in 1964, and soon there were nearly 100 projects organized in communities across the country. In 1966 Roger Bacon, the field coordinator and consultant for Vera wrote the following pessimistic observation after visiting twenty projects across the nation:

> The five years since the Manhattan bail project has seen pretrial release projects of every shape and form springing up throughout the country. Since little was known about pretrial release projects at that time, this was envisioned as the best way to proceed. The theory was, let experimentation

be the key to success. At some future point we will sit down, analyze the strengths and weaknesses of each project and determine what the best procedure is. Well, that time has come now and unfortunately, this determination cannot be made with any degree of certainty. . . . In fact we have not even answered the basic question, are pretrial release projects really necessary? If we were to release all defendants on their own recognizance, how many would return?

Six additional years have passed since Roger Bacon's memo and still the necessary experimentation and improvement in the knowledge and operation of bail reform projects have failed to materialize. As a result of the riots in our cities, the rising crime rate, and the demand for preventive detention legislation, bail reform projects have seen their operations suffer accordingly.

In introducing the subject of bail reform projects, it is imperative that one examine the very difficult, yet basic question: what type of defendants are these projects being designed to serve? Are these projects mainly interested in obtaining RORs for as many defendants as possible regardless of economic capabilities, or are they designed to aid mainly the indigent defendant who is financially incapable of buying his pretrial freedom? In trying to answer this question, one arrives at the realization that these reform projects are being strangled by an irreconcilable contradiction of purpose (which has not been satisfactorily solved in any city). On the one hand, all reform projects need to prove themselves to the community by recommending clients whose pretrial behavior will not threaten the continued existence of the project. Since most projects are only five or six years old, they are still continuing to win the public's support and are therefore cautious about recommending a defendant for ROR. Projects with this policy are more likely to release only the better class of defendants who satisfy their middle-class standards. These defendants may be able to afford to pay the required bond but being ROR'd by the bail project, two major objectives are accomplished: (1) The bail project is able to take a swipe at the bonding industry by beating them to a blue ribbon candidate—one who is unlikely to forfeit. (2) Since these defendants are least likely to forfeit bail, or commit additional crimes, the project has an excellent chance to improve its image before the public. By maintaining good press relations, the project can insure its continued existence which can often be translated into an expanded staff operating from an increased budget.

The second half of the contradiction involves the assumption that these bail projects were primarily designed to serve the poor defendant who would not be able to obtain his pretrial release, except for a ROR. Unfortunately the defendants who are most in need of the project's recommendation are also the group least likely to satisfy the project's middle-class standards which require a certain degree of familial, residential, and job stability.

As cities attempt to deal with these conundrums and contradictions in the operation of their bail reform projects, two explanatory variables seem to emerge which best determine which type of clientele they are fated to serve. The first variable affecting the quality of client is the length of time between the defendant's arrest and when a bail project can arrive on the scene to interview him and recommend his release. Table 6-1 indicates the various amounts of time it takes in our major cities for a bail project to reach a defendant as well as the percentage of defendants which the project ROR's.

Table 6-1 clearly shows that those projects which are able to reach the defendants the quickest are most likely to be releasing the greatest percentage on their own recognizance. Even more important is the fact that individuals who are not indigent[8] and can afford to pay bail will do so at the earliest opportunity in order to avoid the discomfort and humiliation of detention. These individuals will only be benefited by a bail reform project if they are interviewed and are able to obtain their release within a very short time following their confinement. It is difficult to imagine a defendant who knows he can raise the necessary bail through a bondsmen or with the help of family and friends, to be willing to wait around more than a very short while to be interviewed by the project. Even after he is interviewed by the bail project, he may still not be recommended for release and all this time will have been wasted. In discussions with bail project directors, it was learned that most defendants would not wait for more than a half day for the bail project if they were also able to raise the necessary bail. This impatience characterizes the majority of defendants, even though they could save several hundred dollars simply by waiting another few hours for the bail project to reach them. The terrible conditions in our jails—overcrowding, homosexual attacks, filthy sanitation, and inadequate ventilation—are probably the greatest cause for this impatience.

It can be argued that even though a project may not formally state a policy of releasing only indigents, they have purposely set up their operations so as to achieve this result. This type of reasoning is difficult to refute but at the same time is nearly impossible to validate. Because of the tremendous

Table 6-1
Length of Time Until Defendants Interviewed by the Bail Project

City	Average Number of Hours Until Reached by Project	% Defendants ROR'd
Indianapolis	4.5 hrs.	14.4%
Washington, D.C.	18.0 hrs.	31.4%
San Francisco	18.0 hrs.	21.5%
Baltimore	24.0 hrs.	7.2%
Los Angeles	28.0 hrs.	5.0%
Chicago	30.0 hrs.	3.6%
Atlanta	36.0 hrs.	4.1%
St. Louis	60.0 hrs.	4.0%

backlog of court cases, as well as the understaffed bail projects, it seems more reasonable to reject this argument on practical grounds. In other words, due to their hectic working environment, bail projects are incapable of implementing such a policy objective with any degree of certainty. The delays in reaching the defendant are caused by so many other factors than the policy intentions of the bail project that it is difficult to imagine that this single factor could significantly affect the delay period.

A second explanatory variable which affects the clientele of a bail project is the use of a standardized point system which stresses family, community, and economic stability. By satisfying each of these middle-class criteria, the defendant may accumulate a sufficient number of points to be recommended for ROR. These standards severely limit the project's ability to release indigents because of their inability to achieve the required number of points to obtain a recommendation for release. Caleb Foote and others on the staff of the *University of California Law Review* have criticized the limitations of the community ties standard by writing the following:

> This philosophy is erroneous and unfair because the ROR standards reflect middle class values which do not consider the characteristics of either the poor or the young. Unemployment and underemployment are high among arrestees, residential instability and transience are characteristic as are prior records. . . The use of these middle class standards also contains a built-in cultural bias against certain minority groups.[9]

It is quite ironic that the bail reform movement, which has always been believed to have as its underlying goal the pretrial release of defendants who were detained solely because of their poverty, has developed a procedure for determining eligibility for ROR which operates directly to the detriment of such people. It was found that defendants who are forced to rely upon the bail project to obtain their release have only a one in four chance of accumulating the sufficient number of points needed to secure the project's recommendation. Again, it is urged that this low rate is caused by the application of middle-class standards to lower-class lifestyles. The mere fact that a defendant is detained and unable to post bond usually indicates his deprived economic condition.

In addition to the question of whether bail projects should serve all economic classes or strictly the indigent, these reform programs must also grapple with the problem of whether they should be helping only defendants accused of less serious crimes or if all categories of defendants should be eligible to receive their recommendation.[10] Even though most projects work only with felonies and serious misdemeanors, when one examines their operating procedures, many reform programs are prohibited from interviewing certain categories of excluded offenses. (See Chapter 7 for a detailed discussion.)

It may further be concluded from this discussion of how and why bail projects select certain types of defendants and discriminate against others, that these reform programs have not proven to be the hoped for panacea to the ills of the detained indigent defendant.

Before moving on to the additional alternative reforms for the traditional pretrial release system which are currently advocated, a short series of descriptive sketches of various bail reform projects, observed in operation for a week to ten days each, will be presented. These sketches will emphasize the unique features of each city's bail project and allow the reader to capture the flavor and variety of the bail reform movement. The following sketches and all further descriptions of bail reform projects are based on visits during the years 1970 and 1971. Therefore many names and other facts may have changed in the past three years. For example, today Philadelphia has a legitimate project to replace their "quasi-project" visited in December of 1970. Despite this time lag, however, the author feels that the bail reform movement described in this and the next two chapters is a valid and accurate picture.

Washington, D.C. The issue of preventive detention has currently eclipsed the topic of bail reform in the nation's capital. Nevertheless, the city's project releases an extremely high percentage of defendants on the recommendation of the Bail Agency staff, while maintaining a 2.3 percent forfeiture rate. The Bail Agency is headed by an extremely competent director, Bruce Beaudin. The investigative and supervisory staff are highly intelligent and well-motivated law and graduate students. They work full time at the agency and go to school in the evenings.

The Bail Agency interviews defendants the following morning after they are arrested and then verifies this information (facts on the community, economic, and family stability of the defendant) and is ready to make a recommendation to the judge when the defendant appears before him at 1:30 P.M. A unique feature of the city's Bail Agency is its role in supervising any conditions of release which the judge may attach to defendants released on their own recognizance. The court may require the defendant to obtain a job, return to school, report to the Bail Agency on a regular basis, keep out of certain areas of the city, or observe a curfew.[11]

San Francisco. The San Francisco project is often regarded as the most successful one in the country and serves as a model for many other cities attempting to join the bail reform movement. Its major strength appears to be the motivation, competence, and experience of its staff which is comprised of a full-time staff of four, twelve VISTA volunteers, six part-time student helpers, and two trainees from the Neighborhood Youth Corps.[12] After observing the project in operation for ten days, one is impressed by the dedication and expertise exhibited by the staff.

Despite the project's obvious success, it faces a serious problem: an impending financial crisis. The Ford Foundation, which has funded the project for a total of $137,000 a year, has threatened to terminate its grant. If the city of San Francisco does not pick up the project's expenses, it will cease operation. Although the bail project has saved San Francisco a great deal of money, the city's financial crisis, plus the short-sightedness of several key municipal officials, has caused the future of the project to be rather questionable.

Baltimore. Baltimore was the only city in the country to have its bail project sponsored by the State's Attorney's Office (prosecuting attorney), the prosecutorial arm of the criminal court system. Initially a VISTA project, it was extremely successful and in 1968 became a permanent responsibility of the city court under the direction of the Superior Court of Maryland, Balitmore City Division. The current project is staffed by former probation officers, social workers, and other former law enforcement officers. The project has devised an excellent system of supervision of released defendants during the pretrial period. As a result of this system, along with its broad list of excluded offenses, this project has one of the lowest forfeiture rates in the country.

The project appears overly concerned with its public image, and would probably sacrifice recommending more defendants for release in order to keep their forfeiture rate at its unrealistically low level of 0.7 percent some four full percentage points below the national average. It is tragic that a project which has firmly gained the public's support and achieved financial security with the city fathers has been unable to convince itself that the time for caution has ended. This project has a great opportunity to become a maximally effective program if it will only give itself the chance.

Los Angeles. This bail reform project is very similar to Baltimore with respect to its funding, staffing, and conservative nature. It is funded regularly by the Superior Court of Los Angeles County and has experienced no financial problems since its beginning in 1963. The large investigative staff is constantly being increased and presently has twenty-eight men. Almost all investigators are former policemen or probation officers. The weakest point of the program is the supervision of the defendants after they have been released during the pretrial period, although the forfeiture rate at 4.4 percent is not alarming. (The reason for this is the care with which the staff interviews and recommends release.) The project staff is aware of its negligible supervision and is presently planning a program to set up regional offices in the community which will supervise the defendant during this pretrial period.

An interesting development in bail reform in Los Angeles is the formation of a second ROR operation by private citizens. Its goal is to stimulate community interest in recognizance release, and it operates outside the official criminal justice system. This ghetto-based organization is entitled the "Community Justice Center." It is funded by HEW and staffed by young black activists. The CJC serves as a gadfly advocate for those behind bars, and a rallying point for judges, attorneys, and law professors interested in reforming and humanizing the pretrial release procedures. Its impact is difficult to measure, yet coincidentally, and perhaps without direct relationship, the superior court's bail project has doubled the size of its investigative staff in the past year and hired its first minority group investigators.[13]

St. Louis. In comparing the St. Louis project to the Washington project, one can truly sense the tremendous disparities which may exist within the amorphous meaning of "bail reform projects." Both cities have nearly equal populations and both suffer from a rising crime rate, yet the Washington project, with a staff of more than thirty, is able to release more than twenty times as many defendants as the St. Louis project with its meager four-man staff.

The most common explanation for the ineffective operation of the St. Louis project, which dates, in its present form, from 1968, is the public distrust of the program exacerbated by the local newspapers who staunchly oppose it. The judges, who believe the public is antagonistic toward the bail reform movement, have refused to support the bail reform program. The superior court judges, voting *en banc*, decided that they did not have the power to release defendants on their own recognizance, according to their interpretation of the law.

In addition to operating in such a hostile environment, the St. Louis project is also hampered by numerous procedural obstacles. The most severe problem is the very long period of time, usually three to four days, before the project can begin to interview the defendant. Most defendants are unwilling to wait that long a period of time for their release and nearly all the acceptable candidates for ROR have had friends or family raise the necessary funds to have a bondsman put up their bail. There are also a very large number of excluded offenses over which the program is not allowed to interview. A final problem which inhibits the project's operation is the requirement that each released defendant must have a court-approved sponsor. The judges have used this rule to eliminate many potential sponsors whom they believe to be poor risks.

There are currently plans for the Justice Department's LEAA to contribute large sums of money to allow the probation department to sponsor and administer the reform project. This would allow for the investigative staff to be increased 100 percent. However, until the judges change their attitude and the procedures are radically altered, little hope for significantly improving the project's operations can be foreseen.

Atlanta. Atlanta is a very small project—a veritable one-man operation releasing approximately thirty defendants per month. The project is an arm of the court and former directors have been characterized as political appointees. In addition to having a single investigator, the project is also handicapped by being limited by an extensive list of excluded offenses. If a defendant has been arrested for a felony in the previous two years the project will usually refuse to recommend him. The project seems to be mainly for the indigent first offenders who are accused of committing property crimes.

The project operates out of the Fulton County Jail and is not able to interview defendants until three or four days after their arrest. A Vera-type of interview sheet is used but the point system is weighted so as to overemphasize the seriousness of the present charge and the defendant's past criminal record. When the defendant is released, he fills out a card to have himself notified of his

upcoming court date. He is also requested to call or report in to the project periodically; however, the supervision is haphazardly administered. The forfeiture
rate of 8.3 percent is fairly high and probably is a reflection of the smallness
and laxness of the operation rather than the product of any procedural flaw.

Most of the public officials in Atlanta are not overly concerned with the
bail project, principally because it has proven to be such an ineffectual reform
mechanism. The public seems to hold no strong opinion for or against the project and it could be described in the terminology of Bachrach and Baratz as a
"non-issue."[14] The only group which continues to oppose the bail reform
project is the police department which has fought it from its inception. The
arresting officer plays a key role in the determination of the bail amount at
the commitment hearing in municipal court, and the police simply dislike
seeing defendants they arrest back on the streets while awaiting trial.

Chicago. Although operating under the Illinois 1966 Bail Reform Act
which strongly encourages release on recognizance, the Chicago project is
meagerly staffed and only minimally effective, with a very high forfeiture
rate (19 percent). In a city of three-and-a-half-million people, the bail reform
project operates with a staff of four men, yet manages to conduct 7,000 interviews a year while recommending nearly 900 individuals for release. With so
small a staff and so many prisoners to interview, it is no wonder that there is
complete absence of any supervision of the defendants once they are released
and awaiting trial.[15]

The responsibility for the failure of the bail reform project to be adequately
staffed lies primarily with its sponsoring agency, the Circuit Court of Cook
County. The presiding judge, the Honorable John Boyle, has been charged by
critics of the Cook County court system, with turning down federal funds which
might possibly help enlarge the project's operations. The reason for this refusal
is the reluctance of the judge to relinquish control over the project's operation
and avoid sharing power with outside sources.[16]

Indianapolis. The Indianapolis bail project is the only program visited
which specializes in misdemeanors rather than felonies. The original rationale
for this, as stated by Bail Commissioner (Project Director) Jim Droege, was that
it was easier to get the public's and the court's approval of the project by first
dealing with less serious crimes. Then after establishing themselves as a responsible organization, they would move into the area of felonies. Mr. Droege's
reasoning proved correct: after two years of success with misdemeanors, they
are gradually getting into considering felonies. The project's size has doubled
during this period, and there are now eight investigators in addition to the
director, secretarial staff, and statistician. (It should be noted that the project
keeps the most accurate and complete statistics of any project visited.)

The most unique features of the project are the speed with which it
reaches the defendants and its power to release the defendant without obtaining
the judge's approval. The bail project has offices right in the lockup area of the

city jail and is able to interview the defendants within hours after their arrest. The staff usually see the defendant immediately after he has been photographed and fingerprinted. In their race with the bondsmen to get to the best prospects for release, the bail project is usually the victor. The project's authority to release defendants who have qualified on their point system and have had their information verified, is an extraordinary grant of discretion by the courts and is unique to this project. Although the release of the defendant is only until his court appearance the following day, the judges in almost all cases allow the defendant to continue on recognizance release in the charge of the project. The project also has an excellent supervisory system which has resulted in the forfeiture rate of only 2.9 percent. It will be interesting to see if the project will continue to have the same degree of success and power as it begins to handle the more serious crimes.

Quasi Projects. Two of the cities visited proclaimed they were operating bail projects; however after observing their activities for a week, the best they could be called were "quasi projects." The reason for this terminology is that each supposed reform project failed to completely satisfy the definitional requirements of a bail reform project as were initially stated in this chapter. They have been included in this series of sketches to illustrate how far cities will stretch the concept of bail reform. It is hypothesized that cities engage in this type of deception in order to present themselves as being in the forefront of judicial reform, while at the same time operating only token projects which may stifle any further cries for altering the system. It is noteworthy that since these projects were visited during the winter of 1970-71, both cities have received federal grants and are presently operating viable bail reform projects, as effective as any in the country.

Detroit. The Neighborhood Legal Services has a project which employed two senior law students to attempt to aid the court in providing information on certain defendants whom they believe to be good candidates for release on their own recognizance. These two law students work with the arraignment officer who makes recommendations to the judge in all felony cases as to the amount of bond or possible issuance of a personal bond. Each arresting officer presents to the arraignment officer the warrant, arrest record, and prior record of the defendant. This is done in the morning before the 11 A.M. arraignment court. The two law students quickly look through the records of the newly arrested defendants and go over to interview and verify Vera criteria for a few of the defendants they believe to be good prospects for release who were initially overlooked. They then return and present this information to the arraignment officer before the court convenes. They may also work on the problem of bond reduction if personal bonds appear out of the question. During the arraignment court these students sit by this officer and serve as a source of information concerning background on the defendant if the judge wishes to make inquiries in this area.

The NLS-sponsored bail project does not engage in supervising the defendants if they are released except to send a letter requesting the defendant to call back to their offices. They are basically an administrative aid for the arraignment officer and a fact source for the arraignment court judge.

Philadelphia. When the Philadelphia Bail Project, headed by Edmund DePaul, ran out of funds in 1967 and the city refused to finance the project, the Defender Association of Philadelphia attempted to fill this gap in services to the indigent defendant. The Defender Association sponsored a group of law students from the University of Pennsylvania, subsequently replaced by Villanova University law students who operated a bail reduction program which included applications for release on recognizance which is called nominal bond in Philadelphia.

Each Defender Association lawyer filed a bail application for his client at the preliminary arraignment, if bail was not made. The application resembled the Vera format and covered the defendant's roots in the community, his prior record, and a brief factual statement of the present case. The law students obtained this information from the defendant and then attempted to verify the client's community ties. After verification, they made an informal application to the District Attorney's Office for a bail hearing to have the amount reduced or a nominal bond granted.

The Common Pleas Court of Philadelphia has received a large grant from the federal government to begin a city-run bail reform project beginning in the early months of 1971. The project also contains a new cash bail deposit system modeled after the Illinois 10 percent Bail Deposit Provision, as well as a pretrial diversion program, to be discussed in the last section of this chapter. The entire program will be directed by the Probation Department and the Court Administrator's Office.

Citation and Stationhouse Release

Bail reform projects modeled after the Vera Foundation's Manhattan program are only one of several promising alternatives to the traditional system of money bail. Another set of alternatives to be examined are those procedures used by the police to release defendants for less serious crimes without detaining them in jail or the stationhouse. The two procedures most commonly employed are the citation program and stationhouse release. The citation program permits the police to issue a summons to appear to the defendant when he is apprehended on the street. By not taking the defendant into custody, the police save a great deal of time in transporting the offender to the police station and detaining him there. The citation procedures are identical to those used by the police in ticketing traffic offenses. This on-the-spot citation is mainly used for crimes involving traffic or local ordinance violations. This program is used most efficiently in Contra Costa County, California, where extensive use and efficient procedures have made it a model program. These citations, or "summons to appear" as they are called in California, are issued in nearly all misdemeanor cases unless the police believe an arrest must be made to protect the community or the processes of court. Summons are the norm in petty theft, minor assault, and municipal ordinance cases. After the defendant is arrested, the police officer calls in to a computer-based Intelligence Network System which tells him within a minute if the defendant is wanted for another crime. If he is not, he is immediately issued the summons and released until his court date.[17]

Despite the obvious savings in police time, these citation programs have not been very well received by police forces in other parts of the country. The police citation program was originally started by the Vera Institute of Justice with the New York City Police Department, and proved workable. Unlike the bail reform projects which were copied by many communities around the nation after Vera's initial project in Manhattan in 1961, the citation program failed to capture the imagination and confidence of police forces.

In nearly every city investigated, there is presently a provision for the police to utilize a citation or summons procedure, yet there was virtually no implementation of this reform measure, with the possible exception of limited usage in Philadelphia and San Francisco.

If the offender must be arrested and taken to a police station for booking, he still may be spared detention if he can obtain stationhouse release. This second reform measure aiding the police in eliminating unnecessary pretrial detention was also originated by the Vera Institute and was first used in 1964 by the New York City Police Department. It is used for all misdemeanors and a few less serious felonies. After arrest the defendant is brought to the stationhouse where he is interviewed to see if he possesses sufficient community ties to qualify as a good risk under the Vera scale. If the interviewer believes him to be a good risk, a recommendation is made to the precinct captain who has discretionary authority to release or detain the accused. If released, he is presented with a summons notifying him of when he is to appear in court.[18]

In addition to New York, only Washington, D.C. was found to use the stationhouse release program on a regular basis. Their program closely approximates the New York operation with the exception of having an investigator from the D.C. Bail Agency interview the offender over the phone. Upon completion of the phone conversation, the investigator then attempts to verify the information and calls the precinct officer back to give him the agency's recommendation. The primary rationale for this program (which was included in the 1967 act creating the Bail Agency) is to permit the police to release an arrestee on personal recognizance when the courts are not in session (such as weekends, when the jails are at their busiest). The implementation of the program has been limited because of funding and staffing inadequacies, plus the reluctance of the police to refer cases. Nevertheless, the police in Washington in 1969 referred 1037 cases to the Bail Agency which resulted in the release of

681 defendants. However, this is not a very impressive figure when one considers that there were 50,000 offenders potentially eligible for release under this program.[19]

Pretrial Diversion

The concept of pretrial diversion has a much broader focus than any of the other bail reform innovations examined thus far. It has the potential for being the only alternative to pretrial detention which is not content to merely place the defendant back into his old environment. Pretrial diversion attempts to provide the defendant with an assist toward achieving some social and economic viability through the application of intensive short-term manpower training. The program offers itself to the criminal justice system as a flexible and rehabilitative vehicle and a serviceable alternative to the traditional dispositional possibilities. It attempts to intervene in the system and rehabilitate young offenders before they become hardened to a life of crime.

Pretrial diversion originated with the Vera Institute in New York, which along with Washington, D.C.'s "Project Crossroads," constitute the only two cities operating experienced programs. It is encouraging to note that Philadelphia, Detroit, and Atlanta have recently initiated similar programs. Also, the Justice Department has begun work with the Labor Department to set up on an experimental basis, pretrial diversion programs in Alburquerque (for Indians), San Antonio (for Mexican-Americans), Boston (for blacks), Cleveland (for blacks), and Minneapolis (for poor whites) for specialized ethnic groups.

Washington, D.C.'s Project Crossroads was found to be a most impressive model for other cities who might attempt this far-reaching and necessary reform program. The project's enrollment criteria are that the participants must be between sixteen and twenty-six, residents of the Metropolitan area, currently unemployed, underemployed, or their job jeopardized because of their arrest. Additional requirements are that the defendant must have qualified for personal recognizance under the D.C. Bail Agency and has no previous adult conviction or incarceration for more than one year as a juvenile.[20]

Each new participant in the program is assigned a community worker-counselor who is responsible for the participant and evaluates his performance for the court. Contact between the two must be at least once a week on a personal basis and over the telephone as frequently as possible. The project, through its worker-counselors, acts as a middleman between participants and local social welfare service organizations.

Project Crossroads also provides employment and educational services. The employment staff helps arrange job interviews and works to ensure that a suitable placement has been made. Education is handled largely through VISTA volunteers who conduct programs four evenings a week. They tutor participants seeking to pass high school equivalency exams, remedial reading, job test preparation, and armed forces qualifying tests.

At the completion of the prescribed ninety-day period, the counselor may recommend to the court either dismissal of pending charges based on satisfactory project participation and visible self-improvement; extension of the work period to allow more time for the project to work with the individual; or reversion of the defendant to normal court processing, without prejudice, because of unsatisfactory performance in the program. Also the participant may be removed from the program any time during the ninety-day period because of chronic uncooperativeness or the commission of a new offense.[21]

The district's project has fourteen paid staff and seven VISTA volunteers who work in the three operational components of the program: counseling, employment services, and education. In addition, the VISTA volunteers have recruited and coordinated a volunteer staff of about forty-five tutors to provide individualized instruction to project participants. The program can only be criticized for the limited number of participants which it has been able to help. This, of course, is due to insufficient staffing and funding and is in no way the fault of the dedicated men and women currently working in the program. Since its beginning in April 1968, through September 1970, the project's statistics indicate a total of 825 youths to have been enrolled in the project. Charges against 468 enrollees have been dropped, while 285 were returned to normal court processing, primarily because of unsatisfactory program performance. The project summarizes its accomplishments by stating in their October 1970 report: "In keeping with the manpower orientation of the project, approximately 1000 job and training placements have been made for participants, including non-enrollees, and over 6000 hours of remedial education and text coaching was provided by volunteer tutors under the direction of the project's VISTA workers." [22]

Third Party Release

An alternative program based on the traditional English system of bail and personal sureties is the concept of third party release. This procedure releases the defendant to the custody of a willing private third party, who must be approved by the court. Examples of persons customarily used as personal sureties are the defendant's attorney, minister, employer, landlord, or school or union official. The major drawback to this program is the difficulty in constructing some workable sanction to be imposed upon the surety in case the defendant fails to appear. Some standard of supervisory neglect would have to be established. In any event, it is almost inconceivable to be able to develop a suitable sanction which can be applied to such respectable citizens as ministers, lawyers, and educators which at the same time would serve as a viable deterrent to forfeitures.

As a result of the difficulty in operating this type of a system, as well as a general opposition to its innovative format, only 35 percent of the public officials surveyed were willing to state a belief in the workability of third party release.

Twenty-eight percent of the respondents were either unable or unwilling to reach a decision on this issue.

In Washington, D.C., one of the very few cities contemplating using third party release, the Bail Agency reported that because of insufficient personnel it has not been able to develop a coordinated third party custodial program. The Bail Agency also concluded that individual custodians such as friends or members of the family are practically useless. They recommend instead the use of sponsoring organizations, the next variation to be discussed.[23]

Two cities which have been able to establish a third party release program with workable sanctions are Albuquerque, New Mexico and Tulsa Oklahoma. The Tulsa project, under the leadership of Ollie Gresham, has been very effective since its beginning in 1963. It releases a defendant into the custody of his attorney. To qualify, an attorney has to agree that "he will not knowingly request the release of a person previously convicted of a felony or, within six months, of an offense involving moral turpitude." Failure to produce his client in court when required, results in removal of the attorney's name from the approved list. In the first year of operation the Tulsa program released almost 200 defendants a month and had the names of only 13 attorneys removed from the list during the year because of client forfeitures.[24]

Community Release

Community release is a variation of the third party release program. Although it is in the experimental stages presently, it appears to have great future possibilities. As noted in the discussion of third party release, the Washington, D.C. Bail Agency had rejected third party individual custodian release because several community organizations are presently doing an excellent job of serving as surety for released defendants.

The community release procedure closely resembles the third party concept but instead of an individual custodian, a responsible community-based organization like the Woodlawn Organization in Chicago or Black Man's Development Center in Washington is used. These organizations have the staff to adequately supervise the defendant and can become authority figures to control the misconduct of the defendant. They also have the strength and objectivity which individual custodians, particularly family and friends, are lacking. In addition to Washington, the only other cities found to be attempting to implement community release programs are Detroit and Pittsburgh. In Detroit a program was scheduled to begin in the spring of 1971 which is considering the use of community volunteers to supervise defendants which the bail reform project (also to be initiated at this time) releases. The program, under the direction of the city's probation department, will rely on various service, church, and neighborhood organizations to provide volunteers and oversee the program.[25]

Pittsburgh had started an excellent community-based organization in the spring of 1972. Unfortunately the project, calling itself "Community Release Agency," and directed by Dorothy Richardson, was prohibited from operating in the city by the court of common pleas. In an obvious power play, the judges of this court, who had recently countered the CRA threat by establishing their own bail reform agency, decided that there was no need for two projects in the same city. Their rationale for outlawing the CRA was that it was planning to use a few ex-convicts as field workers and supervisors. Despite the fact that CRA received over $200,000 from state and federal sources (nearly $100,000 more than the Common Pleas Court sponsored bail project), it was forced out of existence. The real tragedy is that hundreds of defendants will be deprived of the opportunity to use the CRA program and have been helplessly exploited as unknowing pawns in a political game where they are always the losers.[26]

Daytime Release

A final alternative to be discussed is daytime release. It is designed for those defendants who are too poor a risk to be granted full-time release. They may be allowed to leave the jail during the day so as to continue on their jobs while awaiting trial or in order to help prepare their defense. Such daytime release projects are quite common for convicted and sentenced offenders but are almost never used during the pretrial release period.

The only instance of daytime release for a pretrial detainee uncovered in any of the cities visited was an isolated case in Chicago. In an interview with a Chicago attorney who was interested in bail reform, he disclosed that one of his clients had been released to him on certain days for six-hour periods so that they could more adequately prepare his defense. The case involved a very serious crime resulting in a possible twenty to forty-year sentence. The defendant spoke only Spanish so the preparation of the defense and investigation and location of witnesses, all of whom also spoke Spanish, was dependent upon the lawyer's close personal contact with his client.[27]

Like the concept of third party release, daytime release met very chilly reception from the public officials who responded to the mailed attitudinal questionnaire. Only 42 percent were willing to agree that daytime release was a good alternative to the present system. It was generally thought to be too difficult to implement on a regular basis.

7

The Institutions and Procedures of Bail Reform

In Chapter 6 it was reported that in 1966 Roger Bacon, the field coordinator for the Vera Institute of Justice, traveled around the country inspecting bail reform projects in over twenty cities. The result of this tour led him to bemoan the fact that the bail reform movement seemed to be floundering. His pessimistic evaluations concluded that "the problems posed several years ago . . . Who is best suited to administer pretrial release projects? What kinds of crimes and defendants should they cover? What do you do when a defendant does not meet your criteria for release on recognizance? Who do you present this information to? Do you use objective or subjective criteria? – are still unsolved today."[1]

This chapter will attempt to answer these questions through an examination of the institutional framework and operational procedures which are currently utilized in our nation's bail reform projects. The first half of this chapter will concentrate on the funding, staffing, and supervisory practices found in these projects and comprise their institutional setting. The second half will be devoted to a discussion of the daily operation of the projects, focusing upon such topics as the time lag between arrest and interview, the jurisdictional restrictions, the verification process, and the system of supervision once the ROR has been granted. The chapter will close with a presentation of the statistical output from these projects.

The primary source of information for this evaluation of the bail reform movement will be the intensive studies conducted in eight cities which are operating viable bail reform projects. In addition to seven-to-ten-day observation periods in each city, over 100 interviews were conducted with knowledgeable individuals on this topic. To supplement this rather narrow sample of projects, the results of a mailed survey of an additional thirty projects will also be included.

In order to compare these bail reform projects so as to see what effect the variety of institutions and procedures may exert upon the project's operational effectiveness, some basis of comparison had to be constructed. In this chapter the projects are compared on the basis of the percentage of defendants released on the recommendation of the bail project from the total number of defendants qualified for possible ROR by the project. The resulting figure will be termed the "release rate." An additional measure of comparison also to be used in evaluating their effectiveness is the project's forfeiture rate. The difficulties and validity of this statistic have been elaborated upon in great detail in Chapter 4. It is the underlying assumption of this evaluation that because of the human and public costs of pretrial detention, the greater the percentage of defendants ROR'd by the project, the more effective its operation.

With a single exception, all statistics are taken from the year 1969. Each yearly statistic for the number of defendants released by each project was an exact figure gathered from the project's annual reports in every city except one. The exception was Atlanta, where the project never maintained statistical records. Their yearly release figure was an estimate which was agreed upon by the bail project director and the supervisor and founder of the program, Judge Luther Alverson. Since the project released approximately thirty defendants per month, it is believed that this small figure can be estimated fairly accurately.

The second half of the computation for determining the percentage of defendants released on recommendation of the project is the total number of defendants in each city who fall within the jurisdiction of the project. Because of the difficulties in determining this figure, two separate types of procedures had to be devised. In half of the cities visited (Washington, Detroit, Philadelphia, Atlanta, and Indianapolis) the precise number of defendants who qualified for ROR through the bail project was available. These figures were usually provided by the clerk of the criminal court.

In the second group of cities (St. Louis, Baltimore, Chicago, San Francisco, and Los Angeles) there were no exact statistics and the totals had to be estimated. The estimates were based on data taken from the Federal Bureau of Investigation's *Uniform Crime Reports for 1969.* The total number of defendants was computed for each city by taking the total crime index[2] for each city and multiplying it by the national clearance rate, which was set by the FBI at 20.9 percent for 1969. The 20.9 percent figure represents the percentage of index crimes where a suspect was arrested by the police, charged, and taken into custody to await appearance before a judge.[3]

The FBI crime index was used because the seven index crimes are nearly identical with the categories of crimes over which each bail project has jurisdiction. All five cities in the second group had jurisdiction over felonies and the more serious misdemeanors. By using one nationalized statistical report such as the FBI Crime Reports, the study is assured of a greater degree of consistency.

The Institutional Framework

Table 7-1 offers the reader a clear introduction and summary picture of the institutional picture as exemplified by the variety of organizations and individuals who are involved in running these reform projects.

Table 7-1
Staffing, Supervision, and Direction of Bail Projects

City	Staff	Supervision	Director
Washington	Law students and graduate students	D.C. Court of Criminal Appeals	Bruce Beaudin (Lawyer)
St. Louis	Probation Officers	State Probation Department	James Brackman (Prob. Officer)
San Francisco	VISTA Vols. and graduate students	San Francisco Inst. for Criminal Justice[a]	Kenneth Babb (Sociologist)
Los Angeles	Court Staff Investigators	Superior Court	Bill W. Box (Ex-Probation)
Baltimore	Court Staff Investigators	Supreme Bench of Baltimore	Richard Motsay (Ex-District Attorney)
Atlanta	Law student	Circuit Court of Fulton Company	Larry Thomas (Law student)
Chicago	Law students and graduate students	Circuit Court of Cook County	Marshall Pigeon (Lawyer)
Indianapolis	Law students	Criminal Justice Planning Comm.	Jim Droege (Law professor)

[a]A nonprofit corporation created primarily to facilitate funding of the project from private as well as public sources.

Investigative Staff

As Table 7-2 points out, the sheer size of the investigative staff does not strongly influence either the release rates or the forfeiture rates of the bail projects. Of the top four projects in staff size, San Francisco and Washington are maximally effective[4] but the remaining two, Los Angeles and Baltimore, are only moderately successful. However, if the projects are insufficiently staffed, as in the bottom four cities, they are unable to ROR a significant percentage of their defendants. These four smallest cities in staff size released an average of only 4.1 percent. In summary, the staff size appears to be important only if it is small, for this will preclude the operation of an effective project. However, by merely increasing the size of the staff, there may be no guarantee that the effectiveness will increase proportionally.

The size of the staff is most crucial to the operation of a bail project when the supervisory agency requests that all potential defendants be interviewed. Without a sufficient staff, the project expends all of its time and energy interviewing defendants, many of whom will ultimately decide to pay a bondsman rather than wait for the project to complete its investigation and verification. As noted in Chapter 6, this is the dilemma which faces the Chicago Bail Reform Project. With a staff of only four men, they have been directed to consider any

Table 7-2
Size of the Investigative Staff

City	Staff Size	Release Rate	Forfeiture Rate
Los Angeles	28	5.0%	7.4%
Washington	26	31.4%	2.3%
San Francisco	18	21.5%	2.3%
Baltimore	12	7.2%	0.7%
Indianapolis	8	14.4%	2.9%
St. Louis	4	4.6%	3.1%
Chicago	4	3.6%	19.0%
Atlanta	1	4.1%	8.3%

defendant who requests an interview. It is no wonder they do not have the time to supervise defendants after they are released, and consequently have the greatest forfeiture rate of any of the projects visited.

In addition to the mere size of a project's staff, the type of individual serving as a member of the project's investigative staff is also a significant factor in the project's effectiveness. These staff members are able to influence the direction, style, vigor, and effectiveness of the project. The best way to identify the types of individuals working in bail projects is to classify them as to whether they are volunteers or full-time court personnel. It is also helpful to know their former occupations prior to their joining the bail project.

It is reported in Table 7-3 that in the projects observed, those using volunteer staffs were clearly the most effective, recommending the release of 19 percent of the eligible defendants while maintaining a forfeiture rate of less than 3 percent. In the larger national survey, 41 percent of the projects (twelve cities) were using volunteer staffs. The most common sources of volunteer help were law students (five cities) and VISTA volunteers (three cities). The other three projects obtained their help from a variety of community organizations.

It should be noted that these students or volunteers devote full time to the project and attend school in the evenings or on a part-time basis. The criticism of using law students on a part-time basis is that they often lose interest in the project after the initial enthusiasm has waned. Also, they tend to place their studies above their responsibilities to the project. As a result, during certain times of the year such as finals week, when academic pressures are being exerted, they cannot be counted on to perform their job at the bail project.[5]

The Chicago and Atlanta projects, although staffed by part-time law students, do not contradict the original hypothesis (projects with volunteer staffs are more effective) even though their projects operate with an extremely low release rate. The rationale for distinguishing them is that their low release rate are caused primarily by their undersized staffs rather than the source of the

Table 7-3
Bail Project Effectiveness and Source of Staff

City	Source of Staff	Release Rate	Forfeiture Rate
Washington	Law students and graduate students	31. %	2.3%
San Francisco	VISTA volunteers and graduate students	21.5	2.3
Baltimore	Former police and probation officers	7.2	0.7
Indianapolis	Law students	14.4	2.9
St. Louis	Probation officers	4.5	3.1
Los Angeles	Former police and probation officers	5.0	7.4
Atlanta	Law student	4.1	8.3
Chicago	Law students and Graduate student	3.6	19.0

staff. Four investigators for the entire city of Chicago and one solitary law student for all of Atlanta indicate shadow projects which were erected more for political reasons than humanitarian concerns. Thus, if one were to control for the size of the investigative staff, projects with noncourt staff investigators are releasing more defendants than projects with court staff investigators and are still able to maintain low forfeiture rates.

Why do those projects staffed with volunteers, students, and VISTA workers seem to be effective, especially when compared to the work of full-time court investigators? The explanation most frequently given by bail project directors was that their volunteer and student staff members strongly believed in the purpose of bail reform and carried on their jobs with a missionary-like zeal. Because the education of law students in the field of criminal law is usually defense-oriented, these young law students come to the project with a keen sense of the injustices currently plaguing the criminal justice system. These feelings are manifested in a liberal release policy by most students, weighting the balance toward the freedom of the individual over the protection of society.[6]

Despite the proven ability of volunteers and students to operate effective bail projects, the majority of reform programs in this country employ regularly paid officers of the court. The most common categories of these full-time paid staffs were probation officers (ten cities), court clerks and administrators (five cities), and bail investigators appointed by the judge (three cities).

The reason why full-time court staff investigators operate in projects which have a low release rate is that they are by their training, prosecution-oriented, and very cautious in estimating the eligibility of a defendant for recognizance release. It is also conjectured that one who has been a member of the criminal justice system for a period of time will lack the initiative and spirit necessary to an innovative type of venture such as a bail reform project. Often in their late thirties and forties, these full-time court staff investigators view their work in the bail project as simply a nine to five job. Their primary concern is to serve the court in such a manner as to ensure their job security. They realize that the easiest way to "rock the boat" is to release defendants who fail to appear or commit additional crimes while awaiting trial. The fear of releasing such defendants continually haunts these investigators and influences their strict standards for release. Most of these former police and probation officers sincerely feel an obligation to protect the public, a belief which was firmly instilled in them during their previous training and experiences working with criminals.

Supervision and Direction

Most bail projects are administered by a two-level form of supervision. Immediately above the investigative staff is a director who is in charge of the day-to-day operation of the project and makes all of the nonpolicy decisions. Above this director is the supervisor of the project who decides all major policy questions such as the jurisdiction and size of the project. If one wishes to alter the direction of the project or modify its style, the office of the project's supervisor should be the focal point of these attempted changes. In most cities the bail project is supervised either by the chief judge of the criminal court or the entire court itself. Table 7-4 illustrates what types of officials are found at these two levels of command in the eight bail projects visited.

Based on the variety of supervisors and directors which were observed controlling our nation's largest bail projects, four patterns of relationships were found to exist between the two groups. These patterns represent the variety of leadership styles operating at the juncture of both of these groups. These patterns are shown in Figure 7-1, which also presents an example of each category of pattern.

		SUPERVISION	
		Close	Distant
	Strong	Baltimore	San Francisco
DIRECTION			
	Weak	Chicago	Los Angeles

Figure 7-1. Patterns of Supervision and Division

Table 7-4
Directors and Supervisors

City	Director	Supervisor	Release Rate
Washington	Bruce Beaudin, Lawyer	D.C. Court of Appeals	31.4
San Francisco	Ken Babb, Sociologist	San Francisco Inst. for Criminal Justice	21.5
Indianapolis	Jim Droege, Law Professor	Criminal Justice Planning Comm.	14.4
Baltimore	Rich. Motsay Lawyer	Supreme Bench	7.2
Los Angeles	Bill Box Probation Officer	Superior Court	5.0
St. Louis	Jim Brackman Probation Officer	State Probation Dept. and Circuit Court	4.6
Atlanta	Larry Thomas Law Student	Judge Alberson, Circuit Court	4.1
Chicago	Marshall Pidgeon Lawyer	Judge Boyle, Circuit Court	3.6

The first pattern is symbolized by the San Francisco project, where there is a strong and capable director, and the sponsoring agency does not supervise or provide any help other than financial. The sponsoring agency is the San Francisco Institute for Criminal Justice, a nonprofit corporation created primarily to facilitate funding of the project from private as well as public sources. The director of the project when it was visited in 1970 was Kenneth Babb, a sociologist holding a doctorate from Cambridge University and an extremely capable administrator who completely dominates operation of his highly successful bail project.[7]

The second pattern is most clearly found in Baltimore, where the project is headed by a strong and capable individual, but who, in turn, is controlled by the policy decisions of the Supreme Bench of the City of Baltimore, the sponsoring agency. Director Richard Motsay is a former assistant state's attorney who has been with the project since its creation in 1966. He perceives his main job to be selling the project to the public and appears to be more involved in public relations than concerned with the daily routines of the projects operation. It is interesting to note that over a third of the project's annual report was devoted to a review of Motsay's speaking engagements and other activities designed to improve the civic image of the project. Since the project has been in operation for five years and is generally well received by the public, it seems that Director Motsay could better spend his time in pressuring the Supreme Bench to expand the jurisdiction of the project. Because the Supreme Bench has never been challenged on this issue, it is very difficult to speculate on its reaction. However, after five years of stagnation the project should at least attempt to confront the sponsoring agency on the possibility of expansion.

Los Angeles offers a good example of the third pattern, where the director is simply an administrator but is not closely controlled by the sponsoring agency, in this case the Superior Court of Los Angeles County. The director or OR unit supervisor, as he is called, is Bill Box, Jr., who works closely with the superior court. Box is a capable administrator and directs the largest full-time staff of investigators in the nation (with the possible exception of New York City whose project is in a constant state of turmoil). Because of his narrow role, Supervisor Box is categorized as an administrative director rather than a strong director such as Kenneth Babb. In Los Angeles any impetus for change must come from the superior court judges. With the help of such men as Judge Hayden, the project has been able to expand in staff size and will soon branch out into regional offices with an enlarged jurisdiction.

The final pattern of supervision is found in Chicago. This pattern is characterized by a weak director and a very strong sponsoring agency which controls all policy decisions, major and minor. The bail projects in this pattern have so small an investigative staff (Chicago has a four-man staff) that the director cannot possibly devote full time to administrative details as in the third pattern. The project, despite its small size, has a two-tier level of command. The lower level is run by Tom Royce, who handles the daily operation of the project. He is in charge of the remaining three members of the project's staff, while Marshall Pidgeon, a lawyer representing Judge Boyle's office, is technically director of the project and Royce's superior. Pidgeon also directs the Cook County work release program and other court-supervised activities. He appeared, in an interview with the author, to be out of contact with the detailed functioning of the bail project. Royce, the senior staff investigator, is slightly older and more experienced than his fellow staff members, having been with the project since its beginning. He is a former probation officer who is currently studying at night to become a lawyer. Because of such an undersized staff and the tremendous numbers of interviews these four men must conduct (over 7,000 last year), he is forced to help as much as possible in interviewing the ever-increasing number of defendants.[8]

After reviewing the patterns of supervision and glancing again at Table 7-4, its seems clear that the attitudes and beliefs of these men who direct and supervise the nation's bail projects are crucial to their success. It is also apparent that the personalities and ideas of these men vary a great deal, regardless of the similarity in occupation.

In attempting to determine the relationship between a bail project's pattern of supervision and the effectiveness of its program, interviews, observations, and statistical reports indicate that the lower the level of supervision, the more effective the project. Table 7-5 measures the possible relationship between the degree of supervision and the effectiveness of the program.

Table 7-5
The Degree of Supervision and Its Importance

City	Supervisor	Degree of Supervision	Release Rate
Washington	D.C. Court of Appeals	1	31.4
San Francisco	San Francisco Institute for Criminal Justice	1	21.5
Indianapolis	Criminal Justice Planning Comm.	2	14.4
Baltimore	Supreme Bench	3	7.2
Los Angeles	Superior Court	3	5.0
St. Louis	State Probation Department and Circuit Court	2	4.6
Atlanta	Judge Alverson, Circuit Court	4	4.1
Chicago	Judge Boyle, Circuit Court	5	3.6

NOTE: The term "degree of supervison" will be operationalized in this table by constructing a scale of supervision running from 1 to 5 possible points. The higher the amount of points assigned to a project, the greater and closer the degree of supervision. The decision as to what degree of supervision is to be found in each project is based on the author's interviews and observations in each of the cities and is therefore a subjective conclusion.

The supervisors and directors possess a great potential for either facilitating or inhibiting improvements in bail projects. The attitudes, beliefs, and personalities of these men may have crucial significance to the effectiveness of a bail project. Other variables may be important, but unless the supervisor is convinced of the necessity of reform, it will probably be doomed to failure.

Funding and Institutionalization

Bail projects may be either publicly or privately funded. Only nine (30 percent) of the bail projects surveyed are funded by private agencies such as foundations (2), bar associations (4), private legal aid societies (1) and a small group of miscellaneous organizations not associated with the government (3). The major reason for the scarcity of privately funded projects is simply their expense. In a city of half a million, the annual budget for a ten-man bail project will run close to a quarter of a million dollars. Another explanation is that while these private organizations are willing to sponsor and fund a project during its formative stages, after the project has proven itself as a reliable and efficient operation, they believe it is the obligation of the city or state to carry on the funding and sponsoring activities.[9]

124   FREEDOM FOR SALE

Twenty-one bail projects (70 percent) are sponsored by governmental
agencies. The two most common sponsors are the local court system (9) and
the probation department (8). The remaining projects are sponsored by an
assortment of public legal service groups and public defender organizations
designed to serve the indigent defendant. Most projects are institutionalized
to the degree that they are supervised by the city or county court system
and also have their appropriations controlled by these public institutions. A
summary of these various funding and supervising institutions is found in
Table 7-6.

In evaluating the implications of whether a bail project should be funded
publicly or privately, a paradox has emerged. Where the funding is public and
part of the court's annual budget rather than private or federal monies, the
bail projects are guaranteed financial security, but often operate in a very
cautious and conservative manner, releasing a much lower percentage of defendants than their staff size and budget would seem to permit. This is especially
true in projects such as Chicago and Atlanta where the court directly controls
the size of the project's budget. On the other side of the paradox are found
those bail projects which are privately funded. Although they generally are
more effective than the publicly funded projects, they are financially insecure
and (with the exception of San Francisco), have either folded completely
(Philadelphia and Oakland) or have become absorbed by the court system
(Baltimore and Washington).

Table 7-6
Funding Sources

City	Funding Source	Release Rate	Degree of Supervision
Washington	D.C. Courts Budget (Congress)	31.4%	1
San Francisco	OEO and San Francisco Foundation	21.5	1
Baltimore	City Court's Budget	7.2	3
Indianapolis	Court Budget and LEAA grant	14.4	2
St. Louis	State Budget of Probation Department	4.6	2
Los Angeles	Superior Court's Budget	5.0	3
Atlanta	Court Budget	4.1	4
Chicago	Court Budget	3.6	5

The explanation for the existence of such a paradox is twofold. First, the bail projects which are publicly funded through the court system's budget are conservative in operation because they believe (and in most cases correctly) that the courts which are paying their salaries design them to be extremely careful in their recommendations for release. They realistically understand that if poor risks are released and fail to show or commit additional crimes while released both the project and the sponsoring court system will feel intense pressure from politicians, newspapers, and a generally alarmed public.

The paradox is also explained by the fact that these privately funded projects are only considered to be the pilot programs and are planned to be eventually absorbed into the local court system. The private foundations and federal agencies contribute money to help the newly created bail project get off the ground and prove itself to the city fathers. This proof is manifested in great savings in human costs and the costs to the city budget since it is very expensive to house a defendant and build new jails. Privately funded projects usually are staffed by law students and other volunteer groups who are highly motivated. With an enthusiastic staff and an inevitably short life span, these privately funded projects often work with seemingly reckless abandon, the end result being a very effective program, releasing large numbers of defendants.

The choice should not be between a publicly or a privately funded project. It is the responsibility of the city to absorb the bail project and finance it once it has proven itself as an effective and reliable program. The real problem is the degree of autonomy granted to the bail project once the city has decided to take over and fund the private agency. If a bail reform project is to prosper, it needs financial security which only the public treasury can and should provide. At the same time it is providing this security, the city should be careful to allow the bail reform project sufficient independence in its daily operation, recruitment policies, and other policy decisions. It is clear from the projects visited that as the courts attempt to impose closer financial and policy-making control over the projects, the more conservative and less effective the bail project becomes.

Operational Procedures

Beyond the institutional framework, the bail project's operational procedures are often the key variable affecting the project's success or failure.

Time Lag between Arrest, Interview and ROR

The time lag between arrest and when the bail project is able to interview and release the defendant is an extremely important operational variable. This time period not only affects the number of defendants a bail project is able to release

but also determines the quality of the clientele which the project may serve.
(See Chapter 6 for a detailed explanation of this problem.) The longer the wait
until the project reaches the defendant, the greater chance that defendants will
make financial arrangements to obtain their release, and reject the help of the
project. As Table 7-7 indicates, it is also important to realize that a time lag
does not only exist between arrest and interview but may also be found between
interview, recommendation to the judge following verification, and finally
release.

The inability of most projects to reach their clients within a reasonable
period of time is caused by a series of obstacles—some planned, some accidental.
One reason for this delay is the frequently poor location of the bail project.
In Atlanta the project is not allowed to interview the defendant until he has
been taken from the local police station to the county jail. This does not occur
until after the defendant's preliminary arraignment at the police station where
bail will be set. It is usually not until the next day after the commitment that
the defendant is transported from the temporary downtown lockup to the
county jail, a six mile distance. Once the defendant has been interviewed in the
jail and the information verified, the project's staff must drive the six miles
back into the city to receive the judge's approval. This adds another four hours
to an already two-day delay.

A second reason for this delay is the cumbersome procedural requirements
established by the supervising agency. The Los Angeles project is hampered by
such difficulties because their supervising agency, the Superior Court of Los
Angeles County, does not allow defendants to receive OR applications until
after their arraignment in municipal court, which takes place forty-eight hours
after their arrest. The defendants are then given the next day to complete the

Table 7-7
The Time Lag

City	Interview	Recommendation	Release	Release Rate
Indianapolis	3	3.5	4	14.4%
Washington	12	14	18	31.4%
Baltimore[a]	12	14	16	7.2%
San Francisco	20	40	42	21.5%
Chicago[a]	24	30	48	3.6%
Atlanta[a]	40	42	48	4.1%
Los Angeles	70	76	78	5.0%
St. Louis[a]	240[b]	242[b]	246[b]	4.6%
	48[c]	50[c]	72[c]	

NOTE: All figures in hours have been approximated by bail project officials

[a]Project does not operate on weekends

[b]Figures for St. Louis Circuit Court

[c]Figures for St. Louis Court of Criminal Causes

applications which are picked up the following day (it is now over three days since their arrest) by the OR staff and are evaluated and taken to the judge conducting the preliminary hearing. According to OR unit statistics for 1969, only one applicant in twelve was able to gain his pretrial release through an OR staff recommendation.[10]

Closely linked to the problem of delay caused by procedural requirements is the fact that projects are often forced to make concessions to the sponsoring agency in order to receive the necessary court backing to initiate their program. These concessions take the form of procedural handicaps such as found in St. Louis, where the bail project is prohibited by the city's circuit court from interviewing defendants until after they have been arraigned. This occurs approximately ten days after arrest. Bail projects, in their initial enthusiasm, carelessly compromise away to the courts and bondsmen these procedural limitations which undercut their attempts at judicial reform. Projects often attempt to justify these concessions by stating an optimistic belief that once they prove to the courts how effective their projects are operating, these restrictions will be removed. The history of bail reform, however, has not demonstrated this hoped-for, enlightened reappraisal by the supervising agency. The actual pattern has been just the reverse, with those projects bound by the most stringent procedural requirements exhibiting the slowest amount of growth and often regressing to even lower levels of effectiveness.

A final reason for this time lag is administrative delay. This delay is fostered by the inefficiency and carelessness found in any large bureaucracy. The administrative delays inherent in this system, however, may be even more aggravated when an agency such as a bail reform project incurs the wrath of other, more powerful agencies in the system. An example of the harm done by this antagonism was discovered in San Francisco. The bail project was able to interview defendants within a day but many defendants had to wait an additional twenty-four hours until the police supplied the project with the necessary information to verify the defendant's past record. Other administrative difficulties were reported by the San Francisco Committee on Crime which stated that "the police have recently imposed new limitations on interview times permitted to the project staff. Some staff members have remarked that they have had to wait lengthy periods in the morning before the police have brought the prisoners out for interviews."[11]

Although it is generally advantageous to decrease the time between arrest and when the project interviews the defendant, there may also be some draw-backs to reaching the defendant too quickly—for example, within the first six hours following his arrest. One problem which might arise in projects which are understaffed and forced to quickly interview large numbers of defendants is that only the highly qualified defendants will be released on the project's recommendation. Left behind are large numbers of adequately qualified defendants who were passed over because of the small size of the investigative staff and the time constraints. Also, by engaging in a race with the bondsmen for the best prospects for release, the project is risking the increased hostility of the already-embittered bondsmen. Bondsmen have friends in key political offices and if irritated sufficiently, they can do a very competent job of sabotaging the operation of the project. If the primary objective of the bail project is to help the indigent defendant, it is probably not being accomplished. By speedily interviewing and releasing defendants, the project is releasing many people who have the funds to use a bondsman but prefer to be released through the project to save the expense of a bondsman's fee. Meanwhile, the less qualified but financially impoverished defendant is forced to remain in jail. The project will conduct many interviews of defendants who change their mind and use a bondsman or pay the cash bond instead of waiting an additional three to four hours until the information is verified and the judge has been contacted to approve the recommendation. The interviews which are conducted shortly after arrest are viewed by defendants as simply a possible means of release or a way to pass away an hour while waiting for their family to arrive with the necessary funds. Thus the project which rushes into the interview stage will waste time on defendants who are not sincerely interested in using the project, while the indigent defendants may be deprived of even an opportunity to apply for ROR.

Criteria for Release: Objective v. Subjective Evaluation

In determining whether a defendant should be recommended for release all projects studied used the Vera Institute criteria for release. (An example of these criteria is found in Appendix E.) The Vera Institute based a defendant's release upon the following criteria: prior criminal record, family ties, employment record, residential stability, and a small allowance for the interviewer's discretion.

In using these criteria to evaluate each defendant's potential for release, the bail project may apply them in either a subjective or objective manner. Of the projects visited, six evaluated these criteria objectively, using a strict point system. A defendant earns a number of points by exhibiting job stability, residential stability, and heading a family. He may lose points because of his past criminal record and a faulty appearance record. If he reaches the required number of points, the project will recommend him to the proper authority for release on his own recognizance. The information is gathered through an interview and verified by phoning family, employers, and/or character references. The subjective system, used in Chicago and Los Angeles, is very similar to the objective approach. It asks the same types of questions relating to the defendant's background. The difference is that no final point totals are used and the interviewer's recommendation is based upon his interpretation of the defendant's likelihood of appearing for trial. He relies on the background information but is given broader scope in the final decision.

Proponents of the objective system argue that it eliminates the individual biases of the interviewer and permits him to quickly analyze and determine if the defendant should be recommended for release. Several bail project directors indicated that they preferred the objective system because it appeared that the point system rather than the investigators were actually releasing the defendants. Therefore, when a recommended defendant failed to show or committed an additional crime, the point scale could be blamed instead of the faulty judgment of the investigator. A further advantage to the objective system is that it seems to release more defendants, at least in the small sample of cities surveyed. The cities using the objective system released an average of 15.7 percent of the defendants, nearly four times as many as the cities using the subjective approach, 4.3 percent.

The subjective system of evaluation, however, is not without its advocates. The Los Angeles bail project offers a good example of an efficient subjective system. The applications for release, which contain the same type of Vera criteria, are picked up by the OR unit investigators upon completion by all interested defendants. They are then evaluated and stacked by the strength of this quick evaluation. The best risks are placed on top of these stacks. The investigators then interview the maximum number of defendants off the top of the stack who can be processed before the defendant's next court appearance. The interview notes and verified personal data from the application are then studied. Based on the defendant's attitude during the interview and strength of the background information, he may be recommended for release. As was noted previously, only one application in twelve was recommended and released. The investigative staff are all ex-police officers with an average of twenty years' service on the force before coming to the project. They appear to feel very competent in subjectively evaluating the defendant's attitude due to their many years of experience in dealing with similar individuals.[12]

The proponents of a subjective system argue that it is better able to capitalize on the experience and knowledge of the investigative staff. This is especially true in a project such as in Los Angeles. One may question the use of a subjective system where the investigative staff are eighteen to twenty-one-year-old students or VISTA volunteers whose only experience has been to sit in a classroom or hitchhike across the country. Another advantage of the subjective system is that it makes the investigator feel more responsible for releasing a defendant and may therefore compel him to be more careful in whom he choses to recommend. This argument may be countered by stating that this care in determining release easily turns to caution and then to extreme conservatism, with the result that very few defendants will be recommended. A final argument is that there is always going to be some leeway for subjective choice even in the objective system, so one might as well recognize its presence and try to work with it in a forthright manner.

The last argument offered by proponents of the subjective system raises the interesting question: What difference does it really make whether a bail project is operated objectively or subjectively? Ed DePaul, former director of the Philadelphia Bail Project, revealed in an interview that this controversy has resulted only in a great deal of confusion. He explained this by stating: "The subjective projects are operating with a mental measure or standard by which they evaluate defendants and in the supposedly objective system there is considerable discretion in the granting or denying of points."[13]

It seems impossible to completely eliminate subjective decisions even in supposedly impartial objective programs. Jim Droege, director of the Indianapolis Bail Project, which uses an objective point system, agreed on this point and presented several examples from his project where subjective decisions had to be made. Most information on the defendant's background such as length of residence and job stability do not fall neatly into one of the point slots. One is frequently dealing with periods of time which fall between categories and must therefore rely on his common sense and intuition to dispose of these constantly recurring subjective decisions. He also noted that there is great variation among the projects, and even the individual investigators, as to how hard or easy they will evaluate defendants.[14]

Bail project directors, in an attempt to justify their operations against charges that their criteria for release reflect only middle-class standards unobtainable by indigent defendants, can only reply that there must be some standard of evaluation, and the community ties concept was the best that could be developed. Also, when one considers the alternative as being the traditional system of pretrial release based on paying a financial bond, these criteria do not seem quite so harsh. Most bail projects are aware of the discriminatory effects of the community ties standard and have attempted to work around them as best they can by using a loose interpretation and flexible application of this standard to the point system. Despite the strength of this criticism and the desire of the bail project to eliminate this weakness, there are no innovative release criteria currently being developed to replace the original Vera standards.

Jurisdictional Restrictions: Excluded Offenses

Many bail projects have reacted to the necessity of protecting society by limiting their jurisdiction to only crimes against property or other less serious forms of criminal behavior. These projects believe that the more serious the crime charged, the greater likelihood that the defendant will either forfeit or commit additional crimes during his pretrial release. An example of such a list of excluded offenses is provided by the Atlanta project which is permitted by the Fulton County Superior Court to handle all felonies *except* murder, robbery, drugs, violent crimes, sex crimes, lottery, and any crime where a bond of over $5000 is set. Like most projects with similar lists of excluded offenses, they find themselves releasing primarily defendants accused of either burglary or larceny. The Atlanta project estimated that approximately 80 percent of the defendants they release fall into either of these categories.[15]

This myth linking severity of criminal charge and pretrial behavior continues despite documented evidence found in Table 7-8 that there is no relationship between the defendant's pretrial behavior and the crime of which he is accused.

The bail projects selected for study have been categorized as falling into one of the five following groups, based on the number of offenses which the project has excluded from their jurisdiction: (1) no excluded offenses; (2) most serious violent crimes and crimes involving capital punishment; (3) any crime against a person and where guns are involved; (4) categories two and three, plus additional offenses such as narcotics violations; and (5) only misdemeanors. Table 7-8 illustrates the relationships between these categories of jurisdiction, the release rate, forfeiture rate, and the degree of supervision over the projects by the sponsoring agency.

This table indicates that in the projects studied, those projects which had the narrowest jurisdiction (highest categories in Table 7-8 indicating the greatest number of excluded offenses), also seemed to be the projects under the greatest degree of supervision by their sponsoring agency. A possible explanation for this relationship is that in projects where the court is closely involved in supervising their operation, the courts are very apprehensive about the project releasing defendants accused of the more serious offenses. By their close supervision, the court systems are often linked with the project in the public's mind. The court system is aware of this public image and therefore does not wish to take any chances on releasing potentially dangerous defendants whose future misconduct would jeopardize the public's respect for the court's judgment and

Table 7-8
The Importance of Excluded Offenses

City	Category of Excluded Offenses	Forfeiture Rate	Release Rate	Level of Supervision of Projects
Washington	I	2.3%	31.4%	I
San Francisco	I	2.3%	21.5%	I
Los Angeles	II	7.4%	5.0%	II
Baltimore	III	0.7%	7.2%	III
Chicago	III	19.0%	3.6%	V
Atlanta	IV	8.3%	4.1%	IV
St. Louis	IV	3.1%	4.6%	IV
Indianapolis	V	2.9%	14.4%	II

[a]The operational definitions explaining the levels of supervision by the sponsoring agency are to be found at the end of this chapter's section, "The Model Program."

lose confidence in the bail project which the court sponsors. A final point is that the courts, by limiting the jurisdiction of the project, will have a smaller and therefore more manageable project under their control.

It is surprising, then, to examine the statistics in Table 7-8 which show that the projects excluding the most offenses are the least effective—that is, have the lowest release rates with the highest forfeiture rates. Of the three cities in categories I and II where almost no offenses are excluded, the average release rate of 19 percent was over four times that of the four cities in categories III and IV, which exclude the most offenses. The most telling figure is the forfeiture rate, since one of the major rationales for excluding the more serious offenses is a belief that these defendants have a greater proclivity for failing to appear in court. In the three cities with the least number of excluded offenses, the average forfeiture rate of 3.9 percent is exactly half that of the rate for the four cities with the most excluded offenses, 7.7 percent. Thus merely by shrinking the jurisdiction of a project the improvement of the project's predictive ability is not guaranteed and may even negatively affect its success.

The true significance of the findings in Table 7-8 are that they offer empirical proof that the crime of which a defendant is accused is not a valid predictor of his likelihood of forfeiting. A defendant, therefore, should not be categorically excluded from release by a bail project solely on the basis of the crime of which he is accused. If bail projects are forced to continue to exclude large numbers of serious offenses from their jurisdiction, they will limit themselves to an extremely small number of potential clients, nearly all of whom will be burglars, thieves, and other perpetrators of property crime. An even more serious effect of these exclusionary tactics is their handicapping of the project's operation and assurance of its failure as a viable bail reform alternative.[16]

Verification

Verification is the process by which a bail reform project attempts to validate the information which the defendant has given them during the interview concerning his community ties and prior record. It is an important process in the operation of a bail reform project since most judges refuse to release any defendant whose background information has not been verified. It is not important as an explanatory operational variable since all projects use roughly the same verification procedure—phone calls to character references and employers.

Having to conduct the verification process over the phone presents many difficulties to both the interviewer and the defendant. Most projects will refuse to recommend any defendant whose background information cannot be verified. Thus references who do not have phones or those at work during the day (when most projects make their calls) will not be able to verify the information and the defendant will remain in detention. This discriminates against those references who are financially unable to afford a phone or who work during the day or possibly hold two jobs and are even unavailable in the evening. These references are often prone to frequently change their residence because of inadequacy of funds required for residential stability which adds to the difficulty. The delay in attempting to reach references by phone forces the defendant to remain in jail for long periods of time until these references are contacted. This period of waiting may extend to days if the reference is especially difficult to reach. In most projects, if the staff is unable to reach the reference in two attempts, they will simply give up and deny to the defendant the project's recommendation for release.

Another serious problem in verification by phone is the difficulty of the investigator to elicit truthful and unprompted answers from the reference. Many staff investigators who were interviewed by the author admitted that the phone call to the reference is often a meaningless formality. It is usually a *pro forma* confirmation of an earlier judgment made by the investigator following his interview with the defendant. A frequently advocated reform would be to have the defendant sign a sworn statement that all the information he gave was the truth and any falsification would result in contempt of court. Investigators who have been on the job for over a year were especially skeptical of the necessity of the phone calls to references. They rely on their experience and intuitive insights, in addition to the police officer's arrest record and the defendant's prior record.

Additional problems in verification are caused by some projects requiring more than two references. The average number of references for the cities studied was two. With three or more persons to be contacted, it often takes the investigators over a day to reach all the references, while the defendant impatiently languishes in jail. Administrative delays in receiving copies of the defendant's prior record are also a trouble spot. As noted earlier, the San Francisco police may take a full day to send the defendant's record to the bail project.

Supervision of the Defendant

As bail projects attempt to insure that as many of their clients as possible will show up on their appointed court dates, they have developed various supervisory techniques to be utilized during the pretrial period. These techniques range from a formal note to the defendant informing him of his upcoming court date to complex procedures designed to remove the defendant from his old neighborhood and find him a job in another section of town. It is up to the project to notify the court when the defendant has violated any of these more elaborate conditions of release. The bail projects studied supervise their clients on varying levels, as the following list describes them in descending order of thoroughness.

I.   (a) Additional phone calls and a letter during the pretrial period.
      (b) Defendant required to phone in or drop into project on a regular basis.
      (c) Project actively searches for defendant if he fails to show.
      (d) Supervises a variety of special conditions.
      (e) Attempts various employment and rehabilitative services for the defendant.
II.   Includes (a) through (d) listed in category I.
III. Includes (a) through (c) listed in category I.
IV.   Defendant is required to phone or drop by office on a regular basis.
V.   Additional phone call or letter during the pretrial release period.
VI.   Repeat court notice at time of release.
VII. None.

Table 7-9 illustrates the relationship between the level of supervision of defendants during the pretrial release period and the percentage of defendants failing to appear. Other variables also included in this table for their possible relevance are the size of the staff and the length of time from arrest to trial.

The table clearly shows that as the project increases its supervision over the defendants, it is able to achieve a lower forfeiture rate. The two additional variables, size of staff and amount of court delay, were not found to be nearly as significant as the amount of supervision. The size of the investigative staff is weakly related to a project's supervisory success, but the Los Angeles project shows that mere size is not sufficient to guarantee a low forfeiture rate if conscientious supervision is not practiced.

Table 7-9
Supervision of Defendants during Pretrial Release

City	Level of Supervision of Defendants	Forfeiture Rate	Size of Staff	Time from Arrest to Trial (in mos.)[a]
Baltimore	I	0.7%	12	4–5 mos.
Washington	II	2.3%	26	5–6 mos.
San Francisco	III	2.3%	18	3 mos.
St. Louis	IV	3.1%	4	3–4 mos.
Los Angeles	V	7.2%	28	3 mos.
Atlanta	V	8.3%	1	2 mos.
Chicago	VII	19.0%	4	4–5 mos.

[a]These monthly averages are the products of numerous interviews with knowledgeable public officals involved in the administration of justice in each city.

How are these bail projects, operating without the various advantages claimed by the bondsmen, able to supervise clients so effectively so as to consistently maintain forfeiture rates below the bonding business? (For a statistical comparison, see Table 8-2 in Chapter 8.) One strategy used is to operate the bail project on a more decentralized basis, with the investigative staff working from regional offices around the city. Baltimore, the project with the lowest forfeiture rate in the study, operates out of the nine municipal police districts, placing an investigator who is familiar with the area in charge of each district. Los Angeles is just completing an eighteen-month trial project using regional offices for their investigative staff, and initial returns indicate their forfeitures have been drastically reduced.[17] By placing their investigators in the community, the Los Angeles project was able to recommend more defendants for release and was also able to supervise them more closely after their release. In both San Francisco and Baltimore the investigative staff goes out into the neighborhoods and conducts a thorough search for missing defendants. Since most forfeitures are technical or involuntary, a large percentage of the initial forfeitures are easily contacted and returned for their next court date. Most police and project directors agree that very few defendants intentionally attempt to flee town in order to avoid their next court appearance. The police in Baltimore and Los Angeles work closely with the bail project staff to retrieve these defendants. The police supply information to the project. When the defendant is located, the investigators are notified by the police and the project staff returns the defendant to court. This unusual cooperation found in these two cities may be partially explained by the fact that most of the project's staff are former law enforcement officers who still have friends on the force.

A unique problem is faced by the Washington, D.C. Bail Agency in their supervisory task because they have been given the job of enforcing conditions of release assigned by the District of Columbia District Court. Nearly every defendant released on his own recognizance has a set of conditions which the court may require of his pretrial behavior. The defendant may be told to stay away from a complaining witness, to return to school, to call the agency at specified times during the week or to appear in person at other times, to observe a curfew, or stay out of a certain section of the city. The difficulties inherent in this procedure were succinctly critiqued in the May 1970 *Report of the Judicial Council Committee to Study the Operation of the Bail Reform Act in the District of Columbia*, in the following statement: "It is a simple statement of fact that the Bail Agency is inadequately staffed to supervise the defendants on these conditions, and even when it does supervise conditions, the U.S. Attorney's Office will not prosecute these offenders."[18]

Table 7-10 is a procedural summary chart allowing the reader to compare in detail the various procedural variables discussed so far.

Table 7-10
Summary Chart of Procedural Variables

City	% Δ's Released	% Δ's Forfeited	Average Time From Arrest to ROR	Size of Staff	Verification Process	Supervision	Level of Supervision[a]	Excluded Offenses[b]
Washington	31.4	2.3	18 hrs.	26	Phone and sometimes followup	Court of Appeals	II	I
San Francisco	24.7	2.3	18 hrs.	18	Phone and field-word and references	San Francisco Bar	III	I
Baltimore	7.2	0.7	24 hrs.	12	Strictly phone calls	Supreme Bench	I	IV
Los Angeles	5.0	7.4	24 hrs.	28	Phone calls and subjective reasoning	Superior Court	V	II
Atlanta	4.1	8.3	36 hrs.	1	Strictly phone calls	County Circuit Court	V	V
St. Louis	4.6	3.1	60 hrs.	4	Phone calls and intuitive reasonsing	Circuit Court	IV	V
Chicago	2.9	19.1	30 hrs.	4	Phone calls and intuitive reasoning	Circuit Court	VII	IV
Indianapolis	4.0	2.9	4.5 hrs.	8	Strictly phone calls	Criminal Court	–	VI

[a]See Page 134 for operational definition.
[b]See Page 131 for explanation of categories.

The Outputs: Current Capabilities of
Bail Projects

How many defendants are gaining their pretrial freedom by being released
on their own recognizance through a recommendation of the bail project? What
percentage of those defendants interviewed for possible ROR by a bail project
are eventually recommended? Table 7-11 presents a statistical summary of the
administration of pretrial release in seventy-two cities which will answer these
and additional related questions.

Percentage of Defendants Interviewed for
Possible ROR

The majority of cities surveyed either do not have bail projects or do not
utilize release on recognizance on a regular basis. Forty cities (55 percent)
reported that fewer than 10 percent of all defendants are interviewed for
possible ROR. Of the remaining thirty-two cities, every one, with two exceptions, operates a bail project which is actively attempting to interview sizeable
numbers of defendants.[19] Ten cities interview more than 90 percent of all
defendants. The next largest group is composed of more modest programs
which interview 30 to 39 percent of all defendants. The remaining cities are
evenly distributed between the remaining three intervals, with two to three
cities within each category. Thirty-six percent of the respondents were unwilling
to comment whether these figures represent any type of trend during the past
five years.[20] Of the respondents, however, who were willing to comment on
the past five years, 63 percent replied that the percentage of defendants
being interviewed for possible ROR was increasing.

Percentage of Defendants Recommended
for ROR

Being interviewed does not guarantee that a defendant will be recommended
for ROR. The recommendation is usually made by the bail project or the
designated court official who is responsible to the judge for this information.
Identical with the previous question, forty cities (55 percent), either because
they do not have bail projects or do not use release on recognizance as a regular
form of pretrial release, recommended ROR in less than 10 percent of the
possible cases. Of the cities which did attempt to interview defendants, most
were highly selective. Eight cities recommended only 10 to 19 percent, and
seven cities recommended 20 to 29 percent. The remaining 10 percent intervals
from 30 to 90 percent each contained three to four cities. Only one city believed
they had experienced a decrease in the percentage of recommendations for ROR

Table 7-11
Statistical Summary of Administration of Bail in Seventy-Two City Survey

Number and Percentage of Cities in Each Category

% of Total Defendants	Interviewed for ROR	Recc'd for ROR	ROR'd	Used Bondsmen	Detained	Rearrested		Forfeited	
						1. ROR'd	2. Money Bail	1. ROR'd	2. Money Bail
0-9%	55% (40)	55% (40)	34% (25)	6% (4)	36% (26)	79% (57)	66% (48)	87% (63)	80% (58)
10-19%	3% (2)	11% (8)	18% (13)	4% (3)	39% (28)	13% (9)	18% (13)	11% (8)	13% (9)
20-29%	1% (1)	10% (7)	13% (9)	7% (5)	14% (10)	6% (4)	6% (4)	1% (1)	4% (3)
30-39%	10% (7)	6% (4)	10% (7)	14% (10)	7% (5)	3% (2)	7% (5)	—	3% (2)
40-49%	3% (2)	6% (4)	11% (8)	26% (19)	1% (1)	—	3% (2)	—	—
50-59%	4% (3)	4% (3)	9% (6)	17% (12)	3% (2)	—	—	—	—
60-69%	4% (3)	3% (2)	1% (1)	7% (5)	—	—	—	—	—
70-79%	3% (2)	1% (1)	1% (1)	6% (4)	—	—	—	—	—
80-89%	3% (2)	3% (2)	1% (1)	10% (7)	—	—	—	—	—
90-99%	14% (14)	1% (1)	—	4% (3)	—	—	—	—	—
National Average for 72 Cities	28%	19%	21%	40%	16%	6.4%	8.2%	2.8%	3%

during the previous five years while 64 percent of those responding found the
percentage of favorable recommendations increasing.

Percentage of Defendants Released on Recognizance

The average number of defendants in this survey who gained release on
their own recognizance was slightly over 20 percent. Defendants were able to
achieve ROR through two means. First, the large majority of defendants ROR'd
were interviewed and recommended for release by a bail reform project. The
judge would then go along with the project's recommendation and release the
defendant on his own recognizance. The second method of ROR was when a
judge did not rely on a recommendation from a bail project but made an
independent judgment of the defendant's qualifications for ROR. Liberal judges
in cities without bail reform projects may even ROR more defendants than a
judge operating with a conservative bail reform project.

The 20 percent ROR rate found in Table 7-11 includes both methods of
release. This explains the confusing statistic in that table which shows a greater
percentage of defendants being ROR'd than those who were recommended by
bail projects. Judges, as we have noted, may act on their own initiative and
ROR any defendant, with or without the recommendation of the local bail
reform project. It was encouraging to see that 77 percent of the cities believed
that during the past five years there had been a steady increase in the percentage
of defendants ROR'd. This is only a relative improvement, and advocates
of bail reform are highly critical of the failure of the present judicial system
to ROR only 20 percent of the total number of defendants awaiting trial.[21]

What types of cities seem to be releasing the greatest percentages of defendants on their own recognizance? Considering the demographic factors affecting
the administration of bail, Table 7-12 summarizes the results of this analysis.
The survey found the following four demographic variables to be exerting some
influence upon the operation of a pretrial release system: city size, nonwhite
population, poverty level, and the crime rate.

Although the use of a simple correlation matrix can indicate only the
strength of the relationship between two variables and can offer no guidelines
as to causal relationships between these variables, it is an acceptable statistical
test for measuring the relationship between the demographic characteristics
and the bail system's statistical outputs. Table 7-12 clearly shows that cities
with small black populations, low poverty levels, and experiencing lower than
the national average crime rate, are the most likely to release a larger percentage
of defendants on their own recognizance.

Several of these relationships are difficult to explain. The high crime rate
and low ROR percentage appears to be the most understandable relationship.
Cities with high crime rates are usually more conscious of protecting society

Table 7-12
Statistical Output and Demographic Variables

	Population		Nonwhite Population		Poverty Level		Crime Rate	
	Corr.[a]	s.l.[b]	Corr.	s.l.	Corr.	s.l.	Corr.	s.l.
Defendants ROR'd	−0.2553	0.015	−0.2643	0.012	−3564	0.002	−0.2423	0.043
Defendants Forfeited	−0.0584[c]	0.313	0.1831[c]	0.062	0.0081[c]	0.473	−0.2099	0.038
Defendants Rearrested	0.2540	0.018	0.2840	0.008	0.2295	0.026	0.2395	0.021

[a]Correlations

[b]Significance Levels

[c]Absence of a significant correlation

against the potential harm of accused defendants. These cities, therefore, will be most hesitant to release defendants on their own recognizance, since ROR is characterized as favoring the criminal's freedom over the protection of the community. Analyzing the strong negative correlation between the size of the city's black population and the percentage of defendants ROR'd, it should be remembered that RORs are often based on a number of middle-class standards relating to the stability of the defendant's lifestyle and his community ties. Since many blacks do not subscribe to or emulate these middle-class standards, it is difficult for many lower-class blacks to satisfy these ROR criteria.

8

Bail Reform: Conclusions and Prognostications

In the two previous chapters, bail reform has been discussed in terms of its objectives and the institutional and operational variables which have influenced the development of this movement. Chapter 8 focuses upon the realities of the bail reform movement, beginning with an examination of its realistic capabilities for helping indigent defendants obtain their pretrial freedom as compared with the traditional cities.

Bail Reform Cities v. Traditional Cities: What Difference Do They Really Make?

What difference do bail reform projects actually make in the administration of bail? Are cities operating these projects clearly distinguishable from those less progressive traditional cities which rely primarily on the judgment of the magistrate or judge for the granting of ROR's?[1] Since these reform projects are presently the principal alternative to the money bail system, it is crucial to determine if these projects really do make any difference to the average defendant.

Based on the analysis of the traditional and reform bail programs discussed in previous chapters, the following hypotheses are offered for validation: (1) Bail reform projects are more effective than traditional systems. (2) The bail reform cities are able to maintain forfeiture and rearrest rates for their released defendants that are equal to, and frequently lower than, those found in the traditional cities who rely mainly upon bondsmen for the selection and supervision of released defendants. (3) The volume of business for bondsmen in bail reform cities has markedly decreased since these projects came into existence. Table 8-1 offers a statistical comparison between reform and traditional cities, the results of which appear to validate all of these hypotheses.

Table 8-1 clearly indicates that reform cities are much more likely to operate effective bail systems than their traditional counterparts. Nearly 60 percent of the bail reform cities are operating programs which possess an effectiveness rating above the national average while only 38 percent of the traditional cities are functioning above this same level. This effectiveness rating has been operationally defined by the author to mean the ability of a

141

Table 8-1

Reform v. Traditional: A Comparison of Statistical Output

Dependent Variables (Statistical Output)	Traditional Cities	Reform Cities
1. Effectiveness Rating		
Below National Average	25 (62%)	13 (42%)
Above National Average	14 (38)	18 (58)
2. Percent ROR'd		
Below National Average	24 (67)	15 (47)
Above National Average	12 (33)	17 (53)
3. Forfeiture Rate		
Below National Average	17 (50)	16 (53)
Above National Average	17 (50)	14 (47)
4. Rearrest Rate		
Below National Average	16 (45)	15 (52)
Above National Average	19 (55)	14 (48)
5. Percent Using Bondsmen		
Below National Average	14 (46)	23 (72)
Above National Average	16 (54)	9 (28)
6. Percent Detained		
Below National Average	14 (40)	17 (55)
Above National Average	21 (60)	14 (45)

project to release as many defendants as possible on their own recognizance, while at the same time maintaining a forfeiture rate below the national average.[2] The effectiveness rating is a critical variable since it is a measure of not only the ability of a bail system to release large numbers of defendants, but also the system's ability to control the forfeiture and additional crime rate at the same time.

Although advocates of bail reform simply assume that their program will guarantee increased percentages of ROR'd defendants, critics of these reform projects believe that the reform cities have not appreciably increased the percentage of RORs. The critics argue that ROR is still the prerogative of the judge since he controls the number of RORs, regardless of the presence of a bail reform project. It is true that judges in traditional cities have the authority to ROR, and in many cases do actually use this procedure without the prompting of a reform project, but Table 8-1 shows that one's chances of being ROR'd are much greater in a city operating a reform project. The table reveals that only a third of the traditional cities have an above average ROR percentage while well over half of the reform cities are above this level. Table 7-11 disclosed that the national average of ROR's was 21 percent. However, when one controls for whether the city is reform or traditional, a visible contrast emerges. Reform cities ROR'd 24 percent of all defendants while the traditional cities ROR'd only 16 percent. These figures take on added significance when it is realized that the reform cities are ROR'ing defendants accused of more serious crimes while the overwhelming number of defendants ROR'd in traditional cities are misdemeanants.

It has also been hypothesized that bail reform cities are able to supervise and control the pretrial conduct of defendants just as well as the traditional cities who rely on the expertise and diligence of bondsmen. The bondsmen for years have claimed that they operate an elaborate and effective system of pretrial supervision which is far superior to that administered by the idealistic and inexperienced staff of a bail reform project. Through their many years of experience and their comprehensive network of assistants and fellow bondsmen, they believe they are capable of maintaining a successful supervisory program resulting in an exceedingly low forfeiture rate. Are the claims of these bondsmen valid? Table 8-2 contrasts the forfeiture rates between bondsmen and bail projects in four cities and arrives at least a partial answer to this question.

For these four cities where adequate statistics on the bondsmen were available, two important findings are evident. First, the forfeiture rate for the bondsmen in the four cities casts grave doubts on the supposed superiority of their supervisory techniques. Second, and most important, it illustrates that in all but one city (and even here it was only a 1 percent difference) the bail projects are able to operate with a much lower forfeiture rate.

Based on earlier findings, it is not surprising to find the results of the seventy-two-city survey presented in Table 8-1 indicating that the traditional cities are not quite as effective as reform cities in maintaining below average rearrest rates. This table showed more than half of the reform cities have rearrest rates below the national average while only 45 percent of the traditional cities were able to make this claim.

The third hypothesis also appears to be validated by the statistics reported in Table 8-1. Thus, as most would suspect, bail reform cities have been cutting into the volume of the bondsmen's business. Table 8-1 reveals that in 72 percent of the bail reform cities the percentage of defendants using bondsmen is below the national average of 40 percent. Conversely, in 54 percent of the traditional

Table 8-2
Comparison of Forfeiture Rates: Bondsmen v. Bail Projects

City	Forfeiture Rate Bail Projects	Forfeiture Rate Bondsmen
San Francisco	2.3%	5.4%
Atlanta	8.3%	7.0%
St. Louis	3.1%	4.5%
Indianapolis[a]	2.9%	22.0%
Average	4.1%	9.2%

[a]Figures are only for misdemeanors

cities, the defendants are using bondsmen at a rate above the national average. In traditional cities, 46 percent of the defendants use bondsmen, as compared with 36 percent in the reform cities.

This visible drop in business suffered by bondsmen in bail reform cities offers a reasonable explanation for the antagonism between the bail-bonding industry and the bail reform movement. In basic economic terms the bail reform projects offer a viable threat to the livelihood of the bondsmen. By presenting the defendant a chance to obtain his pretrial release without paying the bondsmen 10 percent of the required bond, the reform project is taking away many potential clients from the bondsmen. An additional irritation is that these reform projects, by releasing only defendants who satisfy their middle-class community ties standard, are robbing the bondsmen of the most desirable clients. Thus, if a bondsman wishes to remain in business, he is forced to begin taking clients who are less desirable and who threaten his financial security by being potentially less responsible.

Since it appears that a defendant's chances for ROR do actually increase in a bail reform city, are there certain demographic characteristics which may define these cities? Table 8-3 considers the type of city most likely to be operating a reform project. Despite the absence of the necessary statistical significance, Table 8-3 does point out some interesting trends and relationships between bail projects and the demographic characteristics of their cities. Most bail projects for example are found in our nation's larger cities (populations

Table 8-3
Demographic Characteristics

	Traditional Cities	*Reform Cities*
Population		
Small	34 (87%)	17 (54%)
Large	5 (13%)	14 (46%)
Total	39 (100%)	31 (100%)
Region		
East	24 (82%)	13 (33%)
West	15 (38%)	18 (67%)
Total	39 (100%)	31 (100%)
Nonwhite		
Low	23 (59%)	18 (61%)
High	16 (41%)	15 (39%)
Total	39 (100%)	33 (100%)
Crime Rate		
Low	15 (53%)	9 (43%)
High	13 (47%)	12 (57%)
Total	28 (100%)	21 (100%)

exceeding 200,000). Only one-third of the smaller cities surveyed administered bail reform programs, as opposed to 74 percent of the larger cities. This is a necessary development since the criminal justice systems in larger urban areas are bothered by more severe problems than the less populous localities.

The regional location also seems to have some influence on the frequency of bail reform. Western states, imagined to be imbued with a progressive spirit, freed from oppressive traditions, are more willing to sponsor bail reform projects. Only one-third of the eastern cities had reform projects, while nearly 60 percent of the western cities are currently sponsoring reform programs.

It is often believed that cities with large black populations would be more hesitant to release increasing numbers of defendants on their own recognizance than cities which were predominantly white. The survey found that the size of a city's nonwhite population had no effect on whether a bail project was in operation.

The final demographic variable to be considered is each city's crime rate. Table 8-3 disclosed that traditional cities are slightly more prone to have a crime rate below the national average than the bail reform cities. The difference is not significant enough to state that traditional cities are justified in not having a bail reform project due to the absence of a serious crime rate providing an overload of clientele for the courts. The crime rate is a variable tied closely to other explanatory variables (the size of the city and its median income) and cannot be thought to be exerting an isolated influence upon the necessity for bail reform.

The Model Program

Based on the premise that the optimal goals of a bail reform project are to obtain the release of as many defendants as possible while maintaining a low forfeiture rate, what may be considered a model program for achieving these ends?

Turning first to the institutional framework, the bail project should be staffed primarily by students and volunteers working on a full-time basis during the day. Having a staff of full-time students who work part time for the project has not proved satisfactory. After a period of initial enthusiasm, the interest of the students begins to fade as their school work starts to take precedence over the bail project. Using a full-time staff of court investigators selected under civil service requirements was also found to be inadequate. Because of their investigative experience, which the civil service exams usually seem to favor, former law enforcement officials and probation officers always seem to be in an advantageous position and are overrepresented by such a system of recruitment. The conservatism of these former law enforcement officers and their ideological link with the prosecutorial side of the administration of justice, causes them to be unlikely proponents of viable bail reform.

The size of the staff should be sufficient to both complete the investigations prior to release as well as adequately supervise the defendants during their release.

The staff should be supervised by an individual who is not directly under the thumb of the sponsoring agency. The project director should be a professional, trained in the problems commonly confronting the project's clients. It is impossible to identify what types of professionals are best qualified to become project directors. Kenneth Babb, sociologist and head of the San Francisco project, represents an ideal type of bail project director.

The sponsoring agency, which is usually the court system ultimately responsible for the bail project's direction, should grant nearly complete autonomy to the project in its day-to-day operations. It should, however, reserve to itself the responsibility for providing reliable and sufficient financial aid so as to insure the economic security of the project. It has been shown in numerous cities that the more a sponsoring agency meddles in the operations of a project, the less effective the program becomes. Both the Washington and San Francisco projects appear to operate with the necessary degree of freedom. San Francisco, however, has sacrificed its project's autonomy for financial insecurity. Its experience points to the importance of having regular public funding behind the project.

A second category of variables affecting the bail project's performance is its operational procedures. One of the key variables in helping the defendant is the speed with which the project can interview and release the defendant, following his being taken into custody. The only advice to be offered on this point is simply the sooner the better. The speed in releasing the defendant should not, however, be accomplished by sacrificing reliable verification of the defendant's community ties and prior record. The Indianapolis reform project, which is able to release defendants within four hours after arrest, is still able to accurately verify the background information as their very low forfeiture rate of 2.8 percent indicates.

A continuing debate surrounds the fairness of the community ties standard which is used by nearly all projects. These criteria are criticized as discriminating against minorities, indigents, youth, and transients. Though it is obvious that these groups are harmed by application of these standards, there must be some mechanism by which to distinguish between potential releasees. The Vera scale seems the best alternative which is currently in use. One approach to easing the amount of discrimination against these minority groups is to de-emphasize the importance of the defendant's residential, economic, and familial stability required by most projects. It is unreasonable to require the jail population to be even more stable in their lifestyle than the average middle-class citizen residing outside of the prison walls. The use of third party release programs offers a way by which defendants lacking the necessary stable background can be released in the care of some responsible organization or group of individuals.

One of the greatest obstacles to operating an effective bail project is the narrowing of its jurisdiction by imposing a wide range of excluded offenses. It has repeatedly been shown in this study that there is no positive correlation between the seriousness of the crime of which the defendant is accused and his proclivity toward forfeiting bond. It is recommended that no crimes be excluded from a bail project's jurisdiction, regardless of their severity. As long as the defendant's background and community ties are carefully investigated and he is adequately supervised during his pretrial release period, the seriousness of his crime is an irrelevant consideration.

The verification process, whereby the defendant's interview sheet containing background information is checked for veracity, is conducted in almost all projects by a phone call. The numerous disadvantages of total reliance on a phone call verification system have already been discussed. Bail projects currently use this procedure because it is all they can afford in order to satisfy the judge's demand that some verification be made before they will ROR a defendant. It would be much easier to require the defendant to sign the interview sheet, any falsification of which would be treated as contempt of court. Verification can also take place on a spot-check basis and include personal visits to references and employers.

The most important procedural variable related to maintaining a high effectiveness rating and a low forfeiture rate is the amount of supervision of the defendant during his pretrial release. The project must be sure to clearly notify the defendant of all court appearances as well as having the defendant maintain weekly contact, either through phoning in or appearing in person at the project office. The supervisory techniques utilized by the Baltimore project are a model for all other cities and have resulted in Baltimore's extremely low forfeiture rate of 0.7 percent. In order to provide superior supervision over released defendants and also to serve as more than custodial officers, it is urged that whenever possible the bail project should work with other social service agencies to aid the defendant during the pretrial period. This might take the form of job counseling and placement, or guidance into vocational training programs. It is understood that most bail projects have their hands full merely trying to keep track of the defendants during the pretrial period, let alone serving as a personal job counselor. Nevertheless, pretrial diversion programs such as Project Crossroads in Washington, D.C. offer realistic opportunities for the rehabilitation of defendants.

Social and Political Influences upon Bail Reform

By devoting an entire chapter to the institutional and procedural variables influencing the operation of a bail reform project, one should not imagine that the success or failure of these programs is due entirely to these "internal" variables. Bail projects are also greatly influenced by a number of "external" variables.[3]

Several of these outside pressure groups have previously been discussed. The judiciary, which is often the sponsoring agency for most bail reform projects, can exert a great deal of influence over their operation. This usually includes control over the funding, staffing, and basic policies of the city's reform project. We have already noted the power of Judge Boyle in Chicago and Judge Alverson in Atlanta, as they closely supervise the operation of their respective bail projects. It has also been noted that the police have been able to influence the operation of bail projects. This may be done indirectly by their ability to decide what charge is initially placed against the defendant or directly by controlling the distribution of certain records needed by bail reform projects to complete their background investigation. Even more than the police, the prosecuting attorney decides the offense with which the defendant is to be charged, often altering the police officer's initial decision. The Prosecuting Attorney's Office also works closely with the judiciary who frequently supervise the bail reform project and from this influential position, vis-à-vis the bench, are able to exert pressure on these projects.

In addition to these three groups (judiciary, police, and prosecutors), there are also several external groups which exert influence on bail reform projects. The first of these political and social groups to be examined is the media.

The Press

Like most of the other social and political factors examined, the press can either inhibit or facilitate the bail project's effectiveness. The choice is dependent upon the editorial policy of the paper which is usually a reflection of the attitudes and beliefs of both the publisher and his subscribers. The press is able to mold the image of the bail project for the public. If it wishes to discredit the project, the newspaper will stress the large number of defendants released who forfeit or commit additional crimes while awaiting trial. If the paper desires to create a positive image, it will stress the humanitarian accomplishments of the project, while also pointing to the great monetary savings to the city by having its jail population decreased. Where projects are financed by the city, it is essential for the public to be satisfied with the operation of the project. The press is therefore in a pivotal position to affect the financial security, and, ultimately, the very existence of the project.

In the majority of cities studied, the newspapers played a neutral role and usually gave very little press coverage, in either a positive or a negative direction, to the bail project's operation. The St. Louis and Baltimore papers, however, illustrate the power of the press to affect the bail project's capabilities. In

St. Louis the newspapers are very critical of the bail project. Any major crime that is committed by a defendant awaiting trial is front page news.

The Baltimore papers illustrate the positive support the press can give to a bail project in creating a strong public image. The director of the Baltimore project, Richard Motsay, is a former assistant state's attorney, but he handles press and public relations with the aplomb of a "Madison Avenue executive." The project makes a conscious effort to present a good image to the city, and as a result of the success of this effort, it is probably the most financially secure program in the country. It is enlightening to read the bail project's annual report which devotes half of its pages to recapping all of the public relations work which Director Motsay accomplished in the last year. Motsay, in an interview with the author, showed him a clipping file from the two major local newspapers which contained over fifty articles applauding the work of the project.[4]

Community Organizations

The presence in a city of a group of active and involved community organizations can be an important force in bail reform. These organizations can either perform a watchdog function over a poorly operating project or it can attempt to provide an improved alternative bail reform project to either replace or supplement the current project.[5]

Two examples of civic action groups which are involved in improving existing bail reform projects are found in Chicago and Los Angeles. In Chicago a group calling themselves the Alliance to End Repression has organized the Cook County Special Bail Bond Project. The Special Bail Bond Project has unsuccessfully attempted to try to have Chief Judge John Boyle enlarge the operation of the current bail project. Because of continued opposition to their interfering with the Judge's reform project, the Special Bail Bond Project is currently operating only a supplementary program to aid the court so as to make possible lower bonds and more recognizance releases. The project is entitled "The Holiday Court Verification Program" and lists two major purposes: (1) to provide verified information about the defendant's community ties, and (2) to provide legal representation at the bail hearing. The program is staffed with lawyers and certified law students.[6]

In Los Angeles the most active community-based organization interested in bail reform is the previously mentioned Community Justice Center. This organization is funded by HEW and operates a paralled CR unit in Watts which functions outside of the official criminal justice system. It serves as a gadfly and watchdog over the superior court's OR unit. The CJC staff conducts follow ups on all unreturned applications for the OR unit and also acts as OR investigators in three inner city municipal courts.[7]

The General Public

The influence of the general public is difficult to measure because of its amorphous nature. One of its most obvious characteristics present in all cities studied, however, was the pervasive absence of citizen interest and concern over the issue of bail reform. The few community organizations who are active in bail reform such as those recently mentioned in Los Angeles and Chicago are isolated exceptions to this broad national pattern of disinterest. Detroit, for example, is the largest city in the country never to have had a viable bail reform project by 1970. Even after experiencing one of the worst riots in the nation's history, the citizens of that city failed to exert any noticeable pressure on the judiciary to become more responsive to the needs of the city's poor. All impetus for reforming the criminal justice system has been deferred to the city officials. Although some badly needed reforms have occurred, the city's judicial establishment is all too slow in responding to the many other inequities currently existing, such as unnecessary pretrial detention and inadequate legal aid for the indigent.

The traditional prescription for solving political and social problems in a democracy is to have the populace turn to the polls and let their wishes be known. There are two basic weaknesses for adopting this tactic as a means of rectifying the injustices of the bail system and strengthening the bail reform movement. The first is that the mood of the majority of the nation's voters is anything but sympathetic to the goals of bail reform. As indicated by polls appearing in the March 8, 1971, issue of *Newsweek* (which echoes the attitude survey results of the President's Commission on Law Enforcement in 1968), the majority of Americans desire an even stronger law and order position by the government. They would prefer greater, not less, pretrial detention of defendants awaiting trial.[8]

The second weakness is that those public officials who control the processes which bail reform attempts to change are too well insulated from outside pressures. The police officer and the magistrate wield the greatest day-to-day influence over the administration of bail. These groups operate at such a low level of public scrutiny that they can be relatively confident in carrying on their "business as usual" without fear of arousing public pressures to alter their procedures.

Politicians and City Officials

For many of the reasons already discussed, most politicians have chosen to neglect or, even worse, to denigrate the bail reform movement. It appears that the influence of politicians on bail reform, when it finally does surface, is usually in a negative direction. Preventive detention is an example of the continuing type of interest the public, and, therefore, the politicians, have in the subject of pretrial release. Even this highly volatile issue is a genuine political topic in only a few cities. Because of the national preoccupation with law and order, most politicians have taken a hard-nosed stand against such reform measures as bail reform. It is fashionable to use the term "bleeding heart liberal" in reference to those few political figures who sense the injustices in the traditional methods of pretrial release and support expanded use of bail reform projects.

Indirect Effects of the Bail Reform Movement

One of the most important indirect effects of operating a bail reform project is its indication to the community that the city's court system does care about its unfortunate clientele. If the courts are to maintain their legitimacy in the critical eyes of the communities they serve, they must use such mechanisms as bail projects to convince citizens of their honorable and humane intentions. Almost on a par with the city's welfare department, the judicial process is on display to the public. It must, therefore, be capable of indicating its sincere dedication to their client's best interests and sensitivities. All one has to do is visit a criminal courthouse in any major city and he will not only see hundreds of different cases processed each day, but the halls and courtrooms will be jammed with friends and relatives of the defendants. All eyes are focused on the court system, witnessing the quality of justice dispensed to the defendants. By having an agency like a bail reform project, which serves to at least temporarily extricate the defendant from the humiliation and discomfort of pretrial detention, it offers some hope to the community that there is at least one public agency from which they can receive fair treatment.

An additional indirect benefit from bail projects is that they frequently serve as a catalyst for other reforms. These projects are usually begun on a cautious trial basis, and as they prove themselves workable they open the way for more imaginative and radical alternatives to the traditional bail system. For example, such reforms as pretrial probation and Bonabond, which are currently being undertaken in Washington, D.C., owe their creation to the success and respect earned by the city's bail reform project.

A final advantage derived from these projects is related to relieving some of the workload from the overburdened judges. By questioning the defendant as to his personal background and community ties prior to his appearance before the judge in his preliminary arraignment, the project can provide the judge with vital information, thus allowing the judge to avoid spending time questioning the defendant and receiving unverified information.

There have also been several negative side effects resulting from the operation of bail reform projects. There is a tendency in certain cities to hold their bail project up as a symbol of the court's reform spirit. They may then use this project as a rationalization for not attempting any additional reforms. This type of thinking accounts for the absence of judicial reform in those cities which are operating the least effective bail projects.

If the bail project is not successful during its initial period of operation, it will usually not only drastically shorten its own life expectancy, but will also serve as an excuse for not attempting new judicial reforms or resurrecting earlier ones. In Detroit, the Neighborhood Legal Services sponsored a quasi bail reform project. It was a two-person operation whose ultimate failure was insured from its inception. Such failures discourage future attempts at establishing effective projects and discredit the entire bail reform movement. The lesson to be learned from this is that if a city is tempted to initiate a bail reform project it had better be a good one, because if it is not, it may do more harm than good.

A final negative indirect effect is that bail projects may exacerbate the already strained relations between the court system and the police. By releasing large numbers of defendants quickly and with relatively little inconvenience, the bail project seems to purposely heighten the tension between these two groups. Often the police realize what the bail projects are doing and vent their hostility directly toward them in a series of harrassments described in Chapter 7.

Historical Perspectives for a Realistic
Prognosis: The Future of Bail Reform

The bail reform movement is of relatively short duration, beginning with the Vera project in Manhattan in 1961 and receiving a strong boost with the passage of the Federal Bail Reform Act in 1966. During the ten-year period from 1961 to 1971, there have been over 100 bail reform projects in operation across the country. Except for the initial growth of projects following the Vera project in 1961 and a second period of rapid expansion following the 1966 federal legislation, there has been no continuing trend toward growth and expansion in recent years. Bail reform projects have been initiated, then folded, and then begun again, all within the period of a few years. The effectiveness of these projects has also continually fluctuated, with little appearance of improvement. As new directors and sponsoring agencies replaced earlier leadership officials, and as new procedures and limitations were either added or dropped, the effectiveness of the project wavered and reflected this instability. Examples of this erratic behavior by bail projects are found nationwide. Projects in Philadelphia and Detroit were both forced to close down approximately five years ago after a few years in operation and then within the past two years, they have both been able to receive federal monies which have allowed them to start on a second round of bail reform.

How does one explain this instability? Why has the bail reform movement been unable to sustain a continued development and improvement in the operation of these projects? One explanation is that the bail reform movement was never able to organize or have available a sufficiently large or efficacious group of citizens urging support of their program. Like penal reform, the constituent group most directly effected by bail reform are those individuals who come in contact with the law. Not only does this group lack numerical strength, but they are also poor, uneducated, and most detrimental of all, undesirable in the eyes of the majority of citizens. Aside from their friends and family and a scattering of sympathetic law professors, judges, and social service groups, defendants awaiting trial have no one interested in their welfare. In addition to this absence of positive support to be mounted in their behalf, there are a group of social and political pressures directed against them to ensure they will be detained in jail and thereby contribute to the maintenance of a safe and secure community.

A second explanation is related to the financial problems of the last decade and their effect on bail reform. It has been the typical mode of operation for beginning bail projects to start as pilot projects. These projects were designed to be autonomous from the court system as much as possible. They were usually staffed by law students, VISTA volunteers, or some variety of volunteer help. The funding was not to be from the city in order to preserve the independence of the project, but rather from private or federal sources. During the project's trial years it was to prove itself to the city, who eventually was to pick up the funding. Thus most projects had to rely initially on short-term grants of one or two years from organizations like the Ford Foundation, local bar associations, and the Office of Economic Opportunity. As these initial trial periods came to a close, the projects waited to be absorbed into the city's annual budget. The financial crises of municipal governments prohibited all but a few of the more solvent cities from continuing the bail reform experiment. The excellent project in Philadelphia under Ed DePaul, as well as the token effort in Oakland were both discontinued because of these financial pressures. The San Francisco project, currently one of the most effective in the nation, is facing an impending financial crisis, and possible dissolution. Unless the city fathers change their mind or the federal government takes a renewed interest in funding the project, it may collapse in the near future.

Many projects did not collapse, however, and once given a chance to prove to their communities that they are actually capable of saving the city many thousands of dollars, the projects slowly began being incorporated into the city's budget. It soon became obvious that with the ever increasing number of defendants brought before the city's criminal courts, either the project was going to be adopted by the city's budget or a new jail was going to have to be built (or at least an annex added on to the present facility). Also, bail projects followed the lead of Baltimore's Project Director Richard Motsay, who recognized the importance of public relations in selling the project to the city. This can be accomplished by appearance on the mass media as well as cultivating a friendly press to print sympathetic stories concerning the project's good deeds.

When the cities began to fund these bail projects, they also demanded the predominant role in determining how these projects were to be operated. As bail projects became institutionalized, they became less viable means for reform. Staffed with court staff investigators who were frequently former policemen or probation officers, the projects became very cautious and were releasing fewer defendants. This retrenchment was accelerated by the emergence in 1968 of law and order and rising crime rates as dominant political issues in a presidential election year.

With such a disappointing ten-year history and the present national attitudes toward law reform, it is quite difficult to foresee a very bright future for the bail reform movement. There are some isolated examples of new and better projects reemerging, as well as several legislative battles looming over the establishment of state bail reform agencies. It is also encouraging to see that several cities (Memphis, Atlanta, Philadelphia, and Detroit) have expanded the scope of their original projects to include a type of pretrial diversion program. It is believed that these programs are the greatest advance and most forward looking development in the brief history of bail reform. The federal government has also become interested in pretrial diversion and is funding experimental programs in five cities located in various regions of the country.

Currently three state legislatures are attempting to establish bail reform agencies in the major cities of their states: Indiana (Indianapolis), Georgia (Atlanta), and Missouri (St. Louis). Except for the Indianapolis Bail Agency, these projects seem doomed to failure. It is the third time such legislation has been attempted in both Missouri and Georgia. Although the proreform forces seem optimistic, it would be more prudent to expect the bondsmen to flex their lobbying muscles again and knock down the legislation as they have so handily done in the past. Whether victorious or not, however, these legislative battles do give some excellent publicity to the bail reform movement and might pave the way for some local experimentation.

A final pessimistic comment is that the financial crisis of the cities, which has been alluded to earlier, seems to be worsening. It is tragic to see one of the model projects in the nation on the verge of collapse due to the financial dilemma which is currently plaguing their city's treasury. Even though it has been made clear that the project is saving San Francisco $300,000 a year, the city will probably be unable to raise the necessary $84,000 to sustain the project.[9]

Until the attitudes of the judiciary (who control the majority of bail projects) and the public in general change, and the economic plight of the cities has been relieved, there is little cause for optimism concerning bail reform. At best projects will probably continue to exist on a year-to-year basis. The isolated instances of improvement such as the new projects in Philadelphia and Detroit, will continue to be overshadowed by the large number of projects collapsing, retrenching, or merely managing to present a token effort.

9 Conclusion

The preceding chapters have attempted to realistically portray the nation's system of pretrial release as well as the viability of alternative reforms. The picture which emerged from this comprehensive and empirical investigation was one filled with pessimism and despair. Rather than editorialize within these earlier chapters, it was believed that the facts presented were able to illustrate the inadequacies and injustices of the present bail system. It will be the purpose of this concluding chapter to move beyond the descriptive statistics and narrative passages, to deal with some of the basic issues surrounding the country's pretrial release system.

Critique of the Current Bail System

It should be made clear at the outset that in critiquing the contemporary bail system, a distinction must be made between a discussion of the weaknesses of the way the courts have implemented the statutes which they are theoretically supposed to follow and a criticism of the statute itself.

The statutory purpose of bail is to guarantee the appearance of the defendant at his trial. It is not to be used as punishment against a defendant believed to be guilty. The judiciary, prosecutor, and even the public defender, however, all seem to believe that once an individual becomes enmeshed in the criminal justice system, his guilt may be assumed. All of their subsequent behaviors and attitudes toward this defendant are controlled by this assumption. As a public defender in Chicago indicated in a recent interview: "It's our court . . . It's like a family. Me, the prosecutor, the judges, we're all friends. I drink with the prosecutors. I give the judge a Christmas present, he gives me a Christmas present. And you learn technique . . . you can plead your man guilty and deal for reduced charges or probation or short time."[1] David Sudonow, continuing this line of reasoning, concludes in his article on public defenders that "The P.D.'s activity is seldom geared to securing acquittals for clients. He and the District Attorney, as co-workers in the same courts, take it for granted that the persons who come before the courts are guilty of crimes and are treated accordingly."[2]

Because of this unanimity in perspective toward defendants entangled in the criminal justice system, public officials are perfectly willing to distort or sidestep statutory provisions in order to maintain the stability of this system. Not only is bail manipulated in an informal type of preventive detention, but the various statutory instructions to the judiciary as to how to conduct a proper bail hearing are also ignored. These statutes clearly order judges to inquire as to the facts of the crime, the background of the defendant, his financial condition, his past record and additional questions considered relevant to the determination of bail. In courtroom after courtroom these statutory provisions were forgotten. In Chicago, which is controlled by the progressive and comprehensive Illinois Bail Reform Act, judges in the Holiday Court were found to be spending fifty-four seconds per defendant. How complete an investigation can be made into a defendant's background in this time period? In not one courtroom did the author ever hear the judge ask the defendant how much bail he thought he could afford!

The problems of bail cannot be solved simply by the passage of additional legislation which aims at correcting the present inadequacies of our bail system. In states such as Illinois and Florida which possess excellent statutes regulating all aspects of pretrial release, the day-to-day administration of bail in various cities violates virtually every provision of that legislation. If these statutes are not implemented, and they presently do not seem to be, than it is irrelevant to applaud their efforts and abate criticism and reform. The real battle for reforming the bail system will have to be fought in the hearts and minds of those public officials—judges, prosecutors, and public defenders—who are responsible for its operation. In addition, reforms must be made within the entire criminal justice system so as to permit these improvements to take place.

This entire problem can be viewed most clearly with regard to the state's attempted regulation of the bail-bonding industry. Elaborate statutes have been passed in recent years which on paper guarantee the close supervision of bondsmen and eradication of previous undesirable behavior. This study, however, has found these statutes to have little effect on the bondsmen's illegal activities. The main cause for this problem is the inability of the State Insurance Commissions, who usually are given the responsibility of controlling bondsmen, to actively dedicate themselves to their assigned tasks. In St. Louis, Missouri, for example, it was discovered that over 90 percent of all forfeitures were not collected and simply tossed out by the court. With little fear of legal reprimand or financial penalities, it is no wonder that so many bondsmen continue to engage in illegal activities, often subverting legislative attempts at reforming their vocation.

The major response of reform groups to correct the ills of this malfunctioning bail system has usually been the establishment of a bail reform project which is designed to aid the court in releasing defendants on their own recognizance. After reviewing the progress made by these projects since their inception in 1961, they can no longer be viewed sanguinely as the answer to the many serious weaknesses of the nation's system of pretrial release. There is a great deal of truth in the criticisms of men like Law Professor Caleb Foote of the University of California who comes very close to describing the bail reform movement as a sham. It seems to ignore those people it was designed to serve, that is, the indigents whose financial condition forces them into pretrial incarceration, while it satisfies the conscience's of judges and public officials who wish to be identified with reform programs benefiting "the disadvantaged."

Despite the good intentions of bail reform projects, they continue to utilize release criteria which can be met only by middle-class defendants, a small and statutorily unintended recipient. By stressing a stable family, residential, and economic lifestyle, as well as penalizing defendants for past experiences with the law, these projects are unable to help the indigent, transient, or youth who fill our nation's pretrial detention facilities. Instead they are able to recommend the release of approximately 15 percent of those defendants falling within their project's jurisdiction. This 15 percent are usually citizens who in all likelihood could have paid their own bail but are able to obtain release on their own recognizance and save this expense.

In summary, these projects have accomplished two things, neither of them related to their stated objectives: (1) by releasing an insignificant percentage of defendants, they have ingratiated themselves to the judiciary as a showpiece of the court's progressive spirit while at the same time failing to cause a radical change in the pretrial release system—a change which might cause a feared imbalance or collapse of the precariously constructed criminal justice system; and (2) they have seriously shaken the bonding industry by robbing it of its most desirable clients and thereby forcing the bondsmen into taking greater risks. Their new clients, coming from a less desirable class of defendants (recidivists, transients, youths, and first offenders) represent the necessity for a greater amount of pretrial supervision since they have a greater likelihood of forfeiting. These criticisms of bail reform are not meant to discredit the movement. It is conceded that these projects were conceived to fill a much needed void in the criminal justice system. But in evaluating their performance in providing aid to the indigent defendant in obtaining his pretrial release, this study must sadly conclude that the movement is inadequate.

The shattering of this illusion of bail reform projects as a panacea to the ills of the nation's pretrial release system is just one of several shibboleths which this study has attempted to explode. Another myth, which this book has tried to put to rest, is the belief that there is a relationship between the seriousness of a defendant's crime and his predilection for skipping town. It has traditionally been thought that the more serious the crime a defendant is accused, the greater the chance that he will forfeit bail. Therefore, in order to detain these defendants within the required jurisdiction, a bail will be set in the amount which is thought to be sufficient to serve as a deterrent from forfeiting. The result is a bail schedule where the greater the seriousness of the crime, the higher the amount of bond.

Chapter 4 presented the results of the national survey which clearly refutes this supposed relationship. According to bondsmen, one of the best risks for bail are defendants accused of murder, the most serious of crimes, at least in terms of the punishment associated with conviction. Very often these crimes are acts of passion by individuals who are immediately penitent over their irrational conduct, and often have no prior history of criminal activity. Several bondsmen also commented that professional criminals such as burglars, who frequently require the services of bondsmen, are also excellent pretrial risks, since they can realistically foresee the future use of bonding services and therefore do not wish to alienate them. As far as defendants thought to be the poorest risks, the bondsmen generally agreed that first offenders, who may panic as their inevitable day of reckoning approaches, are the most likely to forfeit. Also noted as bad risks are shoplifters, junkies, and any other type of recidivist whose mental condition is unstable and unpredictable.

Another myth relating to bondsmen which was challenged in this study is the portrayal of bondsmen as individuals who possess above average abilities in predicting pretrial behavior and who also have at their command an elaborate network of cronies and informers who can quickly retrieve forfeiting defendants. Due to his judgment and his system of control, it is believed that the bondsman provides the court with an exceptional procedure for supervising defendants during their pretrial release. Chapter 4 conclusively indicates that not only do bail reform projects overshadow and outshine the bondsmen in their ability to maintain low forfeiture rates, but in the majority of cities surveyed, the reform projects were much more successful than the bondsmen in keeping their forfeiture rate below the national average.

A final myth which pervades not only the nation's pretrial release system, but its entire legal system is the political neutrality of the judiciary. Supposedly apolitical and concerned only with the objective administration of justice in strict accordance with present statutes and past precedents, judges are pictured as being above the petty squabbles which seem to debilitate our criminal court system. Based on this examination of bail and its reform, the judiciary is deeply mired in the political struggles within the criminal justice system and frequently involved in broader confrontations with the public as well as other governmental institutions. This study is not attempting to slap the hands of the judiciary for engaging in such mundane machinations, but rather to point out the realities of their political activities, particularly with respect to their influence on policies related to the administration of bail. Although Chief Judge Boyle in Chicago, with his close friendship with Mayor Daley, emerges as an archetype of a politically-involved judge, every city visited possessed members of the judiciary who were active in either stifling or recharging the city's bail reform program. As so often results in political infighting, the ultimate issue often becomes lost in the ensuing power struggle as face-saving and ego-tripping suddenly appear as the all-consuming interest. The recent struggle in Pittsburgh between a judicially sponsored bail reform plan and a community-sponsored proposal has resulted in a power conflict where no victor emerged and the city's indigent defendants continued to suffer as the real losers.

Some Final Reflections and Prognostications

The most disturbing aspect of this country's approach to the problem of pretrial release has been its unwillingness to confront the basic inequities perpetrated upon defendants. Simply stated, public officials have blindfolded themselves to the blatant economic discrimination which is practiced by our nation's bail system. We have adopted the English law of bailment into our judicial system, never bothering to question or challenge the basic assumptions of this seventeenth-century legal concept which was contained in the English Bill of Rights (1689). These premises which form the foundations for the past and present bail system are directly related to the idea that the most important thing governing man's behavior is his undying allegiance to the "holy buck." Thus, if we wish to be humane and fair, and allow a defendant to await his trial outside of a pretrial detention facility, the court must be given some assurance that he will eventually appear for his trial. Bail is a system which attempts to permit this pretrial freedom while at the same time using economic pressures to guarantee the appearance of the defendant at the required time. By forcing a defendant to buy his pretrial freedom, the more serious the accusation the higher the price, the courts reason that this instinctual fear of losing this money deposit will be sufficient to prevent the defendant from fleeing town.

This type of reasoning, which rationalizes the necessity and existence of the money bail system, can be challenged on both logical as well as constitutional grounds. The money bail system is illogical because it denies pretrial freedom to those defendants who are least capable of forfeiture, while granting release to those defendants who are actually most likely to be able to afford leaving the jurisdiction and escaping prosecution. If a defendant has bail set at $1,000 and cannot even afford a $100 bondsman's fee, how will he be able to afford a plane or bus ticket out of town? Yet defendants accused of white-collar crimes or members of organized crime syndicates, who are able to post $25,000 and $50,000 bonds, are granted release. Does the court then believe that someone who is capable of raising such an enormous bond will then run out of financial backing and be unable to come up with an extra hundred dollars which will be necessary to purchase plane tickets to a distant location?

An additional questionable assumption of the traditional bail system is that the defendant will fear loss of his money more than loss of his freedom if convicted; a loss which might be avoided by forfeiting bond. How many defendants are so greedy as to be willing to sacrifice a year or more in prison rather than lose a thousand dollars to the court? Since most defendants use bondsmen, they do not have to be concerned with the total amount since the 10 percent fee paid to the bondsmen is not refundable, anyway. If the defendant skips town it will be the bondsman who will be held responsible by the court for the full amount. In any event, it seems highly improbable that a defendant contemplating forfeiting bond in order to avoid prosecution will be deterred from his flight merely because he does not want to lose his financial investment of the original bond.

The Supreme Court of the United States has never dealt directly with the constitutionality of the nation's money bail system. Their pronouncements on the subject of bail have only been in relation to the provision of the Eighth Amendment which states that "excessive bail shall not be required." This simply means, as was enunciated in the Supreme Court's most famous bail related case of *Stack v. Boyle,* that bail is excessive when it is set at "a figure higher than an amount reasonably calculated" to fulfill the purpose of assuring the presence of the accused at his trial.[3] Since the Eighth Amendment does not make admission to bail an absolute right in all circumstances, it seems a waste of time to engage in a oft-repeated debate concerning the inferences and legislative intent of our founding fathers regarding the establishment of an absolute right to bail.

The basic constitutional flaw in this nation's bail system is not the continual violation of the Eighth Amendment's prohibition against excessive bail, but rather the blatant economic discrimination inherent in this system which seems to clearly contradict the equal protection clause of the Fourteenth Amendment. It is difficult to imagine a more obvious example of economic discrimination. Defendants are permitted to buy their pretrial freedom by raising the necessary bond while those disadvantaged defendants unable to afford bond are forced to be detained in jail. The numerous costs of this pretrial incarceration have been previously documented and range from such divergent unpleasantries as losing one's job to being physically assaulted within the cell block. Our court's have permitted a system of justice which allows one's pretrial freedom to be put up for sale and those defendants unable to pay the price must suffer the dire consequences.

The equal protection clause of the Fourteenth Amendment has been used on occasion to overthrow selected aspects of this nation's criminal justice system which has discriminated against a disadvantaged economic class. The two cases most relevant to the topic of bail are the *Griffin v. Illinois* decision and a recent federal court decision involving the Illinois Ten Per Cent Bail Deposit Provision. In *Griffin v. Illinois* (351 U.S. 12 1956) the United States Supreme Court illustrated its concern for indigent defendants by holding that it was a violation of the equal protection clause and therefore unconstitutional discrimination by the state of Illinois, to furnish free stenographic transcripts of trials only for review of constitutional questions and to indigent defendants under death sentence. The court argued that such a restriction prevented other defendants, unable to purchase a transcript, from exercising their right to appellate review.[4]

In the more recent Illinois case which dealt specifically with the topic of bail, the federal district court declared the state's Ten Per Cent Bail Deposit Provision to be unconstitutional because it violated the equal protection clause. The Bail Deposit Provision statute allows any defendant to pay 10 percent of his bond directly to the court, and when he appears for trial, 90 percent of his deposit would be returned, the remainder being kept to pay the court costs in administering the program. The case grew out of the fact that if the defendant was wealthy enough to pay the entire amount of the original bond to the court, this total sum would be returned to him upon his appearance for trial. The court stated that because defendants who could only afford to use the 10 percent plan would be losing 10 percent of their investment, they were being discriminated against since wealthier defendants who could pay the entire cash bond to the court would be permitted to collect this total amount if they showed up at the proper time.

It is true that both of these cases serve as a sound precedent for future court action attacking the complete concept of money bail as an unconstitutional violation of the equal protection clause. However, the circuitous flanking movements noted in the previous cases raise little hope that the Supreme Court, particularly the Burger Court, will move against so sturdy and time-tested an institution as the American bail system. It is especially frustrating to acknowledge the reality of this position since it appears that the constitution and *stare decisis* stand so clearly on the side of this challenge. Based on the present law and order crisis facing the nation, blinding its legislators and handcuffing its judiciary, the advocates of bail reform must turn to other methods and institutions to accomplish their mission.

A final point to illustrate the ludicrous nature and hypocrisy of the current money bail system involves the question of how the courts arrive at the amount of bail to be set in a specific case. In nearly all courts the judge, with the help of a recommended bail schedule, has total discretion as to the amount of a bond in a felony case. The recommended schedule simply arranges the amount of bond by the seriousness of the charge. However, since the defendant's appearance in court is the primary objective of the bail process, it would seem reasonable that the judge make some inquiries into the defendant's economic capabilities. These inquiries may be directed to the defendant, his family, or employer. The objective of such an interrogation would be to determine what the defendant can afford and then set bail in relation to that amount. Unfortunately, this is rarely if ever done. Either the judge believes these questions are irrelevant, does not care one way or the other, or does not have the time to engage in such frivolities. In any event, bail is set without regard to the defendant's economic condition. A $100 bail for a poor defendant may be the same as a $100,000 bond for a big-time racketeer. Many indigent defendants would be unable to raise bail regardless of the amount while organized crime leaders can usually raise any amount which is set. Where is the fear of financial loss in each of these cases? Where is the punishment inflicted justifiable?

Since a frontal attack on the bail system, based on constitutional verities, appears to be doomed to failure, what alternative reforms may temporarily improve the operation of our country's pretrial release system? One possible alternative which is frequently used in England and utilized in a few isolated jurisdictions in this country (see Chapter 6) is the use of third party release. This reform suggests that a defendant be paroled into the custody of a responsible third party such as his attorney, minister, employer, or any official recognized by the court as satisfying their standards. Currently both Pittsburgh and Detroit are attempting to arrange a procedure whereby defendants are released into the charge of some community-based organization which will be held responsible for the defendant's behavior during this pretrial period.

After spending two weeks studying the English bail system in 1970, the author found it interesting to discover that their courts continue to rely on the original concept of personal surety and frequently use a form of third party release. It was very surprising to discover the limited number of instances where money bail was imposed. If a defendant was to be denied his pretrial freedom, the most common reason was not an inability to raise a financial bond, but rather his inability to introduce the court to a satisfactory third party surety. If he represented such an obvious risk to society if released, there was no sense in going through the sham of setting a bond designed to be so high as to be unobtainable. The success of this third party alternative has been evidenced in this country by the Tulsa, Oklahoma experiment reported by Freed and Wald, where nearly 200 defendants a month are released into the custody of one of 310 participating members of the County's Bar Association.[5]

Preventive Detention

After describing the traditional money bail system as being unfair, unconstitutional, illogical, and simply unworkable, and evaluating bail reform as it currently is practiced as ineffective and deceitful, what is the nation left with as a possible means of determining the pretrial condition of defendants following their arrest? Are we really at the point where one is forced to agree with a disillusioned Oakland public defender who stated in an interview that "it really doesn't make any difference at all. What we should do is grant pretrial release to all defendants and scrap the entire bail system. Only three things can happen to defendants who forfeit. One, they will leave town and become a headache for some other jurisdiction. Two, if they stay in town and continue a life of crime, they will soon be re-arrested and with their previous charge the prosecutor will have a stronger hand in the plea bargaining process. Third, if they remain in town and don't commit any additional crimes, than we can say that we have rehabilitated them by intimidation."[6]

The nation, however, is left with one additional alternative which has been tried unsuccessfully in Washington, D.C. and emerged as a red-herring issue in that city's recent Court Reform Act. This is the concept of preventive detention where the judiciary, after a hearing with full constitutional protections, decides if a defendant presents a threat to society in the form of fleeing the jurisdiction to avoid prosecution or committing additional crimes during the pretrial period. For those defendants identified as bad risks and threats to society, there will be a short period of pretrial detention (sixty days in the District), and then a speedy trial. If the court is unable to go to trial following this sixty-day period, the defendant will be given his pretrial freedom until a court date has been determined.

Critics of preventive detention raise several persuasive arguments in their opposition to this concept. Their major fears are its potential for abuse and more specifically their unwillingness to concede that the court system will be able to identify these bad-risk defendants in any manner which will not deny constitutional rights or more general considerations of fair treatment. In Washington, the only jurisdiction currently possessing such a procedure on its statute books, the U.S. Attorney's Office would be making an oral motion for preventive detention against only those defendants charged with dangerous crimes, crimes of violence or convicted of such a crime within the past ten years or charged with any offense which threatens, injures, or intimidates any prospective witness or juror. All of these terms are defined in other sections of the statute.[7]

The major defense of this type of preventive detention statute evolves from the failure of nearly all other attempts at improving or regulating the pretrial release system. This is not to say that all other alternatives have been tried, or even the few reforms that have been attempted have been given the freedom to realistically be evaluated without a number of encumbrances. But given the country's attitude toward crime prevention, and strong statements against reform measures which are characterized as "coddling criminals," not much else can be expected. For all of its disagreeable elements and potential for misuse, preventive detention still is a more logical approach to determining and controlling a defendant's pretrial freedom than the traditional money bail system. The only individuals being discriminated against are those who have been proven to possess certain antisocial tendencies which will threaten society and ultimately their chances for appearing in court at the required time. The problem seems to be to reformulate preventive detention statutes, more in terms of their ability to detain individuals whose behavior make them a threat to forfeit their court appearance rather than merely identifying them under some unworkably vague rubric as "individuals posing a threat to society."

How well can we expect such a system to work? Since Washington is the only court system legally operating a preventive detention program, they provide the only example of its capabilities. The program in the nation's capital, however, has been rather ineffective, particularly after the nationwide coverage given to earlier efforts in Congress to pass the city's court reform bill containing the controversial preventive detention and no-knock provisions.

Despite the early ballyhoo over preventive detention's potential for abuse and its supposed blatant unconstitutionality, its operation failed of its own accord, strangled by the city's unworkable backlog of cases. There were simply insufficient judges, courtrooms, prosecutors, defense attorneys, and calendar days to put the system into operation. Following its passage into law, the city, because of the various complications just noted, was able to use the preventive detention statute less than a dozen times in the first six months of operation and it has rarely been used since.[8]

It seems that the real villain in the District of Columbia's abortive preventive detention experience is a much broader and serious problem that cannot be corrected by merely ironing out the technical and procedural flaws in the original statute. The major cause of the problem is the court congestion and resulting backlog of cases which has handcuffed and perverted the city's criminal justice system. It is only until we are successful in solving this problem, that there will be any chance of actually improving the nation's system of pretrial release. Like so many other attempts at improving the operation of the criminal justice system, viable change cannot occur simply by placing some type of procedural or administrative bandage over an isolated diseased organ when the entire organism is dying. In the case of the criminal justice system, the disease is a cancerous growth commonly labeled court backlog, court delay, or a clogged assembly line.

The narrow perspective of contemporary attempts at improving the pretrial release system such as bail reform projects are doomed to failure because of their inability or unwillingness to grasp the necessity for a radical overhaul of the criminal justice system. These current reform attempts are merely a series of stopgap measures whose impact is easily absorbed by the larger system. Perceptible changes caused by these reforms eventually emerge as a bulge somewhere else within the system: a bulge whose future growth may doom the original reform as the system seeks to return to a state of equilibrium. The attempt by the New York City courts to grease the sluggish wheels of justice provides an interesting example of this phenomenon. The city devised a Master Calendar Control System employing computers and record miniaturization which speeds up the prearraignment processing of criminal suspects, which saves the time of victims and arresting officers by permitting them to swear out complaints in a police station instead of going to court for the arraignment of suspects. It is true that in the first six months of operation, in the Bronx alone, 44,000 man-hours of work for the police were saved. But the short-sighted style of reform only caused the system to malfunction at some other point. In this instance, because the police now had all this time back on the streets, they were able to increase their arrest rate by 17.8 percent. Where do all of these additional suspects go? Right back into the already congested court system at such an accelerated rate as to cause an even greater backlog than before the program's initiation. One step forward and two steps backward.[9]

The main lesson which must be learned is that if the bail system is to be improved, these improvements must be attempted by taking into consideration their effect on the entire criminal justice system. All parts are interrelated and any alteration or twist at one juncture will cause an equal or even greater reaction somewhere else in the system. Does this pessimistic and demanding diagnosis mean the inevitable collapse of the criminal justice system? Is there any conceivable plan by which the court congestion can be relieved and we can get on to the critical business of repairing and improving the nation's pretrial release system? The most plausible answer is to rid the criminal justice system of certain categories of crimes which have no place in this system and have been among the major culprits in causing this backlog of cases. These are the victimless crimes such as alcoholism, drug addition, gambling, prostitution, and homosexuality which account for at least 60 percent of the court's caseload. It is not within the scope of this book to deal extensively with how these categories of "deviants" should be treated and by which alternative social and medical facilities. All that is being argued is that these individuals do not belong in the criminal justice system and their continued presence results in irreparable harm to not only these misplaced individuals but to the entire criminal justice system.

This recommendation is not unique. Sociologists, judges, public officials, and other knowledgeable and concerned citizens have been advocating this for years. The United States Federal Courts have begun to be persuaded by their arguments and in recent cases both alcoholism and drug addiction have had their criminal stigma removed and ordered to be categorized and treated as a medical problem outside of the court's jurisdiction. Morris and Hawkins in their book *The Honest Politicians Guide to Crime Control* state the problem succinctly by writing:

> The function, as we see it of the criminal law is to protect the citizen's person and property and to prevent the exploitation or corruption of the young and others in need of special care or protection. We think it improper, impolitic, and usually socially harmful for the law to intervene or attempt to regulate the private moral conduct of the citizen. In this country we have a highly moralistic criminal law and a long tradition of using as an instrument for coercing men toward virtue. It is a singularly inept instrument for that purpose. It is also an unduly costly one, both in terms of harm done and in terms of the neglect of the proper tasks of law enforcement.[10]

In closing this analysis of bail and its reform, the reader must be made aware of the importance of an equitable pretrial release system, not merely to the unfortunate defendant, or the criminal justice system, but also to the very core of our ability to maintain our democratic form of government. The following quote from Winston Churchill clearly elucidates this sentiment:

> A calm dispassionate recognition of the rights of the accused . . . the unfailing faith that there is a treasure, if you can only find it in the heart of every man . . . are the symbols, which in the treatment of crime and the criminal mark and measure the stored up strength of a nation.[11]

Appendixes

Appendix A: Bail Questionnaire

GENERAL INSTRUCTIONS:

1. All questions requesting statistical information refer to the year 1968, unless otherwise specified.

2. If you are unable to answer any question, please leave it blank and continue on to the next question.

3. Please read the instructions offered at the beginning of each section of the questionnaire.

PART I. ORGANIZATION AND PROCEDURE IN PRE-TRIAL RELEASE

Instructions: If alternative answers are offered please check your choice

1. What is the approximate *average* time between arrest and the setting of bail?

    Same day _____   Next day _____   More than one day _____

2. What is the approximate average time between arrest and the determination of whether the accused will be released on his own recognizance? (The release of a defendant prior to his trial without his having to put up a money deposit. His release is based upon his being identified as a good risk not to flee or commit further crimes.) _____

3. Is there a system of notification to tell the defendant when he must appear in court?

    Yes _____   No _____

    If yes, how is the notification made?

    Phone call _____   Personal visit _____
    Letter _____   Other (specify) _____

4. Were the pre-trial detainess separated in the detention facility from the inmates who were serving sentences?

   Yes _____   No _____

5. What are the approximate jail costs per day per inmate?

   $1 _____ $4 _____
   $2 _____ $5 _____
   $3 _____   Other (Specify) _____

6. What would you estimate was the average length of time spent in jail before trial for each detained defendant? _____

7. Is the amount of bail which is required for each type of crime specified in either a state or local statute or ordinance?

   Yes _____   No _____

8. Is a bondsman available to help the accused raise the required bail?

   Yes _____   No _____

9. Is a verification system used to check on the validity of the information given by the defendant?

   Yes _____   No _____

PART II. APPROXIMATE STATISTICAL DATA

1. The number of individuals arraigned (brought before a magistrate or judge to determine whether the individual should be released prior to his trial).

   _____

Instructions: In any of the following questions in which an approximate percentage is requested, please use one of the letters listed below which corresponds to a percentage interval. All statistics refer to the year 1968.

   a.   0–9%   f. 50–59
   b.   10–19   g. 60–69
   c.   20–29   h. 70–79
   d.   30–39   i. 80–89
   e.   40–49   j. 90–100

2. % of arraigned individuals interviewed by non-judicial personnel
    for possible release on their own recognizance.   _____

3. % of arraigned individuals recommended by the above non-judicial
    personnel for pre-trial release on their own recognizance.   _____

4. % of arraigned individuals released on their own recognizance.   _____

5. % of arraigned individuals released due to payment of bail.   _____

6. % of arraigned individuals detained in jail prior to trial.   _____

7. % of arraigned individuals who were released prior to their trial
    and failed to show up in court for their trial.   _____

    a. % of arraigned individuals released *on their own recognizance*,
        who failed to show up in court for their trial.   _____

    b. % of arraigned individuals released *on payment of bail* who
        failed to show up in court.   _____

8. % of arraigned individuals who were released prior to their trial
    who were arrested for committing another crime while released.   _____

    a. % of arraigned individuals released *on their own recognizance*
        who were arrested for committing another crime while released
        prior to trial.   _____

    b. % of arraigned individuals released *on payment of bail* who
        were arrested for committing another crime while released
        prior to trial.   _____

9. % of persons detained in jail prior to trial who were found guilty. _____

    a. % of persons released *on their own recognizance* who were found
        guilty.   _____

    b. % of persons released *on payment of bail* who were found guilty. _____

10. % of arraigned individuals who use bondsmen to raise the necessary
    bail.   _____

TRENDS—To indicate trends during the last five years concerning the ten questions just answered, please go over each question again and place one of the following symbols next to the question number:

+ increase,   0 no change,   – decrease

PART III. ATTITUDES TOWARD ADMINISTRATION
OF BAIL IN MY COMMUNITY

Instructions: Please indicate your attitude toward each of the following statements by inserting one of the following symbols in the blank space next to each statement.

+ +   agree strongly
+   agree but not strongly
0   undecided
–   disagree but not strongly
– –   disagree strongly

1. The bondsman plays a crucial role in the administration of bail.   _____

2. The power of the bondsman should be decreased.   _____

3. The presiding judge plays the most significant role in determining the size of the bond.   _____

4. We ought to make more use of preventive detention (i.e., the practice of either denying bail or setting bail at an unattainably high amount in order to imprison a person who might present a particular danger to society if left free before trial).   _____

5. An increased use of preventive detention will help reduce the crime rate regardless of the other effects.   _____

6. The present system of bail, based on the defendant's ability to raise the required bond, is a good procedure for determining pre-trial release.   _____

7. The increasing number of defendants released on their own recognizance is partly responsible for the increasing crime rate.   _____

8. The number of defendants released on their own recognizance has increased *too* greatly in recent years.   _____

9. A defendant's chances for acquittal are influenced by whether or not he was detained in jail prior to his trial. _____

10. The bail amount is regularly manipulated by the courts to accomplish a form of preventive detention. _____

11. A bail reform program which released selected defendants through a standardized fact-finding mechanism is a good system for administering bail. _____

12. A good alternative or modification to the present bail system for some individuals is the third party parole where the defendant is paroled in the custody of a willing private third party such as his attorney or a local minister. _____

13. A good alternative or modification to the present bail system for some individuals is daytime release where the accused is permitted to leave for outside employment during the day but must be required to return to jail at night. _____

14. A good alternative or modification to the present bail system is supervised release where the accused is released conditioned on remaining within the court's jurisdiction and periodic check-ins with the policy, probation office, or court. _____

15. Bail is often set too high for the average man to meet. _____

16. In order to tailor the bail system more closely to the accused's financial capabilities, bail should be lowered to more realistic levels. _____

17. More frequently enforced penal sanctions would deter bail jumpers more strongly than forfeiture of the bond. _____

18. The use of cash bail fixed by statute or court rule in accordance with the crime is a good improvement to the present bail system. _____

19. A great improvement to the current administration of bail issue would be to afford the accused a more prompt trial. _____

20. The prosecuting attorney plays a significant role in determining the size of the bond. _____

21. The detention facilities for pre-trial detainness are overcrowded in our city. _____

PART IV. PRE-RELEASE CRITERIA

Instructions: In determining whether a defendant is to be released prior to trial, how important are each of the following criteria used in evaluating the defendant using the following symbols:

+ + + Extremely important
+ +   Moderately important
+   Slightly important
0   Not important

_____ 1. Present charge

_____ 2. Past criminal record

_____ 3. Likelihood of committing a future crime

_____ 4. Present employment

_____ 5. References

_____ 6. Length of present employment

_____ 7. Living with his family

_____ 8. How long he has lived in the city

_____ 9. How long he has lived at his present address

_____ 10. Has he previously been released on parole or bail, and if so, has he appeared on time.

Are the above criteria weighted according to a point scoring system in your community?

Yes _____   No _____

PART V. BAIL REFORM PROGRAMS

1. Does your city utilize a bail reform program? (A program providing for the release of many persons prior to trial without having to put up a money deposit. Release is based upon being identified as a good risk which is

determined by a standardized fact-finding mechanism such as the objective formula used by the Vera Foundation.)

Yes _____   No _____

If your city does not have a bail reform program as above defined, you need not answer the rest of the questions.

2. What was the starting date of your program? _____

3. Who is the sponsor of controlling agency in the program?

Probation Department _____   The courts _____
Legal Aid Officers _____   Other (specify) _____
Bar Association _____

4. Who interviews defendants for factual information relevant to pre-trial release?

Probation officers _____   Only Judges _____
Law students _____   Other (specify) _____
VISTA volunteers _____

5. What is the source of funds for financing the project?

City _____   Bar Association _____
State _____   Other (specify) _____
Federal _____

6. What types of crimes does your program have jurisdiction over?

Felonies _____   Misdemeanors _____
Lesser felonies _____   Other (specify) _____

7. Has the bail reform project been expanded since its beginning?

Yes _____   No _____

Thank you again for your cooperation.

Appendix B: City Classification

Reform Cities

Albuquerque, New Mexico
Austin, Texas
Baltimore, Maryland
Berkeley, California
Clinton, New York
Cleveland, Ohio
Colorado Springs, Colorado
Columbus, Ohio
Crown Point, Indiana
Denver, Colorado
Des Moines, Iowa
Detroit, Michigan
Herkimer, New York
Houston, Texas
Indianapolis, Indiana
Long Beach, California

Los Angeles, California
Madison, Wisconsin
Martinez, California
New York City, New York
Oakland, California
Reading, Pennsylvania
Redwood, Califronia
St. Louis, Missouri
Salt Lake City, Utah
San Francisco, California
Santa Barbara, California
Seattle, Washington
Syracuse, New York
Tulsa, Oklahoma
Washington, D.C.

Traditional Cities

Atlanta, Georgia
Boise, Idaho
Boston, Massachusetts
Cedar Rapids, Iowa
Charleston, West Virginia
Chattanooga, Tennessee
Corpus Christi, Texas
Dallas, Texas
El Paso, Texas
Flint, Michigan
Gainesville, Florida
Galveston, Texas
Glendale, California
Hackensack, New Jersey
Holidaysburg, Pennsylvania
Jackson, Mississippi

Jacksonville, Florida
Kansas City, Kansas
Lancaster, Pennsylvania
Memphis, Tennessee
New Orleans, Louisiana
Ogden, Utah
Oklahoma City, Oklahoma
Pasadena, California
Philadelphia, Pennsylvania
Rockville, Maryland
San Antonio, Texas
San Diego, California
San Mateo, California
Spokane, Washington
Trenton, New Jersey
Wichita, Kansas

Illinois Cities

Bloomington
Chicago
Decatur
Elgin

Galesburg
Kankakee
Springfield
Waukegan
Wheaton

177

Appendix C: Individuals Interviewed

The following is a list of individuals interviewed during the eleven-city survey. A few persons interviewed asked that they remain anonymous, and the writer has honored their request.

Atlanta, Georgia

Hon. Luther Alverson, Superior Court of Fulton County
Susan Black, Office of Bond Clerk
Jack Boyle, District Attorney's Office
Foy Devine, Attorney, Activist in Bail Reform Legislation
Hon. Daniel Duke, Criminal Court of Fulton County
Hon. Jack Ethridge, Superior Court of Fulton County
Al Horn, Defense Attorney
John Knuckle, District Attorney's Office
Rogers Hornsby, Bondsman
Hon. T.C. Little, Municipal Court
Hon. John Langford, Juvenile Court of Fulton County
James L. McGovern, Director of Atlanta Commission on Crime
Leroy Stenchcombe, Sheriff, Fulton County
Larry Thomas, Bail Project Director
Jess Watson, Public Defender
Glenn Zell, Defense Attorney

Baltimore, Maryland

John Camou, Pre-Trial Release Project
Hon. Meyer Cardin, Supreme Bench, City of Baltimore
Joseph Gibbons, Pre-Trial Release Project
Hon. Robert Hammerman, Circuit Court of Baltimore City, Division for Causes
Steve Harris, Legal Aid Bureau
Frederick Invernizzi, Director, Administrative Office of the Courts
Hon. I. Sewell Lamden, Chief Judge, Municipal Court
Joseph Matera, Director, Legal Aid Bureau

Richard Motsay, Director, Pre-Trial Release Project
Hon. Charles Moylan, Maryland Court of Special Appeals (former State's
    Attorney for the city)
Gordon Walker, Bondsman
James White, Defense Attorney

Chicago, Illinois

Thomas P. Cawley, First Assistant Public Defender
Kermit Coleman, Attorney, A.C.L.U.
Larry Diamond, Alliance to End Repression
Hon. Louis Giliberto, Magistrate's Court, Supervisor of Surety Section
Thomas Grippando, Community Legal Council
Rev. John Hill, Director, Alliance to End Repression
Hans Mattick, Center for Studies in Criminal Justice
Elmer Kissane, Chief of Criminal Division, State's Attorney's Office
Donald McIntyre, Research Director, Chicago Council of Lawyers, American
    Bar Foundation
Ralph Meyberg, Former OR Division Investigator
Patrick Murphey, Legal Aid Bureau
Marshall Patner, Attorney, Businessmen for the Public Interest
Marshall Pidgeon, Director of OR Division
Tom Royce, Cook County Bail Project (O.R. Division)
Warren Wolfson, Defense Attorney

Detroit, Michigan

Hon. George Crockett, The Recorder's Court
H.Y. Duplessis, Deputy Chief, Probation Department
Hon. Robert E. DeMascio, Presiding Judge, The Recorder's Court
Charles B. Goldfarb, Bondsman
Ernest Goodman, Private Attorney
James S. Henahan, Chief Probation Officer
Maurice Kobel, Arraignment Officer
Clarence Laster, Pre-Trial Conference Division, Office of the Prosecuting
    Attorney
Hon. James H. Lincoln, Judge of Probate, Juvenile Division
Michael J. O'Connor, Wayne County Office of the Prosecuting Attorney,
    Chief of Recorder's Court Department
Louis Simmons, Private Attorney
Myzell Sowell, Public Defender's Division

Indianapolis, Indiana

Larry Champion, Prosecuting Attorney's Office
Hon. John Davis, Criminal Division, Marion County Court
James Droege, Bail Project Director
Al Farb, Bondsman
Hon. Harold N. Fields, Marion County Juvenile Court
Judge Sharp, Municipal Court of Marion County
Larry Whitney, Bail Project Researcher (Statistician)
Frank E. Wright, Bondsman

Los Angeles, California

Owen Boone, Intake and Detention Control, Juvenile Division
Richard Buckley, Public Defender
Hon. Leo Freund, Division 64, Municipal Court
Irving Glasser, Bondsman
Sam Gordon, Assistant to the Executive Officer, the Superior Court
Gordon Jacobson, District Attorney's Office
Alan Ostroff, Assistant Supervisor of the OR Unit

Oakland (Alameda County), California

John Ballestresse, Bondsman
Hon. George Brunn, Alameda County, Berkeley
J.F. Coakley, District Attorney
Edward Hooley, Public Defender
D.L. Kukendall, Probation Department
Sam Strellis, Attorney, Former Public Defender
Captain Richard Young, Berkeley Police Department, Supervisor OR Unit

Philadelphia, Pennsylvania

G. Richard Bacon, Executive Secretary, Pennsylvania Prison Society
Richard Max Bocko, Assistant District Attorney
Peter Buffum, Staff Sociologist, Pennsylvania Prison Society
Allen Davis, Private Attorney
Edmund DePaul, Defense Attorney, Former Bail Project Director
Ephraim Gomberg, Executive Vice President of Philadelphia Crime Commission
David Kairys, Defender's Association
Paul Michel, Assistant District Attorney

Herman Pollock, Defender's Association
Michael Rotko, Assistant District Attorney
Judge Spaeth, Philadelphia Court of Common Pleas
Martin Vinikoor, Office of District Attorney, Juvenile Court
Jean White, Office of Court Administrator, Common Pleas Court
Vincent Ziccardi, Defender's Association

St. Louis, Missouri

Jack Bantle, Circuit Attorney's Office
James Brachman, Director of Nominal Bond Project
Hon. G.A. Buder, Circuit Court
Irving Croupen, Bondsman
Andrew Freeman, Circuit Clerk for Criminal Causes
Ellen Hanson, National Juvenile Law Center
Charles Mann, Social Worker, former director of bail project
Hon. Theodore McMillan, Juvenile Court
Joseph Noskay, Public Defender
James Sauter, Defense Attorney
Barney Wippold, Journalist
Herman Wood, Director of Institutional Services, St. Louis County Jail

San Francisco, California

Kenneth Babb, Bail Project Director
John Ballestresse, Bondsman
Edward Mancuso, Public Defender
Hon. Francis Mayer, Juvenile Court
John Nico, Deputy Public Defender
Irving Reichert, San Francisco Committee on Crime
Gregory Stout, Defense Attorney

Washington D.C.

Bruce Beaudin, Director of Bail Agency
Jim Davis, Project Crossroads
Paul Fenton, U.S. Congress, Counsel for House Committee on the Judiciary
Ronald Goldfarb, Attorney and Author
Hon. Orman Ketcham, Juvenile Court
William McDonald, Georgetown University Law Center
Hon. Tim Murphy, Court of General Sessions
John G. Perazich, Legal Aid Society
Richard Perlman, Director of Research, Juvenile Court
Joe Trotter, Project Crossroads
Chuck Work, U.S. Attorney's Office, Court of General Sessions

Appendix D: San Francisco Bail Project Pretrial Release Criteria

TO BE RECOMMENDED FOR RELEASE ON OWN RECOGNIZANCE, A DEFENDANT NEEDS:

1. A Bay area address where he can be reached, *AND*

2. A total of five points (verified by references) from the following

RESIDENCE
3 Present address one year or more
2 Present residence 6 months, *OR* present and prior 1 year
1 Present residence 3 months, *OR* present and prior 6 months

1 Five years or more in Nine Bay Area Counties

FAMILY TIES
3 Lives with family, *AND* has contact with other family members in area
2 Lives with family, *OR*, has contact with family in the Bay Area
1 Lives with a nonfamily person

EMPLOYMENT
3 Present job one year or more
2 Present job 3 months, *OR* present and prior job 6 months
1 Current job, *OR* intermittent work for 1 year
1 Receiving unemployment compensation or welfare
1 Supported by family, or savings

PRIOR RECORD (within the last 15 years)
2 No convictions
1 One misdemeanor conviction
0 Two misdemeanor convictions, *OR* one felony conviction
-1 Three or more misdemeanor convictions, *OR* two or more felony convictions
-2 Four or more misdemeanor convictions, *OR* three or more felony convictions

Appendix E: Variation in Bail and its Reform: A National View

After concluding an examination of how seventy-two cities administer their respective pretrial release systems, one is forced to confront a pair of very difficult questions. Is there a recognizable pattern of variation in the operation of these bail systems? If variation does exist, what individual or group of variables may explain these differences? The first question can be answered with a weakly affirmative answer. This survey has uncovered a plethora of procedures and styles utilized in administering a city's bail system. However, despite the variety in institutional and operational variables, the actual outputs of these systems such as ROR, forfeiture, and rearrest rates, are not experiencing a very high degree of variation.

An example of this phenomena of varying procedures and similar outlets can be seen through a comparison of the Indianapolis and Washington bail systems. Both cities reported that 11 percent of their defendants released prior to trial committed additional crimes, yet their bail systems utilize completely different methods of release and are staffed by judges of differing attitudes. An additionally confusing factor is that cities may be very similar for one category of output but then be divergent for another type of output variable. An illustration of this point is discovered when comparing Washington and Detroit. Both cities have a release rate of approximately 66 percent, however, Detroit is maintaining a forfeiture rate six times that of the District. It was also found that frequently the outputs of each city's system were inconsistent within themselves; for instance, a city like Chicago, having a low detention rate, was plagued at the same time by an above average forfeiture rate. The main problem is that it is impossible to treat a city's pretrial release system as a cohesive unit functioning with a consistent set of outputs and procedures.

Table E-1 illustrates the variation in outputs from the nation's bail systems. The large majority of cities experienced very similar rates of defendant's misconduct. The forfeiture rates were around 3 percent while approximately 7 percent of the released defendants were committing additional crimes. A greater degree of fluctuation was found in the ROR and detention rates, although these statistics also failed to achieve the desired degree of variance to satisfy statistical tests.

Turning to the second question of how can one explain the moderate amount of variation found between bail systems, two sets of variables are

Table E-1
Statistical Summary of Administration of Bail in Seventy-Two City Survey

% of total Defendants	Inter-viewed for ROR	Recc'd for ROR	ROR'd	Used Bonds-men	Detained	Rearrested		Forfeited	
						1. ROR'd	2. Money Bail	1. ROR'd	2. Money Bail
0-9%	55% (40)	55% (40)	34% (25)	6% (4)	36% (26)	79% (57)	66% (48)	87% (63)	80% (58)
10-19%	3% (2)	11% (8)	18% (13)	4% (3)	39% (28)	13% (9)	18% (13)	11% (8)	13% (9)
20-29%	1% (1)	10% (7)	13% (9)	7% (5)	14% (10)	6% (4)	6% (4)	1% (1)	4% (3)
30-39%	10% (7)	6% (4)	10% (7)	14% (10)	7% (5)	3% (2)	7% (5)	–	3% (2)
40-49%	3% (2)	6% (4)	11% (8)	26% (19)	1% (1)	–	3% (2)	–	–
50-59%	4% (3)	4% (3)	9% (6)	17% (12)	3% (2)	–	–	–	–
60-69%	4% (3)	3% (2)	1% (1)	7% (5)	–	–	–	–	–
70-79%	3% (2)	1% (1)	1% (1)	6% (4)	–	–	–	–	–
80-89%	3% (2)	3% (2)	1% (1)	10% (7)	–	–	–	–	–
90-99%	14% (14)	1% (1)	–	4% (3)	–	–	–	–	–
National Average for 72 Cities	28%	19%	21%	40%	16%	6.4%	8.2%	2.8%	3%

Number of Percentage of Cities in Each Category

Table E-2
Successful Bail Systems and Demographic Characteristics

Demographic Characteristics	Forfeiture Rate			ROR Rate		
	Mult. Corr.	R^2	F Level	Mult. Corr.	R^2	F Level
1. Population	0.143	0.021	1.5	0.241	0.058	3.8
2. Nonwhites	0.058	0.003	1.4	0.078	0.006	1.2
3. Median Income	0.033	0.001	1.1	0.016	0.001	0.3
4. Poverty Level	0.018	0.001	1.0	0.009	0.001	0.3
5. Crime Rate	0.017	0.001	0.7	0.003	0.001	0.2
Total	0.269			0.347		

most applicable: demographic and sociopolitical. Examining the demographic variables first, Table E-2 analyzes their effect on the administration of bail. The following demographic variables were thought to exert some influence upon the operation of a bail system: city size, nonwhite population, poverty level, crime rate, and median income.

In applying regression analysis to the study of the seventy-two bail systems surveyed, it was discovered that only one of these demographic variables was able to exert a significant influence. Taken as a group, the size of the city was clearly found to be the most important, although even it failed to achieve a significant level. The conclusion to be drawn from this data is that the problems of bail are national in scope, affecting cities of all types, with the larger cities experiencing a disproportional number of pretrial problems such as forfeitures and additional crimes.

If demographic characteristic offer so little help in identifying the moderate amount of variation between bail systems, can political and social variables provide any clearer explanation? The only variables falling under this general rubric, which appear to affect the operation of a bail system were the following which were discussed in detail in Chapter 2: political linkages of the judiciary, community activism, and the news media. All three variables exert primarily a negative effect. In other words, cities with very politically oriented judges such as Pittsburgh, operate a very ineffective bail system. Also cities where the community is apathetic, as in Detroit, or the newspapers espouse a tough law and order editorial policy, operate similarly ineffective bail systems with high forfeiture rates and low release rates.

Notes

Chapter 1
An Introduction to the American Bail System

1. "1970 National Jail Census" (Washington, D.C.: U.S. Department of Justice, 1970), p. 2.
2. This exception is Washington, D.C. whose new Court Reform Act of 1970 had added an additional purpose which will be discussed in detail in the second section of this chapter.
3. This is a nearly exact restatement of the Rule 46 (c) of the Federal Rules of Criminal Procedure which indicates to the federal judiciary the purpose of bail as well as criteria to be used in setting this amount.
4. It is presently unclear as to what effect the recent Supreme Court decision declaring the death penalty unconstitutional will have on the bail-setting procedures.
5. Georgia Code Title 29, Chapter 9.
6. *Report of the Governor's Commission on Crime and Justice,* Atlanta, Georgia, 1968, p. 103.
7. Federal Rules of Criminal Procedure, 46(c).
8. Michigan Statutes Annotated, #28.892-28.893, 1954.
9. California Penal Code Section 1275 and Illinois Code of Criminal Procedure 110-5 (1964).
10. District of Columbia Court Reform Act of 1970, Public Law 91-358, July 29, 1970, Section 23-1321.
11. For complete analysis, see Paul B. Wice, "Bail Reform in American Cities," *Criminal Law Bulletin* (November 1973), p. 787.
12. District of Columbia Court Reform Act of 1970, Section 23-1322, p. 172.
13. *Ibid.,* p. 173.
14. *Ibid.,* p. 174.
15. Nan C. Bess and William F. McDonald, *Preventive Detention in the District of Columbia: The First Ten Months* (Washington, D.C.: Georgetown Institute of Criminal Law and Procedure, March 1972), p. 69.
16. A confidential interview with a San Francisco defense attorney, August 1970.
17. Arthur Beeley, *The Bail System in Chicago* (Chicago: The University of Chicago Press, 1966), p. 160.
18. They will consciously attempt to charge the defendant with the most serious crime which they believe he might have committed, regardless of knowledge and evidence that a lesser charge would be fairer and more realistic.

19. Confidential interview with an Alameda County Criminal Court Judge, Berkeley, California, August 1970.

20. Donald McIntyre, ed., *Law Enforcement on the Metropolis* (Chicago: American Bar Foundation, 1967), p. 121.

21. Stephen Franklin. "Public Defender Plan Bogged Down in County," *Pittsburgh Post Gazette*, October 2, 1972, p. 6.

22. Rule 749 Bail Bonds, Rules of the Supreme Bench of Baltimore City, November 28, 1969.

23. Confidential interviews in the St. Louis Circuit Court, Criminal Division, Clerks Office, February 1971.

24. Confidential interviews with Atlanta, Georgia bail bondsmen, January 1971.

25. Confidential interviews with Baltimore bail bondsmen, December 1970.

26. Report of the Judicial Council Committee to *Study the Operation of the Bail Reform Act in the District of Columbia*, District of Columbia Circuit, May 1970, p. 15.

27. *Ibid.*

28. It was decided to concentrate on the larger cities with populations exceeding 500,000 because the problems of pretrial release were most severe in these types of communities. Also, the majority of the reform measures have been initiated in cities of this size.

29. Observed in Atlanta Georgia Municipal Court, Commitment Hearings, January 1971.

30. Confidential interview with defense attorney, San Francisco, California, September 1970.

31. Report of the District's Judicial Committee, p. 22.

32. National Bureau of Standards, *Crimes Committed While Awaiting Trial* (Washington, D.C.), p. 161.

33. Alan Davis, "Sexual Assaults in the Philadelphia Prison System and Sheriff's Vans," *Trans-Action* (December 1968), p. 8.

34. *Chicago Crime Commission Annual Report*, 1968.

Chapter 2
The Administration of Bail: The Procedures

1. *Mallory* v. *U.S.* 354 U.S. 449 (1957).

2. Donald McIntyre, ed., *Law Enforcement in the Metropolis* (Chicago: American Bar Foundation, 1968), pp. 81–83.

3. Interview with Myzell Sowell, Defenders Association, Detroit, Michigan, November 1970.

4. Morris Wexler, "A Dialogue on Bail," *Chicago Bar Record*, p. 191.

5. John S. Boyle, "Bail Under the Judicial Article," *De Paul Law Review* 17 (Winter 1968) 267.

6. Lee Silverstein. "Bail in the State Courts—A Field Study and Report," *Minnesota Law Review* 50 (1966) 621.

7. By examining the demographic characteristics of these cities, it was found that larger cities with above average nonwhite populations are the strongest supporters of this criterion. A tentative explanation for this finding is that since the nation's largest cities, who also happen to possess the largest percentages of nonwhites, are experiencing the greatest crime rate increases, any defendant attempting to gain his pretrial release must stress neither the present charge nor past criminal history but something less volatile such as the fact that his past criminal record while awaiting trial is unblemished.

8. President's Commission on Law Enforcement and the Administration of Justice, *Challenge of Crime in a Free Society* (New York: Avon, 1968), p. 319.

9. Confidential interview with judge of the Circuit Court of the City of St. Louis, February 1971.

10. Illinois Criminal Code Court Rules; cited in the Boyle article.

11. Cook County Special Bail Project Report of February 10, 1970 (Mimeographed).

12. *Ibid*.

13. Interview with Warren Wolfson, defense attorney, Chicago, Illinois, February 1971.

14. Interview with members of the Atlanta District Attorney's Office, January 1971.

15. 36th Annual Report of the Defender Association of Philadelphia, 1969–70, p. 10.

16. Interview with Judge Davis, Indianapolis Criminal Court System, November 1970.

17. Interview with Greg Stout, San Francisco attorney, August 1970.

18. Interview with Deputy Public Defender, Chicago, Illinois, October 1970.

19. Interview with Judge Spaeth of the Court of Common Pleas, Philadelphia, December 1970.

20. The San Francisco Committee on Crime, *A Report on the Criminal Court of San Francisco* Part II, San Francisco, February 13, 1970, p. 13.

21. Interview with Charles Work, U.S. Attorney, Court of General Sessions, Washington, D.C., December 1970.

22. One can plainly see the problem of delay as mainly a concern for defendants charged with felonies. Misdemeanors were usually disposed of at either the first court appearance or in a matter of a few weeks. The bail set was also of such a small amount as to permit nearly all defendants to gain their pretrial release. Judges frequently are more prone to grant personal bonds for misdemeanants than felons so often even indigent defendants could obtain their temporary freedom. Unfortunately the author was unable to collect data which could illustrate the difference in length of delay between defendants detained in jail and those who gained their pretrial release. The record keeping of urban court systems is simply not up to this task.

23. Interview with Martin Vinikoor, District Attorney's Office, Philadelphia, December 1970.

24. File memorandum, Pennsylvania Prison Society, June 8, 1970.

Chapter 3
Nonjudicial Actors

1. Marshall Patner, "Memo: Bail in Chicago, the Police Run It," 1969 (Mimeographed).
2. Ibid.
3. Defender Association of Philadelphia, 36th Annual Report, for the year July 1, 1969 to June 30, 1970, p. 18.
4. *Chicago Crime Commission Annual Report*, 1968.
5. Interview with Judge Moylan, former state's attorney, Baltimore, Maryland, December 1970.
6. Confidential interview with public defender, Oakland, California, September, 1970.
7. Interview with Paul Michel, assistant district attorney, Philadelphia, Pennsylvania, December 1970.
8. Paul B. Wice, "Bail Reform in American Cities," *Criminal Law Bulletin* (November 1973), p. 775.
9. Donald McIntyre, ed., *Law Enforcement in the Metropolis* (Chicago: American Bar Foundation, 1968), p. 120.
10. Frederick Suffet. "Bail Setting: A Study of Courtroom Interaction," *Crime and Delinquency* (October 1966), pp. 318–31.
11. Information on the Philadelphia District Attorney's Office was gained from interviews with four members of their staff in addition to a week of observing their operation.
12. Confidential interviews with attorneys in Indianapolis, November 1970 and Atlanta, January 1971.
13. David Sudnow's excellent article on "Normal Crimes: Sociological Features of the Penal Code in a Public Defenders Office," *Social Problems*, 12:255, offers an excellent analysis of the operation of this public defense in its nonadversarial form.
14. Interview with Al Freeman, Indianapolis, November 1970.
15. Fred Barnes, "The Professional Bondsman: Life Isn't What it used to be," Sunday Magazine, *Washington Star*, August 17, 1969.
16. Interview with Hank Edwards, Atlanta, January 1971.
17. In addition to racial breakdown, the bondsmen seemed to be disproportionately represented by Jews with four having Jewish appearing last names The bondsmen were generally over forty with only three less than thirty-eight.
18. "Bail Bondsman Wears Hotpants to Florida Job," *Washington* (Pa.) *Observer Reporter* October 18, 1972, p. 1.
19. *Indianapolis Star*, February 19, 1971, p. 25.
20. Interview with Al Freeman, Indianapolis, November 1970.
21. Interview with Glenn Zell, Atlanta attorney, January 1971.
22. Interview with Irving Richert, research director, San Francisco Crime Commission, September 1970.
23. *Washington Star*, August 17, 1969.
24. *Washington Post*, February 2, 1969.
25. Confidential interview with Detroit, Michigan bondsman, November 1970.

26. *Washington Star*, August 17, 1969.
27. This figure is based on the results of the author's seventy-two city national survey as well as statements presented in the 1965 National Conference on Bail.
28. "California Bail System," *California Law Review* 66 (August 1968) 1134.
29. Ibid. Copyright ©, 1968, California Law Review, Inc. Reprinted by permission.
30. *Atlanta Constitution-Journal*, March 1, 1970.
31. Interview with Glenn Zell, Atlanta attorney, January 1970.
32. *Washington Post*, February 2, 1970.
33. *Washington Star*, August 17, 1969.
34. St. Louis Record's Clerk Office, Court of Criminal Causes.
35. Interview with Al Freeman, Indianapolis, November 1970.
36. *Indianapolis Star*, October 16, 1970 and December 8, 1970.
37. *Indianapolis Star*, July 2, 1970.
38. Interview with Judge Moylan, Baltimore, December 1970.
39. Confidential interview with St. Louis attorney, February 1971.
40. Interview with Al Freeman, Indianapolis, November 1970.
41. Interview with Vincent Ziccardi, Philadelphia Defenders Association, December 1970.

Chapter 4
Pretrial Misconduct: Forfeiture and Additional Crimes

1. Interview with Paul Michel, Philadelphia District Attorney's Office, December 1970.
2. Interview with Judge Tim Murphy of the Court of General Sessions, Washington, D.C., December 1970.
3. Cook County Special Bail Project "Proposal for Holiday Court Inter-viewer—Verification Program," May 4, 1971, p. 7.
4. Interview with Public Defender Hooley, Oakland, California, August 1970.
5. Interview with Judge Davis of the Indianapolis Criminal Courts, November 1970.
6. Norman Lefstein, "Analysis of Metropolitan Police Department's Study Concerning Crime on Bail," January 22, 1969. Preventive Detention Hearings before the Constitutional Rights Subcommittee of U.S. Senate Committee on the Judiciary.
7. United States Department of Commerce, National Bureau of Standards Report, "Compilation and Use of Criminal Court Data in Relation to Pretrial Release of Defendants," Washington, D.C., March 1970, p. 161.
8. Indianapolis Bail Project Report, "Rate of Crime on Bail," January-February 1970, (mimeographed).
9. "Preventive Detention: An Empirical Analysis" *Harvard Civil Rights Law Review* 6 (March 1971) 291.
10. Confidential interview with Detroit bondsman, November 1970.

11.   Information obtained through interviews with men in each city, September 1970–February 1971.
12.   N.H. Cogan, "Pennsylvania Bail Provisions: The Legality of Preventive Detention." *Temple Law Quarterly* 44 (Fall, 1970):51.

Chapter 5
Pretrial Detention Facilities

1.   Daniel Freed and Patricia Wald, *Bail in the U.S.: 1964* (Washington, D.C., Government Printing Office, 1964), p. 39.
2.   Interview with the Pennsylvania Prison Society, Philadelphia, December 1970.
3.   The author found the most abhorrent conditions existing in the central police district cells of Baltimore City. These filthy two-man cells seem to be copied from the torture chambers of a medieval castle. They were damp, dark, and crowded with the constant smell of urine, sweat, and vomit permeating the air.
4.   Confidential interview with members of Sheriff's Department, Fulton County Jail, Atlanta, Georgia, January 1971.
5.   Indianapolis Bail Project Jail Inventory, Final Report, December 14, 1967, mimeographed.
6.   Interview with Pennsylvania Prison Society, Philadelphia, December 1970.
7.   Interview with Charles Mann, St. Louis, February 1971, former chairman of the Technical Advisory Committee of the Government's Citizens Committee on Delinquency of Crime, and the author of the section of the committee's report on the jails of Missouri.
8.   Report of the President's Commission on Crime in the District of Columbia, 1966, GPO, p. 423.
9.   San Francisco Committee on Crime, *A Report on the San Francisco County Jails and City Prison*, August 1969, p. 36.
10.   Commonwealth of Pennsylvania ex. rel. Cephus Bryant v. Edward J. Hendrick, Court of Common Pleas for Philadelphia County, Criminal Trial Division, Sessions 1970, No. 1567, pp. 5–7.
11.   The President's Committee on Law Enforcement and Administration of Justice, Task Force Report on Corrections, 1968, p. 24.
12.   Commonwealth of Pennsylvania, ex. rel. Bryant vs. Hendricks, p. 15.
13.   San Francisco Committee on Crime: Report on Jails, pp. 9–10.
14.   Ibid., pp. 9–13.
15.   Report of President's Committee on Crime in the D.C., p. 423.
16.   Ronald Lee Lang v. Robinson, Testimony of Leroy Cathran.
17.   Task Force Report: Corrections, p. 25.
18.   Cephus Bryant v. Hendricks, p. 21.
19.   Ronald Lee Lang v. Robinson.
20.   Caleb Foote, "Philadelphia Bail Study," *University of Pennsylvania Legal Review* (1954): 1051–52.
21.   Freed and Wald, *Bail in the U.S.*, p. 46.

22. Interview with judge in the Fulton County Superior Court, Atlanta, Georgia, January, 1970.

23. San Francisco Committee on Crime, p. 5.

24. Ibid., p. 49.

25. News item in the *Pittsburgh Post Gazette*, October 17, 1972.

26. Cephus Bryant, p. 10.

27. News item from the *New York Times*, October 25, 1971.

28. *Task Force Report: Corrections*, p. 25.

Chapter 6
Introduction to Bail Reform

1. Paul Wice, "Bail Reform in American Cities," *Criminal Law Bulletin* (November 1973), p. 780.

2. President's Commission on Law Enforcement and Administration of Justice, *Task Force Report: The Courts*, Washington, D.C., 1967, p. 33.

3. San Francisco Committee on Crime. *A Report on the Criminal Courts of San Francisco Part II Bail and OR Release*, February 10, 1971, p. 24.

4. *Pannell* v. *United States* 320 F.2d 693 (D.C. Circ.) 1963.

5. Chapter 3 has presented a complete analysis of these collusive activities.

6. Office of Economic Opportunity, "Roster of Pretrial Release Projects," October 30, 1972, mimeographed.

7. Wayne Thomas, "The Current State of Bail Reform: Bail Projects," Center on Administration of Criminal Justice, School of Law, University of California, Davis, mimeographed p. 7.

8. The definition of this term varies a great deal from court system to court system, but it generally means either those defendants who are unable to post bail or unable to hire a lawyer.

9. "Beyond the Bail System: A Proposal for Reform" 57 *California Law Review* (November 1968): 1112. Copyright © 1968, California Law Review, Inc. Reprinted by permission.

10. Most states by statute have denied pretrial release to any defendant accused of a capital offense, so we are actually speaking of crimes ranging from armed robbery downward in seriousness.

11. *Report of the Judicial Council Committee to Study the Operation of the Bail Reform Act in the District of Columbia*. District of Columbia Circuit Court, May 1970, p. 21.

12. Interview with Kenneth Babb, director of San Francisco Bail Project, September 1970.

13. Charlot Holzkamper, "Own Recognizance" *Intercom* (Winter Issue, 1969): p. 3.

14. Peter Bachrach and Morton Baratz, *Power and Poverty* (New York: Oxford University Press, 1970), p. 44.

15. They are required by Judge Boyle to interview any defendant who would like to be interviewed for possible ROR.

16. Information gathered from interviews with concerned public officials and concerned citizen groups such as the Cook County Special Bail Project. See Appendix C for listing.

17. President's Commission on Law Enforcement and Administration of Justice, p. 41.
18. Ibid.
19. Report of the District of Columbia Bail Agency for the Period of January 1, 1969 to December 31, 1969, mimeographed.
20. Project Crossroads, Report for October 1970. Washington, D.C., p. 7.
21. Ibid. p. 12.
22. Ibid. p. 14.
23. Report of the Judicial Council Committee to Study the Operation of the Bail Reform Act in the District of Columbia, p. 15.
24. Daniel Freed and Patricia Wald, *Bail in the U.S.: 1964*, Washington, D.C. 1964, p. 77.
25. Interview with H.Y. Duplessis, probation officer, Detroit, November 1970.
26. Stephen Franklin and Paul Wice, "Some Thoughts on Bail Bond Reform" *Pittsburgh Renaissance* (March 1973), p. 22.
27. Interview with Warren Wolfson, attorney, Chicago, March 1971.

Chapter 7
The Institutions and Procedures of Bail Reform

1. Wayne Thomas, *The Current State of Bail Reform: Bail Projects*, (University of California, Davis: Center on Administration of Criminal Justice, 1971), p. 7.
2. The FBI lists seven serious crimes as comprising the crime index. These seven crimes are almost always considered felonies in all jurisdictions. Examples of these seven crimes are murder, manslaughter, auto theft, larceny over $50, armed robbery, burglary, and rape.
3. Federal Bureau of Investigation, *Uniform Crime Reports 1969* Washington, D.C., 1969, p. 41.
4. This study has operationally defined effectiveness as the ability of a project to release as many defendants as possible on their own recognizance, while at the same time maintaining a forfeiture rate below the national average.
5. Interview with Edmund DePaul, former director of the Philadelphia Bail Project, December 1970.
6. These past two paragraphs are laden with generalities which contain many exceptions. This analysis should not leave the reader with the mistaken belief that only law students and VISTA volunteers can operate an effective project. There are many capable court staff investigators doing an excellent job. More important, it is not the general source of the staff but rather the caliber of the individual investigator that is crucial. It will also be shown in later sections of this chapter that operational and procedural variables are even more important in explaining how to organize an effective bail project.
7. San Francisco Committee on Crime, *A Report on the Criminal Court of San Francisco Part II Bail and OR Release*, February 10, 1971, p. 16.

8. Interview with members of the Cook County Bail Project, Chicago, March 1971.

9. The Philadelphia project, under the direction of Edmund DePaul and funded by the city's bar association, experienced a brief two-and-one-half-year life span due to the city's unwillingness to assume its obligation once the private funding terminated in 1967.

10. Charlot Holzkamper, "Own Recognizance," *Intercom* (Winter Issue, 1969), p. 7.

11. San Francisco Committee on Crime, p. 19.

12. Holzkamper, "Own Recognizance," p.4.

13. Thomas, *Current State of Bail Reform*, p. 25.

14. Interview with Jim Droege, director of Indianapolis Bail Project, November 1970.

15. Interview with director of the Atlanta Bail Reform Project, Fulton County Jail, January 1971.

16. This chapter has discussed the narrowing of a bail project's jurisdiction in terms of the exclusion of certain offenses, but this is not the only criteria for disqualification, though it is by far the most commonly used. Before leaving this topic, it is necessary to note two additional rationales for disqualification which are occasionally used: (1) automatic disqualification of defendants with a history of drug use or severe emotional instability, and (2) automatic disqualification of defendants with felony convictions. Most projects simply score their point sheets in such a manner as to exclude these undesirables through failure to achieve the necessary points rather than systematically excluding them from the entire operation.

17. Holzkamper, "Own Recognizance," p. 5.

18. *Report of the Judicial Council Committee to Study the Operation of the Bail Reform Act in the District of Columbia*, District of Columbia Circuit Court, May 1970, p. 21.

19. Thirty of these thirty-two cities were listed by the OEO's Pretrial Release Program Directory as presently operating a bail reform project.

20. It is believed that this reluctance to comment on this question is simply because the city in question does not release more than a handful of defendants on their own recognizance and has been following this policy for many years. Therefore the question is virtually irrelevant to the functioning of their city's bail system.

21. What is particularly upsetting to advocates of bail reform is that the large majority of defendants ROR'd are accused of the least serious crimes. This results in the neglect of those defendants who have the greatest to lose by their denial of pretrial freedom because of the lengthy backlog to try felony cases.

Chapter 8
Bail Reform: Conclusion and Prognostications

1. Traditional cities are simply defined as any jurisdiction which is not presently operating a bail reform project.

2. The exact formula for determining the effectiveness rating is two times the percentage of defendants which the project ROR's minus the forfeiture and additional crime rate.

3. It should be remembered that as these various groups and institutions are evaluated as to their possible influence on the bail reform movement, they are not acting in a vacuum but rather may interact among themselves, creating additional influences.

4. Interview with Richard Motsay, director of the Baltimore Bail Reform Agency, December 1970.

5. One might wonder about the presence of right-wing and conservative organizations opposing the work of the bail projects. Despite the great public concern over law and order, this has not manifested itself in the form of any organized efforts to oppose bail reform projects that are releasing defendants back on the streets.

6. "Draft Proposal: Holiday Court Verification Program," Cook County Special Bail Project, February 1970, p. 1. Mimeographed.

7. Charlot Holzkamper, "Own Recognizance," *Intercom* (Winter Issue, 1969), p. 3.

8. "The Public: A Hard Line," *Newsweek*, March 8, 1971, p. 39.

9. San Francisco Committee on Crime, "A Report on the Criminal Court of San Francisco, Part II; Bail and OR Release" February 10, 1971, p. 25.

Chapter 9
Conclusions

1. *Newsweek*, March 8, 1971, p. 29. Copyright Newsweek, Inc. 1971, reprinted by permission.

2. David Sudonow, "Normal Crimes: Socio Economic Features of the Penal Code in a Public Defender Office" *Social Problems*, 12, no. 3, (1965), p. 261.

3. *Stack* v. *Boyle* 342 U.S. 1 (1925).

4. C. Herman Pritchett, *The American Constitution* (New York: MacGraw Hill, 1968), p. 642.

5. Daniel Freed and Patricia Wald, *Bail in the United States: 1964* (Washington, D.C.: Government Printing Office, 1964), pp 76–77.

6. Confidential interview with member of Oakland, California Public Defender Office, August 1970.

7. Public Law 91–358, July 29, 1970, Sec. 23–1322, District of Columbia Court Reform Act.

8. See Chapter 1 for a detailed explanation of preventive detention in the District of Columbia.

9. *New York Times*, November 11, 1969, p. 41.

10. Norval Morris and Gordon Hawkins, *The Honest Politicians Guide to Crime Control*, Chicago: Univ. of Chicago Press, 1970.

11. Wayne LaFave, "Alternatives to the Present System of Bail," *Illinois Law Forum*, vol. 1965, Spring, p. 19.

Bibliography

Books

Bachrach, Peter, and Baratz, Morton. *Power and Poverty*. New York: Oxford University Press, 1970.

Beeley, Arthur L. *The Bail System in Chicago*. Chicago: University of Chicago Press, 1966.

Blumberg, Abraham. *Criminal Justice*. Chicago: Quadrangle, 1967.

Federal Bureau of Investigation. *Uniform Crime Reports*. Washington: Government Printing Office, 1968.

Freed, Daniel, and Wald, Patricia. *Bail in the United States: 1964*. Washington: Government Printing Office, 1964.

Friedland, Martin. *Detention Before Trial*. Toronto: University of Toronto Press, 1965.

Goldfarb, Ronald. *Ransom*. New York: John Wiley, 1965.

Jacob, Herbert. *Justice in America*. Boston: Little, Brown and Co., 1965.

McIntire, Donald M. (ed.) *Law Enforcement in the Metropolis*. Chicago: American Bar Foundation, 1968.

Oaks, Dallen H., and Lehman, Warren. *A Criminal Justice System and the Indigent*. Chicago: University of Chicago Press, 1968.

President's Commission on Law Enforcement and Administration of Justice. *Challenge of Crime in a Free Society*. New York: Avon Books, 1968.

———. Task Force Report: *Corrections*. Washington; Government Printing Office, 1968.

———. Task Force Report: *The Courts*. Washington: Government Printing Office, 1967.

Quinney, Richard. *The Social Reality of Crime*. Boston: Little, Brown, and Co., 1970.

United States Bureau of the Census. *United States City and County Data Book, 1967*. Washington: Government Printing Office, 1967.

Periodicals

Ares, Charles, et al. "The Manhattan Bail Projects: An Interim Report on the Use of Pre-Trial Parole." *New York University Law Review* 37 (1963): 67–95.

Barnes, Fred. "The Professional Bondsman: Life Isn't What It Used to Be." *The Washington Star Sunday Magazine* (August 17, 1969), p. 8.

"Beyond the Bail System: A Proposal for Reform." *California Law Review* 57 (November 1968): 1112.

Boyle, John. "Bail Under the Judicial Article." *DePaul Law Review* 17 (Winter 1968): 267.

"California Bail System," *California Law Review.* 36 (August 1968): 1134.

"Crime and Punishment in America." *The Center Magazine* 3 (May/June 1971): 6.

Foote, Caleb. "Compelling Appearance in Court: Administration of Bail in Philadelphia." *University of Pennsylvania Law Review* 102 (June 1954): 1031.

Holzhamper, Charlot. "Own Recognizance." *Intercom* (Winter 1969). p. 3

Kamin, Alfred. "Bail Administration in Illinois." *Illinois Bar Journal,* 53 (April 1965): 674–686.

LaFave, Wayne. "Alternatives to the Present System of Bail." *Illinois Law Forum* 1965 (Spring): 19.

McCarthy, David, and Wahl, Jeanne. "The District of Columbia Bail Project: An Illustration of Experimentation and a Brief for Change." *Georgetown Law Journal* 53 (Spring 1965): 675.

Nagel, Stuart. "Disparities in Criminal Procedure." *UCLA Law Review* 14 (August 1969): 1272.

"The Public: A Hard Line." *Newsweek* (March 8, 1971), p. 39.

Silverstein, Lee. "Bail in the State Courts—A Field Study and Report." *Minnesota Law Review* 50 (1966): 621–652.

Sudnow, David. "Normal Crimes: Sociological Features of the Penal Code in a Public Defenders Office." *Social Problems* 12 (1964): 250.

Suffet, Frederick. "Bail Setting: A Study of Courtroom Interaction." *Crime and Delinquency* (October 1966): 318–331.

Wexler, Morris. "A Dialogue on Bail," *Chicago Bar Record,* 189–94.

Wice, Paul B. "Bail Reform in American Cities." *Criminal Law Bulletin* (November 1973): 770-797.

Wice, Paul. B., and Franklin, Stephen." Some Thoughts on Bail Bond Reform." *Pittsburgh Renaissance* (March 1973): 22.

Wice, Paul B., and Simon, Rita James. "Pretrial Release: A Survey of Alternatives." *Federal Probation* (December 1970): 60.

Newspapers

Atlanta Constitution-Journal, March, 1970.

Chicago Today, July 16, 1970.

Indianapolis Star, July 2, 1970; October 16, 1970; December 8, 1970; February 19, 1971.

New York Times, October 25, 1971; March 2, 1971; September 27, 1971.

Washington Post, February 2, 1969.

Public Documents and Reports

American Friends Service Committee. "Awaiting Trial in the Allegheny County Jail." Pittsburgh, November, 1971. (Mimeographed.)

Bail and Summons: 1965. Institute on the Operation of Pretrial Release Projects. New York, August 1966.

Bail Commission Annual Report. Judicial Department of the State of Connecticut. (Mimeographed)

Chicago Crime Commission, *Annual Report,* 1968.

"Compilation and Use of Criminal Court Data in Relation to Pretrial Release of Defendants," National Bureau of Standards, United States Department of Commerce, Report 10181, Washington, March 1970.

Cook County Special Bail Project Report of February 10, 1970. (Mimeographed.)

Defenders Association of Philadelphia. *36th Annual Report.* Philadelphia, 1969–1970.

DePaul, Edmund E. "Progress Report, February 9, 1966, to September 8, 1967." Bail Project of the Philadelphia Bar Foundation, 1968. (Mimeographed).

Des Moines Pre-Trial Release Project. Report for 1964–1969.

Detroit Recorder's Court. *Annual Report, 1969.*

District of Columbia Bail Agency. "First Annual Report for Period Ending May 31, 1967." (Mimeographed.)

———. "Report for Period January 1, 1969–December 31, 1969. (Mimeographed.)

———. "Second Annual Report of Period Ending May 31, 1968." (Mimeographed.)

———. "Third Annual Report, Period of June 1, 1968, through May 31, 1969." (Mimeographed.)

"Draft Proposal: Holiday Court Verification Program." Chicago: Cook County Special Bail Project, 1970. (Mimeographed.)

Gibson, Evelyn. "Time Spent Awaiting Trial." *Home Office Studies in the Causes of Delinquency and the Treatment of Offenders.* London: Her Majesty's Stationery Office, 1960.

Indianapolis Bail Project. *Jail Inventory: Final Report.* Indianapolis, December 14, 1967. (Mimeographed.)

———. "Rate of Crime on Bail." January 1970. (Mimeographed.)

———. *Proposed Indiana Bail Reform Act.* Indianapolis, 1971. (Mimeographed.)

Lefstein, Norman. "Analysis of Metropolitan Police Department's Study. Concerning Crime on Bail." Preventive Detention Hearings Before Subcommittee on Constitutional Rights of the United States Senate Committee on the Judiciary on January 22, 1969. Washington: Government Printing Office, March 1970.

National Conference on Bail and Criminal Justice. *Proceedings and Interim Report.* Washington, April 1965.

Office of the Director, St. Louis County Correctional Institutions. "Summary Report of Activities for 1970."

Patner, Marshall. "Memo: Bail in Chicago, The Police Run It." Chicago:
    Businessmen for the Public Interest, 1969. (Mimeographed.)
    . "Memorandum on Bail in Chicago." Chicago: Businessmen for the
    Public Interest, 1970. (Mimeographed.)
Pennsylvania Prison Society. "File Memorandum: Jail Inventory at Holmesburg
    Prison." June 8, 1970.
"Project Crossroads," National Committee for Children and Youth. Wash-
    ington, D.C. October 1970. (Mimeographed.)
"Proposal to Establish a Permanent Pretrial Release Program in San Francisco,"
    Committee on the Administration of Criminal Justice, San Francisco,
    1969.
Report and Evaluation on the Bail Procedures in Chicago's Looting Cases,
    Illinois Division, ACLU, Chicago, 1967. (Mimeographed.)
Report of the Governor's Citizens Committee on Delinquency and Crime,
    Jefferson City, Missouri, December 1968.
Report of the Judicial Council Committee to Study the Operation of the Bail
    Reform Act in the District of Columbia. Washington: District of
    Columbia Circuit Court, May 1970.
Report of the President's Commission on Crime in the District of Columbia.
    Washington: Government Printing Office, 1966.
"Report of Recommendations in the Prerelease Program." Submitted to the
    St. Louis Commission on Crime and Law Enforcement, May 21, 1970.
    (Mimeographed.)
San Francisco Committee on Crime. A Report on the Criminal Court of San
    Francisco, Part II: Bail and OR Release. San Francisco, February 10,
    1971.
    . A Report on the San Francisco County Jails and City Prison. San
    Francisco, August 1969.
Second Annual Report of Pre-Trial Release Division. Baltimore, December
    1970. (Mimeographed.)
"Tentative Draft Proposal: Bail Reform Project." Chicago Council of
    Lawyers, Criminal Justice Committee, 1970. (Mimeographed.)
Thomas, Wayne. "The Current State of Bail Reform: Bail Projects."
    Davis, California: Center on the Administration Justice, 1970.
U.S. Congress, Senate, Committee on the Judiciary. Amendments to the Bail
    Reform Act of 1966. Hearings before the Subcommittee on Constitu-
    tional Rights, 91st Cong., 1st sess. January 21–30, February 4, 1969.
    . Preventive Detention. Hearings before Subcommittee on Constitu-
    tional Rights. 91st Cong., 1st sess., May 20, 21, 22, 27, and June 9, 11,
    17, 18, 19, 1970.
Whitney, Larry G. "Surety Bond Forfeiture Rate in Indianapolis for 1969."
    Indianapolis Bail Project, 1970. (Mimeographed.)
"Youth Awaiting Trial: A Report on Detention and Bail Practices in Baltimore,"
    Baltimore Criminal Justice Commission. March 15, 1963. (Mimeographed.)

Judicial Decisions and State Statutes

California Penal Code, Section 1271.

Commonwealth of Pennsylvania ex rel. Cephas Bryant v. *Edward J. Hendrick*,
Court of Common Pleas for Philadelphia County, Criminal Trial Division,
Session 1970, No. 1567.

Commonwealth of Pennsylvania ex rel. Isaac Hartage v. *Edward Hendrick.*
Supreme Court of Pennsylvania, No. 79, Misc. Docket No. 18, July 31,
1970.

Dash et al., v. *Mitchell et al.,* Motion for Convening of a Three-Judge Court.
Civil Action 3713, 1970, United States District Court for the District of
Columbia.

District of Columbia Court Reform Act of 1970, Public Law 91-358, Section
23-1321.

Georgia Code, Title 29, Chapter 9.

Michigan Statutes Annotated. Numbers 28.892-93. (1954).

Pannell v. *United States.* 320 F.2d. 693 (D.C. Circ.) 1963.

Pennsylvania Bail Rules. Supreme Court Rules Section 400s: Ascertaining
Bail

Supreme Bench of Baltimore City. *Rule 749, Bail Bonds.* November 28, 1969.

Williams v. *United States.* 342 U.S. 8 (1951).

Index

Index

About the Author

Paul B. Wice is assistant professor of political science at Washington and Jefferson College. He received the B.A. from Bucknell University, the M.A. from American University, and the Ph.D. from the University of Illinois. He has contributed articles to the *Criminal Law Bulletin* and other professional journals.